Almighty God,
Father of our Lord Jesus Christ,
grant, we pray,
that we might be grounded and settled
in your truth
by the coming of your Holy Spirit
into our hearts.

What we do not know,
reveal to us;
what is lacking within us,
make complete;
that which we do know,
confirm in us;
and keep us blameless in your service,
through Jesus Christ our Lord.

Amen.

IMMERSE
The Reading **Bible**®

POETS

Tyndale House Publishers, Inc.
Carol Stream, Illinois

CREATED IN ALLIANCE WITH

INSTITUTE FOR
BIBLE READING

Visit Tyndale online at www.immerseBible.com, www.newlivingtranslation.com, and www.tyndale.com.

Visit the Institute for Bible Reading at www.instituteforbiblereading.org.

For information about special discounts for bulk purchases, please contact Tyndale House Publishers at csresponse@tyndale.com, or call 1-800-323-9400.

Library of Congress Cataloging-in-Publication Data

Names: Tyndale House Publishers.
Title: Poets.
Description: Carol Stream, Illinois : Tyndale House Publishers, Inc., [2017] | Series: Immerse : the reading Bible
Identifiers: LCCN 2017051052 | ISBN 9781496424174 (softcover)
Classification: LCC BS1308.A3 N394 2017 | DDC 223/.0520834—dc23 LC record available at https://lccn.loc.gov/2017051052

Printed in the United States of America

25	24	23	22	21	20
8	7	6	5	4	3

CONTENTS

———— ✝ ————

These books contain collections of songs that express the pains and joys of God's people. Through them, we can enter more deeply into Israel's story and also learn to talk to God in the heights and depths of our own experience.

———— ✝ ————

These books of ancient wisdom explore the workings of life in God's good but fractured world. They teach that the Creator has woven his wisdom into his creation and invite us to find and follow God's good way.

—— *Welcome to* ——

I M M E R S E
The Bible Reading Experience

The Bible is a great gift. The Creator of all things entered into our human story and spoke to us. He inspired people over many centuries to shape words into books that reveal his mind, bringing wisdom into our lives and light to our paths. But God's biggest intention for the Bible is to invite us into its Story. What God wants for us, more than anything else, is that we make the Bible's great drama of restoration and new life the story of our lives, too.

The appropriate way to receive a gift like this is to come to know the Bible deeply, to lose ourselves in it precisely so that we can find ourselves in it. In other words, we need to immerse ourselves in it—to read God's words at length and without distraction, to read with deeper historical and literary perspective, and to read through the Bible with friends in a regular three-year rhythm. *Immerse: The Bible Reading Experience* has been specially designed for this purpose.

Immerse: The Reading Bible presents each book of the Bible without the distractions of chapter and verse markers, subject headers, or footnotes—all later historical additions to the text. The *Holy Bible,* New Living Translation, is presented in a single-column format with easy-to-read type. To provide meaningful perspective, book introductions give historical and literary context, and the books are often reordered chronologically or grouped with books that share similar ancient audiences. Every feature in this unique Bible enhances the opportunity for readers to engage with God's words in simple clarity.

A more complete explanation of this unique Bible presentation can be found in the articles that begin on page 329 at the back of this volume.

—— *Introduction to* ——

POETS

THE FIVE COVENANTS GOD MADE WITH HUMANITY—through Noah, Abraham, Moses, David, and Jesus—provide the deep structure of the Bible. The vital historic context for the first four of these covenants— the Flood, the call of Abraham, the Exodus, and the establishment of Israel's monarchy—are found in the *Beginnings* and *Kingdoms* volumes. The words and deeds of the prophets who spoke for God to the people of Israel follow in the *Prophets* volume.

As the Jewish people assembled their Scriptures over time, they included another group of books that they called the Writings. These books from the latter part of the First Testament provide us with a key link to Israel's world during and after the nation's seventy-year exile in Babylon. By the time these books were collected in final form, Israel's political independence had ended and the people were living under the rule of foreign powers. While some of the Jewish people remained in their traditional homeland, many were dispersed throughout the ancient Near Eastern world.

The sages and scribes who wrote and gathered the Writings provided stories, songs, and wise words to God's people to keep them closely tethered to their ancient identity and calling. The unique stories and historical records of the Writings can be found in the *Chronicles* volume. The poetical books from the Writings are collected here in *Poets*.

The first books in this volume (Psalms, Lamentations, and Song of Songs) are collections of song lyrics. These song collections reflect the rich reality of human life and a full range of human emotions. They are closely tied to Israel's life and history, expressing the agony of their trials and the joy of their celebrations. Through the deep sorrow of Lamentations; the joyful exuberance of the love songs of Song of Songs; and the complaints, thanksgiving, exultation, and praise of Psalms, we enter more deeply into Israel's story.

Israel's regular worship calendar—from weekly Sabbath observances to annual festival celebrations—formed a vital part of the nation's ongoing covenant relationship with God. Many of the songs Israel used in worship are preserved in the great collection of lyric poems known as Psalms. And through these songs, we also can learn to find our own voice for talking to God about the heights and depths in our own life journey.

These Hebrew songs are primarily expressed through parallel lines of Hebrew poetry. Most Hebrew poetry is written in groupings of parallel lines (usually two lines, though sometimes three). These lines work together in various ways, often using rich metaphors and other poetic features, to state and then revisit their points. Second and third lines can reinforce, extend, deepen, or even talk back to the opening statements.

The final books in this collection (Proverbs, Ecclesiastes, and Job) come from Israel's wisdom tradition. These books share customary features found in the wisdom writing of other ancient Near Eastern cultures, but they have the invaluable advantage of seeing life from within the context of a covenant relationship with God. They proclaim that "fear of the LORD"—Yahweh, Israel's covenant God—"is the foundation of true knowledge."

These wisdom books explore the workings of life in God's good but fractured world. Their core premise is that the Creator has embedded his wisdom into his creation, and they invite people to find and then follow that good way of life. Wisdom books commend the path of "wisdom" or "righteousness," asserting that the God who created the world is the one who can best instruct us on how to live and flourish within it.

The wisdom books are also written mostly in poetry, though in a greater variety of forms than the lyric poetry of Israel's songs. Proverbs consists almost entirely of couplets (two lines of verse), while Job mostly contains much longer poetic speeches. Ecclesiastes is a mixture of poetry and prose, though the prose receives its shape more from recurring words and imagery (as in a poem) than from the linear progression of a plot line (as in a story).

It is a tremendous gift to us that the Bible is not just a collection of lectures about God. These books of songs and wisdom literature add depth, color, and texture to the biblical narrative. Through the use of beautiful lyric poetry and striking imagery, they help us fully realize that God's truth is truth for us in our lives today. They invite us to see all the struggles, triumphs, and complications of our own lives within the bigger story of God's ongoing work to bring flourishing life and peace to the world he created.

IMMERSED IN PSALMS

THERE ARE MOMENTS in life that need to be expressed with the full strength of human emotion. And nothing serves that need better than putting words to music. So we should not be surprised that ancient Israel had a songbook, used in large gatherings at the Temple and also in smaller settings within local communities. Psalms is a book of song lyrics, and many have musical notations, instructions, and even the names of tunes still attached. The fact that our Scriptures include heartfelt expressions like these, of God's people speaking directly to him, highlights that he wants to hear from us. He wants us to express our deepest longings and feelings to him.

These songs were gathered into the large collection we have today during the time after Israel's exile to Babylon, but many are preserved from earlier times. King David is associated with seventy-three of them, nearly half of the total number. (Our collection now includes 150 psalms, though Psalms 9/10 and 42/43 were each originally written as one psalm but later divided. And one psalm is repeated twice, appearing as both Psalm 14 and Psalm 53.) Whether birthed in the spiritual journey of an individual or the experiences of the community of God's people, all these songs came to be used in the corporate worship of Israel.

But Psalms is more than a songbook. As the collection of Hebrew poems came together, it was shaped into five "books," each closing with a doxology (special words of praise to God). These five books of psalms recall the five books of Moses (the *Torah*) at the beginning of the Bible. Just as the *Torah* was used for instruction and study, Psalms came to be used the same way. In fact, Psalm 1 seems to have been placed first precisely to encourage people to meditate on Psalms as a book of instruction. This shows that these songs that were *sung* in worship could also be *read* as Scripture.

These song lyrics are written in the usual form of Hebrew poetry, with groupings of parallel lines. The second line repeats, contrasts, or intensifies the meaning of the first line. The figurative language in these poems is perfectly suited for forcefully expressing authentic human responses within God's story.

Most of the psalms in the Bible are one of three types: praise, lament, or thanksgiving. Psalms of praise call on people to worship and sing to God, honoring him for his goodness and grace. Songs of lament are prayers to God for deliverance in deeply troubled times. Laments typically begin with an urgent and emotional cry, describing the struggles that the person or community is facing, and then make a specific request for help, almost always ending with expressions of trust in God. Psalms of thanksgiving often begin by reviewing the troubles the poet was experiencing. Then the poet calls upon God and is delivered. Finally, others are invited to share in thanking and praising God.

This collection of psalms also includes some other types of songs. Royal psalms celebrate the role of Israel's king—both the human king and God as the nation's high king. Pilgrim psalms (also called psalms of ascent) were sung by pilgrims making their way up to Jerusalem for one of the great Jewish festivals. Wisdom psalms echo Israel's traditions about following God's instructions to discover the path to flourishing life.

It is important that the psalms are more than just songs of praise. The laments and cries for justice prevent the praise songs from being merely a celebration of the status quo. The life of faith includes the shattering pain of injustice and wrongdoing that calls God's power and goodness into question. In such situations, God's deliverance of his people in answer to their cries leads them to a more profound appreciation of his faithfulness and care. The enduring overall message of the book is that God welcomes the honest expressions of our hearts, reflecting all the challenges of our ongoing relationship with him.

The book of Psalms was very popular in the first century AD and is crucial for understanding the story of Jesus the Messiah. The writers of the New Testament saw the themes of Psalms continuing in the ongoing story of God's people. This can also be true for us today as we read, sing, reflect on, and enter into the same story of struggle, rescue, and restoration. Israel's songbook gives us the words for expressing our own movements through lament and praise and thanksgiving on our journey with God toward a world of justice and peace.

PSALMS

✢

Book One
(PSALMS 1–41)

PSALM 1

Oh, the joys of those who do not
   follow the advice of the wicked,
   or stand around with sinners,
   or join in with mockers.
But they delight in the law of the LORD,
   meditating on it day and night.
They are like trees planted along the riverbank,
   bearing fruit each season.
Their leaves never wither,
   and they prosper in all they do.

But not the wicked!
   They are like worthless chaff, scattered by the wind.
They will be condemned at the time of judgment.
   Sinners will have no place among the godly.
For the LORD watches over the path of the godly,
   but the path of the wicked leads to destruction.

PSALM 2

Why are the nations so angry?
   Why do they waste their time with futile plans?
The kings of the earth prepare for battle;
   the rulers plot together
against the LORD
   and against his anointed one.
"Let us break their chains," they cry,
   "and free ourselves from slavery to God."

But the one who rules in heaven laughs.
    The Lord scoffs at them.
Then in anger he rebukes them,
    terrifying them with his fierce fury.
For the Lord declares, "I have placed my chosen king on the throne
    in Jerusalem, on my holy mountain."

The king proclaims the LORD's decree:
"The LORD said to me, 'You are my son.
    Today I have become your Father.
Only ask, and I will give you the nations as your inheritance,
    the whole earth as your possession.
You will break them with an iron rod
    and smash them like clay pots.'"

Now then, you kings, act wisely!
    Be warned, you rulers of the earth!
Serve the LORD with reverent fear,
    and rejoice with trembling.
Submit to God's royal son, or he will become angry,
    and you will be destroyed in the midst of all your activities—
for his anger flares up in an instant.
    But what joy for all who take refuge in him!

PSALM 3

A psalm of David, regarding the time David fled from his son Absalom.

O LORD, I have so many enemies;
    so many are against me.
So many are saying,
    "God will never rescue him!"   *Interlude*

But you, O LORD, are a shield around me;
    you are my glory, the one who holds my head high.
I cried out to the LORD,
    and he answered me from his holy mountain.   *Interlude*

I lay down and slept,
    yet I woke up in safety,
    for the LORD was watching over me.
I am not afraid of ten thousand enemies
    who surround me on every side.

Arise, O LORD!
    Rescue me, my God!

Slap all my enemies in the face!
  Shatter the teeth of the wicked!
Victory comes from you, O LORD.
  May you bless your people.   *Interlude*

PSALM 4

For the choir director: A psalm of David, to be accompanied by stringed instruments.

Answer me when I call to you,
  O God who declares me innocent.
Free me from my troubles.
  Have mercy on me and hear my prayer.

How long will you people ruin my reputation?
  How long will you make groundless accusations?
  How long will you continue your lies?   *Interlude*
You can be sure of this:
  The LORD set apart the godly for himself.
  The LORD will answer when I call to him.

Don't sin by letting anger control you.
  Think about it overnight and remain silent.   *Interlude*
Offer sacrifices in the right spirit,
  and trust the LORD.

Many people say, "Who will show us better times?"
  Let your face smile on us, LORD.
You have given me greater joy
  than those who have abundant harvests of grain
    and new wine.
In peace I will lie down and sleep,
  for you alone, O LORD, will keep me safe.

PSALM 5

For the choir director: A psalm of David, to be accompanied by the flute.

O LORD, hear me as I pray;
  pay attention to my groaning.
Listen to my cry for help, my King and my God,
  for I pray to no one but you.
Listen to my voice in the morning, LORD.
  Each morning I bring my requests to you and wait
    expectantly.

O God, you take no pleasure in wickedness;
    you cannot tolerate the sins of the wicked.
Therefore, the proud may not stand in your presence,
    for you hate all who do evil.
You will destroy those who tell lies.
    The LORD detests murderers and deceivers.

Because of your unfailing love, I can enter your house;
    I will worship at your Temple with deepest awe.
Lead me in the right path, O LORD,
    or my enemies will conquer me.
Make your way plain for me to follow.

My enemies cannot speak a truthful word.
    Their deepest desire is to destroy others.
Their talk is foul, like the stench from an open grave.
    Their tongues are filled with flattery.
O God, declare them guilty.
    Let them be caught in their own traps.
Drive them away because of their many sins,
    for they have rebelled against you.

But let all who take refuge in you rejoice;
    let them sing joyful praises forever.
Spread your protection over them,
    that all who love your name may be filled with joy.
For you bless the godly, O LORD;
    you surround them with your shield of love.

PSALM 6

For the choir director: A psalm of David, to be accompanied by an eight-stringed instrument.

O LORD, don't rebuke me in your anger
    or discipline me in your rage.
Have compassion on me, LORD, for I am weak.
    Heal me, LORD, for my bones are in agony.
I am sick at heart.
    How long, O LORD, until you restore me?

Return, O LORD, and rescue me.
    Save me because of your unfailing love.
For the dead do not remember you.
    Who can praise you from the grave?

I am worn out from sobbing.
>All night I flood my bed with weeping,
>drenching it with my tears.
My vision is blurred by grief;
>my eyes are worn out because of all my enemies.

Go away, all you who do evil,
>for the LORD has heard my weeping.
The LORD has heard my plea;
>the LORD will answer my prayer.
May all my enemies be disgraced and terrified.
>May they suddenly turn back in shame.

PSALM 7

A psalm of David, which he sang to the LORD concerning Cush of the tribe of Benjamin.

I come to you for protection, O LORD my God.
>Save me from my persecutors—rescue me!
If you don't, they will maul me like a lion,
>tearing me to pieces with no one to rescue me.
O LORD my God, if I have done wrong
>or am guilty of injustice,
if I have betrayed a friend
>or plundered my enemy without cause,
then let my enemies capture me.
>Let them trample me into the ground
>and drag my honor in the dust.   *Interlude*

Arise, O LORD, in anger!
>Stand up against the fury of my enemies!
>Wake up, my God, and bring justice!
Gather the nations before you.
>Rule over them from on high.
>The LORD judges the nations.
Declare me righteous, O LORD,
>for I am innocent, O Most High!
End the evil of those who are wicked,
>and defend the righteous.
For you look deep within the mind and heart,
>O righteous God.

God is my shield,
>saving those whose hearts are true and right.

God is an honest judge.
　　He is angry with the wicked every day.

If a person does not repent,
　　God will sharpen his sword;
　　he will bend and string his bow.
He will prepare his deadly weapons
　　and shoot his flaming arrows.

The wicked conceive evil;
　　they are pregnant with trouble
　　and give birth to lies.
They dig a deep pit to trap others,
　　then fall into it themselves.
The trouble they make for others backfires on them.
　　The violence they plan falls on their own heads.

I will thank the LORD because he is just;
　　I will sing praise to the name of the LORD Most High.

PSALM 8

For the choir director: A psalm of David, to be accompanied by a stringed instrument.

O LORD, our Lord, your majestic name fills the earth!
　　Your glory is higher than the heavens.
You have taught children and infants
　　to tell of your strength,
silencing your enemies
　　and all who oppose you.

When I look at the night sky and see the work of your fingers—
　　the moon and the stars you set in place—
what are mere mortals that you should think about them,
　　human beings that you should care for them?
Yet you made them only a little lower than God
　　and crowned them with glory and honor.
You gave them charge of everything you made,
　　putting all things under their authority—
the flocks and the herds
　　and all the wild animals,
the birds in the sky, the fish in the sea,
　　and everything that swims the ocean currents.

O LORD, our Lord, your majestic name fills the earth!

PSALM 9–10

For the choir director: A psalm of David, to be sung to the tune "Death of the Son."

I will praise you, LORD, with all my heart;
  I will tell of all the marvelous things you have done.
I will be filled with joy because of you.
  I will sing praises to your name, O Most High.

My enemies retreated;
  they staggered and died when you appeared.
For you have judged in my favor;
  from your throne you have judged with fairness.
You have rebuked the nations and destroyed the wicked;
  you have erased their names forever.
The enemy is finished, in endless ruins;
  the cities you uprooted are now forgotten.

But the LORD reigns forever,
  executing judgment from his throne.
He will judge the world with justice
  and rule the nations with fairness.
The LORD is a shelter for the oppressed,
  a refuge in times of trouble.
Those who know your name trust in you,
  for you, O LORD, do not abandon those who search for you.

Sing praises to the LORD who reigns in Jerusalem.
  Tell the world about his unforgettable deeds.
For he who avenges murder cares for the helpless.
  He does not ignore the cries of those who suffer.

LORD, have mercy on me.
  See how my enemies torment me.
  Snatch me back from the jaws of death.
Save me so I can praise you publicly at Jerusalem's gates,
  so I can rejoice that you have rescued me.

The nations have fallen into the pit they dug for others.
  Their own feet have been caught in the trap they set.
The LORD is known for his justice.
  The wicked are trapped by their own deeds.   *Quiet Interlude*

The wicked will go down to the grave.
  This is the fate of all the nations who ignore God.
But the needy will not be ignored forever;
  the hopes of the poor will not always be crushed.

Arise, O Lord!
>   Do not let mere mortals defy you!
>   Judge the nations!
Make them tremble in fear, O Lord.
>   Let the nations know they are merely human.   *Interlude*

O Lord, why do you stand so far away?
>   Why do you hide when I am in trouble?
The wicked arrogantly hunt down the poor.
>   Let them be caught in the evil they plan for others.
For they brag about their evil desires;
>   they praise the greedy and curse the Lord.

The wicked are too proud to seek God.
>   They seem to think that God is dead.
Yet they succeed in everything they do.
>   They do not see your punishment awaiting them.
>   They sneer at all their enemies.
They think, "Nothing bad will ever happen to us!
>   We will be free of trouble forever!"

Their mouths are full of cursing, lies, and threats.
>   Trouble and evil are on the tips of their tongues.
They lurk in ambush in the villages,
>   waiting to murder innocent people.
>   They are always searching for helpless victims.
Like lions crouched in hiding,
>   they wait to pounce on the helpless.
Like hunters they capture the helpless
>   and drag them away in nets.
Their helpless victims are crushed;
>   they fall beneath the strength of the wicked.
The wicked think, "God isn't watching us!
>   He has closed his eyes and won't even see
>   what we do!"

Arise, O Lord!
>   Punish the wicked, O God!
>   Do not ignore the helpless!
Why do the wicked get away with despising God?
>   They think, "God will never call us to account."
But you see the trouble and grief they cause.
>   You take note of it and punish them.

The helpless put their trust in you.
  You defend the orphans.

Break the arms of these wicked, evil people!
  Go after them until the last one is destroyed.
The Lord is king forever and ever!
  The godless nations will vanish from the land.
Lord, you know the hopes of the helpless.
  Surely you will hear their cries and comfort them.
You will bring justice to the orphans and the oppressed,
  so mere people can no longer terrify them.

PSALM 11

For the choir director: A psalm of David.

I trust in the Lord for protection.
So why do you say to me,
  "Fly like a bird to the mountains for safety!
The wicked are stringing their bows
  and fitting their arrows on the bowstrings.
They shoot from the shadows
  at those whose hearts are right.
The foundations of law and order have collapsed.
  What can the righteous do?"

But the Lord is in his holy Temple;
  the Lord still rules from heaven.
He watches everyone closely,
  examining every person on earth.
The Lord examines both the righteous and the wicked.
  He hates those who love violence.
He will rain down blazing coals and burning sulfur
    on the wicked,
  punishing them with scorching winds.
For the righteous Lord loves justice.
  The virtuous will see his face.

PSALM 12

For the choir director: A psalm of David, to be accompanied by an eight-stringed instrument.

Help, O Lord, for the godly are fast disappearing!
  The faithful have vanished from the earth!

Neighbors lie to each other,
  speaking with flattering lips and deceitful hearts.
May the Lord cut off their flattering lips
  and silence their boastful tongues.
They say, "We will lie to our hearts' content.
  Our lips are our own—who can stop us?"

The Lord replies, "I have seen violence done to the helpless,
  and I have heard the groans of the poor.
Now I will rise up to rescue them,
  as they have longed for me to do."
The Lord's promises are pure,
  like silver refined in a furnace,
  purified seven times over.
Therefore, Lord, we know you will protect the oppressed,
  preserving them forever from this lying generation,
even though the wicked strut about,
  and evil is praised throughout the land.

PSALM 13

For the choir director: A psalm of David.

O Lord, how long will you forget me? Forever?
  How long will you look the other way?
How long must I struggle with anguish in my soul,
  with sorrow in my heart every day?
  How long will my enemy have the upper hand?

Turn and answer me, O Lord my God!
  Restore the sparkle to my eyes, or I will die.
Don't let my enemies gloat, saying, "We have defeated him!"
  Don't let them rejoice at my downfall.

But I trust in your unfailing love.
  I will rejoice because you have rescued me.
I will sing to the Lord
  because he is good to me.

PSALM 14

For the choir director: A psalm of David.

Only fools say in their hearts,
  "There is no God."

They are corrupt, and their actions are evil;
    not one of them does good!

The LORD looks down from heaven
    on the entire human race;
he looks to see if anyone is truly wise,
    if anyone seeks God.
But no, all have turned away;
    all have become corrupt.
No one does good,
    not a single one!

Will those who do evil never learn?
    They eat up my people like bread
    and wouldn't think of praying to the LORD.
Terror will grip them,
    for God is with those who obey him.
The wicked frustrate the plans of the oppressed,
    but the LORD will protect his people.

Who will come from Mount Zion to rescue
        Israel?
    When the LORD restores his people,
    Jacob will shout with joy, and Israel will
        rejoice.

PSALM 15
A psalm of David.

Who may worship in your sanctuary, LORD?
    Who may enter your presence on your holy hill?
Those who lead blameless lives and do what is right,
    speaking the truth from sincere hearts.
Those who refuse to gossip
    or harm their neighbors
    or speak evil of their friends.
Those who despise flagrant sinners,
    and honor the faithful followers of the LORD,
    and keep their promises even when it hurts.
Those who lend money without charging interest,
    and who cannot be bribed to lie about the
        innocent.
Such people will stand firm forever.

PSALM 16
A psalm of David.

Keep me safe, O God,
    for I have come to you for refuge.

I said to the LORD, "You are my Master!
    Every good thing I have comes from you."
The godly people in the land
    are my true heroes!
    I take pleasure in them!
Troubles multiply for those who chase after other gods.
    I will not take part in their sacrifices of blood
    or even speak the names of their gods.

LORD, you alone are my inheritance, my cup of blessing.
    You guard all that is mine.
The land you have given me is a pleasant land.
    What a wonderful inheritance!

I will bless the LORD who guides me;
    even at night my heart instructs me.
I know the LORD is always with me.
    I will not be shaken, for he is right beside me.

No wonder my heart is glad, and I rejoice.
    My body rests in safety.
For you will not leave my soul among the dead
    or allow your holy one to rot in the grave.
You will show me the way of life,
    granting me the joy of your presence
    and the pleasures of living with you forever.

PSALM 17
A prayer of David.

O LORD, hear my plea for justice.
    Listen to my cry for help.
Pay attention to my prayer,
    for it comes from honest lips.
Declare me innocent,
    for you see those who do right.

You have tested my thoughts and examined my heart in the night.
    You have scrutinized me and found nothing wrong.

I am determined not to sin in what I say.
I have followed your commands,
which keep me from following cruel and evil people.
My steps have stayed on your path;
I have not wavered from following you.

I am praying to you because I know you will answer,
O God.
Bend down and listen as I pray.
Show me your unfailing love in wonderful ways.
By your mighty power you rescue
those who seek refuge from their enemies.
Guard me as you would guard your own eyes.
Hide me in the shadow of your wings.
Protect me from wicked people who attack me,
from murderous enemies who surround me.
They are without pity.
Listen to their boasting!
They track me down and surround me,
watching for the chance to throw me to the ground.
They are like hungry lions, eager to tear me apart—
like young lions hiding in ambush.

Arise, O LORD!
Stand against them, and bring them to their knees!
Rescue me from the wicked with your sword!
By the power of your hand, O LORD,
destroy those who look to this world for their reward.
But satisfy the hunger of your treasured ones.
May their children have plenty,
leaving an inheritance for their descendants.
Because I am righteous, I will see you.
When I awake, I will see you face to face and be satisfied.

PSALM 18

For the choir director: A psalm of David, the servant of the LORD. He sang this song to the LORD on the day the LORD rescued him from all his enemies and from Saul. He sang:

I love you, LORD;
you are my strength.
The LORD is my rock, my fortress, and my savior;
my God is my rock, in whom I find protection.

He is my shield, the power that saves me,
  and my place of safety.
I called on the LORD, who is worthy of praise,
  and he saved me from my enemies.

The ropes of death entangled me;
  floods of destruction swept over me.
The grave wrapped its ropes around me;
  death laid a trap in my path.
But in my distress I cried out to the LORD;
  yes, I prayed to my God for help.
He heard me from his sanctuary;
  my cry to him reached his ears.

Then the earth quaked and trembled.
  The foundations of the mountains shook;
  they quaked because of his anger.
Smoke poured from his nostrils;
  fierce flames leaped from his mouth.
  Glowing coals blazed forth from him.
He opened the heavens and came down;
  dark storm clouds were beneath his feet.
Mounted on a mighty angelic being, he flew,
  soaring on the wings of the wind.
He shrouded himself in darkness,
  veiling his approach with dark rain clouds.
Thick clouds shielded the brightness around him
  and rained down hail and burning coals.
The LORD thundered from heaven;
  the voice of the Most High resounded
  amid the hail and burning coals.
He shot his arrows and scattered his enemies;
  great bolts of lightning flashed, and they were confused.
Then at your command, O LORD,
  at the blast of your breath,
the bottom of the sea could be seen,
  and the foundations of the earth were laid bare.

He reached down from heaven and rescued me;
  he drew me out of deep waters.
He rescued me from my powerful enemies,
  from those who hated me and were too strong for me.
They attacked me at a moment when I was in distress,
  but the LORD supported me.

He led me to a place of safety;
   he rescued me because he delights in me.
The LORD rewarded me for doing right;
   he restored me because of my innocence.
For I have kept the ways of the LORD;
   I have not turned from my God to follow evil.
I have followed all his regulations;
   I have never abandoned his decrees.
I am blameless before God;
   I have kept myself from sin.
The LORD rewarded me for doing right.
   He has seen my innocence.

To the faithful you show yourself faithful;
   to those with integrity you show integrity.
To the pure you show yourself pure,
   but to the crooked you show yourself shrewd.
You rescue the humble,
   but you humiliate the proud.
You light a lamp for me.
   The LORD, my God, lights up my darkness.
In your strength I can crush an army;
   with my God I can scale any wall.

God's way is perfect.
   All the LORD's promises prove true.
   He is a shield for all who look to him for protection.
For who is God except the LORD?
   Who but our God is a solid rock?
God arms me with strength,
   and he makes my way perfect.
He makes me as surefooted as a deer,
   enabling me to stand on mountain heights.
He trains my hands for battle;
   he strengthens my arm to draw a bronze bow.
You have given me your shield of victory.
   Your right hand supports me;
   your help has made me great.
You have made a wide path for my feet
   to keep them from slipping.

I chased my enemies and caught them;
   I did not stop until they were conquered.

I struck them down so they could not get up;
 they fell beneath my feet.
You have armed me with strength for the battle;
 you have subdued my enemies under my feet.
You placed my foot on their necks.
 I have destroyed all who hated me.
They called for help, but no one came to their rescue.
 They even cried to the LORD, but he refused to answer.
I ground them as fine as dust in the wind.
 I swept them into the gutter like dirt.
You gave me victory over my accusers.
 You appointed me ruler over nations;
 people I don't even know now serve me.
As soon as they hear of me, they submit;
 foreign nations cringe before me.
They all lose their courage
 and come trembling from their strongholds.

The LORD lives! Praise to my Rock!
 May the God of my salvation be exalted!
He is the God who pays back those who harm me;
 he subdues the nations under me
 and rescues me from my enemies.
You hold me safe beyond the reach of my enemies;
 you save me from violent opponents.
For this, O LORD, I will praise you among the nations;
 I will sing praises to your name.
You give great victories to your king;
 you show unfailing love to your anointed,
 to David and all his descendants forever.

PSALM 19

For the choir director: A psalm of David.

The heavens proclaim the glory of God.
 The skies display his craftsmanship.
Day after day they continue to speak;
 night after night they make him known.
They speak without a sound or word;
 their voice is never heard.
Yet their message has gone throughout the earth,
 and their words to all the world.

God has made a home in the heavens for the sun.
It bursts forth like a radiant bridegroom after his wedding.
　　It rejoices like a great athlete eager to run the race.
The sun rises at one end of the heavens
　　and follows its course to the other end.
　　Nothing can hide from its heat.

The instructions of the LORD are perfect,
　　reviving the soul.
The decrees of the LORD are trustworthy,
　　making wise the simple.
The commandments of the LORD are right,
　　bringing joy to the heart.
The commands of the LORD are clear,
　　giving insight for living.
Reverence for the LORD is pure,
　　lasting forever.
The laws of the LORD are true;
　　each one is fair.
They are more desirable than gold,
　　even the finest gold.
They are sweeter than honey,
　　even honey dripping from the comb.
They are a warning to your servant,
　　a great reward for those who obey them.

How can I know all the sins lurking in my heart?
　　Cleanse me from these hidden faults.
Keep your servant from deliberate sins!
　　Don't let them control me.
Then I will be free of guilt
　　and innocent of great sin.

May the words of my mouth
　　and the meditation of my heart
be pleasing to you,
　　O LORD, my rock and my redeemer.

PSALM 20

For the choir director: A psalm of David.

In times of trouble, may the LORD answer your cry.
　　May the name of the God of Jacob keep you safe from all harm.

May he send you help from his sanctuary
　　and strengthen you from Jerusalem.
May he remember all your gifts
　　and look favorably on your burnt offerings. *Interlude*

May he grant your heart's desires
　　and make all your plans succeed.
May we shout for joy when we hear of your victory
　　and raise a victory banner in the name of our God.
May the LORD answer all your prayers.

Now I know that the LORD rescues his anointed king.
　　He will answer him from his holy heaven
　　and rescue him by his great power.
Some nations boast of their chariots and horses,
　　but we boast in the name of the LORD our God.
Those nations will fall down and collapse,
　　but we will rise up and stand firm.

Give victory to our king, O LORD!
　　Answer our cry for help.

PSALM 21

For the choir director: A psalm of David.

How the king rejoices in your strength, O LORD!
　　He shouts with joy because you give him victory.
For you have given him his heart's desire;
　　you have withheld nothing he requested. *Interlude*

You welcomed him back with success and prosperity.
　　You placed a crown of finest gold on his head.
He asked you to preserve his life,
　　and you granted his request.
　　The days of his life stretch on forever.
Your victory brings him great honor,
　　and you have clothed him with splendor and majesty.
You have endowed him with eternal blessings
　　and given him the joy of your presence.
For the king trusts in the LORD.
　　The unfailing love of the Most High will keep him from stumbling.

You will capture all your enemies.
　　Your strong right hand will seize all who hate you.

You will throw them in a flaming furnace
   when you appear.
The LORD will consume them in his anger;
   fire will devour them.
You will wipe their children from the face of the earth;
   they will never have descendants.
Although they plot against you,
   their evil schemes will never succeed.
For they will turn and run
   when they see your arrows aimed at them.
Rise up, O LORD, in all your power.
   With music and singing we celebrate your mighty acts.

PSALM 22

For the choir director: A psalm of David, to be sung to the tune "Doe of the Dawn."

My God, my God, why have you abandoned me?
   Why are you so far away when I groan for help?
Every day I call to you, my God, but you do not answer.
   Every night I lift my voice, but I find no relief.

Yet you are holy,
   enthroned on the praises of Israel.
Our ancestors trusted in you,
   and you rescued them.
They cried out to you and were saved.
   They trusted in you and were never disgraced.

But I am a worm and not a man.
   I am scorned and despised by all!
Everyone who sees me mocks me.
   They sneer and shake their heads, saying,
"Is this the one who relies on the LORD?
   Then let the LORD save him!
If the LORD loves him so much,
   let the LORD rescue him!"

Yet you brought me safely from my mother's womb
   and led me to trust you at my mother's breast.
I was thrust into your arms at my birth.
   You have been my God from the moment I was born.

Do not stay so far from me,
   for trouble is near,

and no one else can help me.
My enemies surround me like a herd of bulls;
    fierce bulls of Bashan have hemmed me in!
Like lions they open their jaws against me,
    roaring and tearing into their prey.
My life is poured out like water,
    and all my bones are out of joint.
My heart is like wax,
    melting within me.
My strength has dried up like sunbaked clay.
    My tongue sticks to the roof of my mouth.
    You have laid me in the dust and left me for dead.
My enemies surround me like a pack of dogs;
    an evil gang closes in on me.
    They have pierced my hands and feet.
I can count all my bones.
    My enemies stare at me and gloat.
They divide my garments among themselves
    and throw dice for my clothing.

O Lord, do not stay far away!
    You are my strength; come quickly to my aid!
Save me from the sword;
    spare my precious life from these dogs.
Snatch me from the lion's jaws
    and from the horns of these wild oxen.

I will proclaim your name to my brothers and sisters.
    I will praise you among your assembled people.
Praise the Lord, all you who fear him!
    Honor him, all you descendants of Jacob!
    Show him reverence, all you descendants of Israel!
For he has not ignored or belittled the suffering of the needy.
    He has not turned his back on them,
    but has listened to their cries for help.

I will praise you in the great assembly.
    I will fulfill my vows in the presence of those who worship you.
The poor will eat and be satisfied.
    All who seek the Lord will praise him.
    Their hearts will rejoice with everlasting joy.
The whole earth will acknowledge the Lord and return to him.
    All the families of the nations will bow down before him.

For royal power belongs to the LORD.
  He rules all the nations.

Let the rich of the earth feast and worship.
  Bow before him, all who are mortal,
  all whose lives will end as dust.
Our children will also serve him.
  Future generations will hear about the wonders of
    the Lord.
His righteous acts will be told to those not yet born.
  They will hear about everything he has done.

PSALM 23
A psalm of David.

The LORD is my shepherd;
  I have all that I need.
He lets me rest in green meadows;
  he leads me beside peaceful streams.
  He renews my strength.
He guides me along right paths,
  bringing honor to his name.
Even when I walk
  through the darkest valley,
I will not be afraid,
  for you are close beside me.
Your rod and your staff
  protect and comfort me.
You prepare a feast for me
  in the presence of my enemies.
You honor me by anointing my head with oil.
  My cup overflows with blessings.
Surely your goodness and unfailing love will pursue me
  all the days of my life,
and I will live in the house of the LORD
  forever.

PSALM 24
A psalm of David.

The earth is the LORD's, and everything in it.
  The world and all its people belong to him.

For he laid the earth's foundation on the seas
    and built it on the ocean depths.

Who may climb the mountain of the LORD?
    Who may stand in his holy place?
Only those whose hands and hearts are pure,
    who do not worship idols
    and never tell lies.
They will receive the LORD's blessing
    and have a right relationship with God their savior.
Such people may seek you
    and worship in your presence, O God of Jacob.   *Interlude*

Open up, ancient gates!
    Open up, ancient doors,
    and let the King of glory enter.
Who is the King of glory?
    The LORD, strong and mighty;
    the LORD, invincible in battle.
Open up, ancient gates!
    Open up, ancient doors,
    and let the King of glory enter.
Who is the King of glory?
    The LORD of Heaven's Armies—
    he is the King of glory.   *Interlude*

PSALM 25
A psalm of David.

O LORD, I give my life to you.
    I trust in you, my God!
Do not let me be disgraced,
    or let my enemies rejoice in my defeat.
No one who trusts in you will ever be disgraced,
    but disgrace comes to those who try to deceive others.

Show me the right path, O LORD;
    point out the road for me to follow.
Lead me by your truth and teach me,
    for you are the God who saves me.
    All day long I put my hope in you.
Remember, O LORD, your compassion and unfailing love,
    which you have shown from long ages past.

Do not remember the rebellious sins of my youth.
  Remember me in the light of your unfailing love,
  for you are merciful, O LORD.

The LORD is good and does what is right;
  he shows the proper path to those who go astray.
He leads the humble in doing right,
  teaching them his way.
The LORD leads with unfailing love and faithfulness
  all who keep his covenant and obey his demands.

For the honor of your name, O LORD,
  forgive my many, many sins.
Who are those who fear the LORD?
  He will show them the path they should choose.
They will live in prosperity,
  and their children will inherit the land.
The LORD is a friend to those who fear him.
  He teaches them his covenant.
My eyes are always on the LORD,
  for he rescues me from the traps of my enemies.

Turn to me and have mercy,
  for I am alone and in deep distress.
My problems go from bad to worse.
  Oh, save me from them all!
Feel my pain and see my trouble.
  Forgive all my sins.
See how many enemies I have
  and how viciously they hate me!
Protect me! Rescue my life from them!
  Do not let me be disgraced, for in you I take refuge.
May integrity and honesty protect me,
  for I put my hope in you.

O God, ransom Israel
  from all its troubles.

PSALM 26
A psalm of David.

Declare me innocent, O LORD,
  for I have acted with integrity;
  I have trusted in the LORD without wavering.

Put me on trial, LORD, and cross-examine me.
    Test my motives and my heart.
For I am always aware of your unfailing love,
    and I have lived according to your truth.
I do not spend time with liars
    or go along with hypocrites.
I hate the gatherings of those who do evil,
    and I refuse to join in with the wicked.
I wash my hands to declare my innocence.
    I come to your altar, O LORD,
singing a song of thanksgiving
    and telling of all your wonders.
I love your sanctuary, LORD,
    the place where your glorious presence dwells.

Don't let me suffer the fate of sinners.
    Don't condemn me along with murderers.
Their hands are dirty with evil schemes,
    and they constantly take bribes.
But I am not like that; I live with integrity.
    So redeem me and show me mercy.
Now I stand on solid ground,
    and I will publicly praise the LORD.

PSALM 27

A psalm of David.

The LORD is my light and my salvation—
    so why should I be afraid?
The LORD is my fortress, protecting me from danger,
    so why should I tremble?
When evil people come to devour me,
    when my enemies and foes attack me,
    they will stumble and fall.
Though a mighty army surrounds me,
    my heart will not be afraid.
Even if I am attacked,
    I will remain confident.

The one thing I ask of the LORD—
    the thing I seek most—
is to live in the house of the LORD all the days of my life,
    delighting in the LORD's perfections

and meditating in his Temple.
For he will conceal me there when troubles come;
    he will hide me in his sanctuary.
    He will place me out of reach on a high rock.
Then I will hold my head high
    above my enemies who surround me.
At his sanctuary I will offer sacrifices with shouts of joy,
    singing and praising the LORD with music.

Hear me as I pray, O LORD.
    Be merciful and answer me!
My heart has heard you say, "Come and talk with me."
    And my heart responds, "LORD, I am coming."
Do not turn your back on me.
    Do not reject your servant in anger.
    You have always been my helper.
Don't leave me now; don't abandon me,
    O God of my salvation!
Even if my father and mother abandon me,
    the LORD will hold me close.

Teach me how to live, O LORD.
    Lead me along the right path,
    for my enemies are waiting for me.
Do not let me fall into their hands.
    For they accuse me of things I've never done;
    with every breath they threaten me with violence.
Yet I am confident I will see the LORD's goodness
    while I am here in the land of the living.

Wait patiently for the LORD.
    Be brave and courageous.
    Yes, wait patiently for the LORD.

PSALM 28

A psalm of David.

I pray to you, O LORD, my rock.
    Do not turn a deaf ear to me.
For if you are silent,
    I might as well give up and die.
Listen to my prayer for mercy
    as I cry out to you for help,
    as I lift my hands toward your holy sanctuary.

Do not drag me away with the wicked—
    with those who do evil—
those who speak friendly words to their neighbors
    while planning evil in their hearts.
Give them the punishment they so richly deserve!
    Measure it out in proportion to their wickedness.
Pay them back for all their evil deeds!
    Give them a taste of what they have done to others.
They care nothing for what the LORD has done
    or for what his hands have made.
So he will tear them down,
    and they will never be rebuilt!

Praise the LORD!
    For he has heard my cry for mercy.
The LORD is my strength and shield.
    I trust him with all my heart.
He helps me, and my heart is filled with joy.
    I burst out in songs of thanksgiving.

The LORD gives his people strength.
    He is a safe fortress for his anointed king.
Save your people!
    Bless Israel, your special possession.
Lead them like a shepherd,
    and carry them in your arms forever.

PSALM 29

A psalm of David.

Honor the LORD, you heavenly beings;
    honor the LORD for his glory and strength.
Honor the LORD for the glory of his name.
    Worship the LORD in the splendor of his holiness.

The voice of the LORD echoes above the sea.
    The God of glory thunders.
    The LORD thunders over the mighty sea.
The voice of the LORD is powerful;
    the voice of the LORD is majestic.
The voice of the LORD splits the mighty cedars;
    the LORD shatters the cedars of Lebanon.
He makes Lebanon's mountains skip like a calf;

he makes Mount Hermon leap like a young wild ox.
The voice of the LORD strikes
　　with bolts of lightning.
The voice of the LORD makes the barren wilderness quake;
　　the LORD shakes the wilderness of Kadesh.
The voice of the LORD twists mighty oaks
　　and strips the forests bare.
In his Temple everyone shouts, "Glory!"

The LORD rules over the floodwaters.
　　The LORD reigns as king forever.
The LORD gives his people strength.
　　The LORD blesses them with peace.

PSALM 30

A psalm of David. A song for the dedication of the Temple.

I will exalt you, LORD, for you rescued me.
　　You refused to let my enemies triumph over me.
O LORD my God, I cried to you for help,
　　and you restored my health.
You brought me up from the grave, O LORD.
　　You kept me from falling into the pit of death.

Sing to the LORD, all you godly ones!
　　Praise his holy name.
For his anger lasts only a moment,
　　but his favor lasts a lifetime!
Weeping may last through the night,
　　but joy comes with the morning.

When I was prosperous, I said,
　　"Nothing can stop me now!"
Your favor, O LORD, made me as secure as a mountain.
　　Then you turned away from me, and I was shattered.

I cried out to you, O LORD.
　　I begged the Lord for mercy, saying,
"What will you gain if I die,
　　if I sink into the grave?
Can my dust praise you?
　　Can it tell of your faithfulness?
Hear me, LORD, and have mercy on me.
　　Help me, O LORD."

You have turned my mourning into joyful dancing.
    You have taken away my clothes of mourning and clothed
        me with joy,
that I might sing praises to you and not be silent.
    O LORD my God, I will give you thanks forever!

PSALM 31

For the choir director: A psalm of David.

O LORD, I have come to you for protection;
    don't let me be disgraced.
    Save me, for you do what is right.
Turn your ear to listen to me;
    rescue me quickly.
Be my rock of protection,
    a fortress where I will be safe.
You are my rock and my fortress.
    For the honor of your name, lead me out of this danger.
Pull me from the trap my enemies set for me,
    for I find protection in you alone.
I entrust my spirit into your hand.
    Rescue me, LORD, for you are a faithful God.

I hate those who worship worthless idols.
    I trust in the LORD.
I will be glad and rejoice in your unfailing love,
    for you have seen my troubles,
    and you care about the anguish of my soul.
You have not handed me over to my enemies
    but have set me in a safe place.

Have mercy on me, LORD, for I am in distress.
    Tears blur my eyes.
    My body and soul are withering away.
I am dying from grief;
    my years are shortened by sadness.
Sin has drained my strength;
    I am wasting away from within.
I am scorned by all my enemies
    and despised by my neighbors—
    even my friends are afraid to come near me.
When they see me on the street,
    they run the other way.

I am ignored as if I were dead,
    as if I were a broken pot.
I have heard the many rumors about me,
    and I am surrounded by terror.
My enemies conspire against me,
    plotting to take my life.

But I am trusting you, O LORD,
    saying, "You are my God!"
My future is in your hands.
    Rescue me from those who hunt me down
      relentlessly.
Let your favor shine on your servant.
    In your unfailing love, rescue me.
Don't let me be disgraced, O LORD,
    for I call out to you for help.
Let the wicked be disgraced;
    let them lie silent in the grave.
Silence their lying lips—
    those proud and arrogant lips that accuse
      the godly.

How great is the goodness
    you have stored up for those who fear you.
You lavish it on those who come to you for protection,
    blessing them before the watching world.
You hide them in the shelter of your presence,
    safe from those who conspire against them.
You shelter them in your presence,
    far from accusing tongues.

Praise the LORD,
    for he has shown me the wonders of his unfailing love.
    He kept me safe when my city was under attack.
In panic I cried out,
    "I am cut off from the LORD!"
But you heard my cry for mercy
    and answered my call for help.

Love the LORD, all you godly ones!
    For the LORD protects those who are loyal to him,
    but he harshly punishes the arrogant.
So be strong and courageous,
    all you who put your hope in the LORD!

PSALM 32
A psalm of David.

Oh, what joy for those
    whose disobedience is forgiven,
    whose sin is put out of sight!
Yes, what joy for those
    whose record the Lord has cleared of guilt,
    whose lives are lived in complete honesty!
When I refused to confess my sin,
    my body wasted away,
    and I groaned all day long.
Day and night your hand of discipline was heavy on me.
    My strength evaporated like water in the summer heat.   *Interlude*

Finally, I confessed all my sins to you
    and stopped trying to hide my guilt.
I said to myself, "I will confess my rebellion to the Lord."
    And you forgave me! All my guilt is gone.   *Interlude*

Therefore, let all the godly pray to you while there is still time,
    that they may not drown in the floodwaters of judgment.
For you are my hiding place;
    you protect me from trouble.
    You surround me with songs of victory.   *Interlude*

The Lord says, "I will guide you along the best pathway for your life.
    I will advise you and watch over you.
Do not be like a senseless horse or mule
    that needs a bit and bridle to keep it under control."

Many sorrows come to the wicked,
    but unfailing love surrounds those who trust the Lord.
So rejoice in the Lord and be glad, all you who obey him!
    Shout for joy, all you whose hearts are pure!

PSALM 33

Let the godly sing for joy to the Lord;
    it is fitting for the pure to praise him.
Praise the Lord with melodies on the lyre;
    make music for him on the ten-stringed harp.
Sing a new song of praise to him;
    play skillfully on the harp, and sing with joy.

For the word of the LORD holds true,
   and we can trust everything he does.
He loves whatever is just and good;
   the unfailing love of the LORD fills the earth.

The LORD merely spoke,
   and the heavens were created.
He breathed the word,
   and all the stars were born.
He assigned the sea its boundaries
   and locked the oceans in vast reservoirs.
Let the whole world fear the LORD,
   and let everyone stand in awe of him.
For when he spoke, the world began!
   It appeared at his command.

The LORD frustrates the plans of the nations
   and thwarts all their schemes.
But the LORD's plans stand firm forever;
   his intentions can never be shaken.

What joy for the nation whose God is the LORD,
   whose people he has chosen as his inheritance.

The LORD looks down from heaven
   and sees the whole human race.
From his throne he observes
   all who live on the earth.
He made their hearts,
   so he understands everything they do.
The best-equipped army cannot save a king,
   nor is great strength enough to save a warrior.
Don't count on your warhorse to give you victory—
   for all its strength, it cannot save you.

But the LORD watches over those who fear him,
   those who rely on his unfailing love.
He rescues them from death
   and keeps them alive in times of famine.

We put our hope in the LORD.
   He is our help and our shield.
In him our hearts rejoice,
   for we trust in his holy name.
Let your unfailing love surround us, LORD,
   for our hope is in you alone.

PSALM 34

A psalm of David, regarding the time he pretended to be insane in front of Abimelech, who sent him away.

I will praise the LORD at all times.
  I will constantly speak his praises.
I will boast only in the LORD;
  let all who are helpless take heart.
Come, let us tell of the LORD's greatness;
  let us exalt his name together.

I prayed to the LORD, and he answered me.
  He freed me from all my fears.
Those who look to him for help will be radiant with joy;
  no shadow of shame will darken their faces.
In my desperation I prayed, and the LORD listened;
  he saved me from all my troubles.
For the angel of the LORD is a guard;
  he surrounds and defends all who fear him.

Taste and see that the LORD is good.
  Oh, the joys of those who take refuge in him!
Fear the LORD, you his godly people,
  for those who fear him will have all they need.
Even strong young lions sometimes go hungry,
  but those who trust in the LORD will lack no
    good thing.

Come, my children, and listen to me,
  and I will teach you to fear the LORD.
Does anyone want to live a life
  that is long and prosperous?
Then keep your tongue from speaking evil
  and your lips from telling lies!
Turn away from evil and do good.
  Search for peace, and work to maintain it.

The eyes of the LORD watch over those who do right;
  his ears are open to their cries for help.
But the LORD turns his face against those who do evil;
  he will erase their memory from the earth.
The LORD hears his people when they call to him for help.
  He rescues them from all their troubles.
The LORD is close to the brokenhearted;
  he rescues those whose spirits are crushed.

The righteous person faces many troubles,
    but the LORD comes to the rescue each time.
For the LORD protects the bones of the righteous;
    not one of them is broken!

Calamity will surely destroy the wicked,
    and those who hate the righteous will be punished.
But the LORD will redeem those who serve him.
    No one who takes refuge in him will be condemned.

PSALM 35
A psalm of David.

O LORD, oppose those who oppose me.
    Fight those who fight against me.
Put on your armor, and take up your shield.
    Prepare for battle, and come to my aid.
Lift up your spear and javelin
    against those who pursue me.
Let me hear you say,
    "I will give you victory!"
Bring shame and disgrace on those trying to kill me;
    turn them back and humiliate those who want to harm me.
Blow them away like chaff in the wind—
    a wind sent by the angel of the LORD.
Make their path dark and slippery,
    with the angel of the LORD pursuing them.
I did them no wrong, but they laid a trap for me.
    I did them no wrong, but they dug a pit to catch me.
So let sudden ruin come upon them!
    Let them be caught in the trap they set for me!
    Let them be destroyed in the pit they dug for me.

Then I will rejoice in the LORD.
    I will be glad because he rescues me.
With every bone in my body I will praise him:
    "LORD, who can compare with you?
Who else rescues the helpless from the strong?
    Who else protects the helpless and poor from those who rob them?"

Malicious witnesses testify against me.
    They accuse me of crimes I know nothing about.
They repay me evil for good.
    I am sick with despair.

Yet when they were ill, I grieved for them.
  I denied myself by fasting for them,
  but my prayers returned unanswered.
I was sad, as though they were my friends or family,
  as if I were grieving for my own mother.
But they are glad now that I am in trouble;
  they gleefully join together against me.
I am attacked by people I don't even know;
  they slander me constantly.
They mock me and call me names;
  they snarl at me.

How long, O Lord, will you look on and do nothing?
  Rescue me from their fierce attacks.
  Protect my life from these lions!
Then I will thank you in front of the great assembly.
  I will praise you before all the people.
Don't let my treacherous enemies rejoice over my defeat.
  Don't let those who hate me without cause gloat over my sorrow.
They don't talk of peace;
  they plot against innocent people who mind their own business.
They shout, "Aha! Aha!
  With our own eyes we saw him do it!"

O Lord, you know all about this.
  Do not stay silent.
  Do not abandon me now, O Lord.
Wake up! Rise to my defense!
  Take up my case, my God and my Lord.
Declare me not guilty, O Lord my God, for you give justice.
  Don't let my enemies laugh about me in my troubles.
Don't let them say, "Look, we got what we wanted!
  Now we will eat him alive!"

May those who rejoice at my troubles
  be humiliated and disgraced.
May those who triumph over me
  be covered with shame and dishonor.
But give great joy to those who came to my defense.
  Let them continually say, "Great is the Lord,
  who delights in blessing his servant with peace!"
Then I will proclaim your justice,
  and I will praise you all day long.

PSALM 36

For the choir director: A psalm of David, the servant of the LORD.

Sin whispers to the wicked, deep within their hearts.
   They have no fear of God at all.
In their blind conceit,
   they cannot see how wicked they really are.
Everything they say is crooked and deceitful.
   They refuse to act wisely or do good.
They lie awake at night, hatching sinful plots.
   Their actions are never good.
   They make no attempt to turn from evil.

Your unfailing love, O LORD, is as vast as the
      heavens;
   your faithfulness reaches beyond the clouds.
Your righteousness is like the mighty mountains,
   your justice like the ocean depths.
You care for people and animals alike, O LORD.
   How precious is your unfailing love, O God!
All humanity finds shelter
   in the shadow of your wings.
You feed them from the abundance of your own house,
   letting them drink from your river of delights.
For you are the fountain of life,
   the light by which we see.

Pour out your unfailing love on those who love you;
   give justice to those with honest hearts.
Don't let the proud trample me
   or the wicked push me around.
Look! Those who do evil have fallen!
   They are thrown down, never to rise again.

PSALM 37

A psalm of David.

Don't worry about the wicked
   or envy those who do wrong.
For like grass, they soon fade away.
   Like spring flowers, they soon wither.

Trust in the LORD and do good.
   Then you will live safely in the land and prosper.

Take delight in the LORD,
   and he will give you your heart's desires.

Commit everything you do to the LORD.
   Trust him, and he will help you.
He will make your innocence radiate like the dawn,
   and the justice of your cause will shine like the noonday sun.

Be still in the presence of the LORD,
   and wait patiently for him to act.
Don't worry about evil people who prosper
   or fret about their wicked schemes.

Stop being angry!
   Turn from your rage!
Do not lose your temper—
   it only leads to harm.
For the wicked will be destroyed,
   but those who trust in the LORD will possess the land.

Soon the wicked will disappear.
   Though you look for them, they will be gone.
The lowly will possess the land
   and will live in peace and prosperity.

The wicked plot against the godly;
   they snarl at them in defiance.
But the Lord just laughs,
   for he sees their day of judgment coming.

The wicked draw their swords
   and string their bows
to kill the poor and the oppressed,
   to slaughter those who do right.
But their swords will stab their own hearts,
   and their bows will be broken.

It is better to be godly and have little
   than to be evil and rich.
For the strength of the wicked will be shattered,
   but the LORD takes care of the godly.

Day by day the LORD takes care of the innocent,
   and they will receive an inheritance that lasts forever.
They will not be disgraced in hard times;
   even in famine they will have more than enough.

But the wicked will die.
    The Lord's enemies are like flowers in a field—
    they will disappear like smoke.

The wicked borrow and never repay,
    but the godly are generous givers.
Those the Lord blesses will possess the land,
    but those he curses will die.

The Lord directs the steps of the godly.
    He delights in every detail of their lives.
Though they stumble, they will never fall,
    for the Lord holds them by the hand.

Once I was young, and now I am old.
    Yet I have never seen the godly abandoned
    or their children begging for bread.
The godly always give generous loans to others,
    and their children are a blessing.

Turn from evil and do good,
    and you will live in the land forever.
For the Lord loves justice,
    and he will never abandon the godly.

He will keep them safe forever,
    but the children of the wicked will die.
The godly will possess the land
    and will live there forever.

The godly offer good counsel;
    they teach right from wrong.
They have made God's law their own,
    so they will never slip from his path.

The wicked wait in ambush for the godly,
    looking for an excuse to kill them.
But the Lord will not let the wicked succeed
    or let the godly be condemned when they are put on trial.

Put your hope in the Lord.
    Travel steadily along his path.
He will honor you by giving you the land.
    You will see the wicked destroyed.

I have seen wicked and ruthless people
    flourishing like a tree in its native soil.

But when I looked again, they were gone!
   Though I searched for them, I could not find them!

Look at those who are honest and good,
   for a wonderful future awaits those who love peace.
But the rebellious will be destroyed;
   they have no future.

The LORD rescues the godly;
   he is their fortress in times of trouble.
The LORD helps them,
   rescuing them from the wicked.
He saves them,
   and they find shelter in him.

PSALM 38
A psalm of David, asking God to remember him.

O LORD, don't rebuke me in your anger
   or discipline me in your rage!
Your arrows have struck deep,
   and your blows are crushing me.
Because of your anger, my whole body is sick;
   my health is broken because of my sins.
My guilt overwhelms me—
   it is a burden too heavy to bear.
My wounds fester and stink
   because of my foolish sins.
I am bent over and racked with pain.
   All day long I walk around filled with grief.
A raging fever burns within me,
   and my health is broken.
I am exhausted and completely crushed.
   My groans come from an anguished heart.

You know what I long for, Lord;
   you hear my every sigh.
My heart beats wildly, my strength fails,
   and I am going blind.
My loved ones and friends stay away, fearing my disease.
   Even my own family stands at a distance.
Meanwhile, my enemies lay traps to kill me.
   Those who wish me harm make plans to ruin me.
   All day long they plan their treachery.

But I am deaf to all their threats.
  I am silent before them as one who cannot speak.
I choose to hear nothing,
  and I make no reply.
For I am waiting for you, O LORD.
  You must answer for me, O Lord my God.
I prayed, "Don't let my enemies gloat over me
  or rejoice at my downfall."

I am on the verge of collapse,
  facing constant pain.
But I confess my sins;
  I am deeply sorry for what I have done.
I have many aggressive enemies;
  they hate me without reason.
They repay me evil for good
  and oppose me for pursuing good.
Do not abandon me, O LORD.
  Do not stand at a distance, my God.
Come quickly to help me,
  O Lord my savior.

PSALM 39

For Jeduthun, the choir director: A psalm of David.

I said to myself, "I will watch what I do
  and not sin in what I say.
I will hold my tongue
  when the ungodly are around me."
But as I stood there in silence—
  not even speaking of good things—
  the turmoil within me grew worse.
The more I thought about it,
  the hotter I got,
  igniting a fire of words:
"LORD, remind me how brief my time on earth will be.
  Remind me that my days are numbered—
  how fleeting my life is.
You have made my life no longer than the width of
    my hand.
  My entire lifetime is just a moment to you;
  at best, each of us is but a breath."   *Interlude*

We are merely moving shadows,
    and all our busy rushing ends in nothing.
We heap up wealth,
    not knowing who will spend it.
And so, Lord, where do I put my hope?
    My only hope is in you.
Rescue me from my rebellion.
    Do not let fools mock me.
I am silent before you; I won't say a word,
    for my punishment is from you.
But please stop striking me!
    I am exhausted by the blows from your hand.
When you discipline us for our sins,
    you consume like a moth what is precious to us.
    Each of us is but a breath.   *Interlude*

Hear my prayer, O LORD!
    Listen to my cries for help!
    Don't ignore my tears.
For I am your guest—
    a traveler passing through,
    as my ancestors were before me.
Leave me alone so I can smile again
    before I am gone and exist no more.

PSALM 40

For the choir director: A psalm of David.

I waited patiently for the LORD to help me,
    and he turned to me and heard my cry.
He lifted me out of the pit of despair,
    out of the mud and the mire.
He set my feet on solid ground
    and steadied me as I walked along.
He has given me a new song to sing,
    a hymn of praise to our God.
Many will see what he has done and be amazed.
    They will put their trust in the LORD.

Oh, the joys of those who trust the LORD,
    who have no confidence in the proud
    or in those who worship idols.
O LORD my God, you have performed many wonders for us.

Your plans for us are too numerous to list.
   You have no equal.
If I tried to recite all your wonderful deeds,
   I would never come to the end of them.

You take no delight in sacrifices or offerings.
   Now that you have made me listen, I finally understand—
   you don't require burnt offerings or sin offerings.
Then I said, "Look, I have come.
   As is written about me in the Scriptures:
I take joy in doing your will, my God,
   for your instructions are written on my heart."

I have told all your people about your justice.
   I have not been afraid to speak out,
   as you, O LORD, well know.
I have not kept the good news of your justice hidden in my heart;
   I have talked about your faithfulness and saving power.
I have told everyone in the great assembly
   of your unfailing love and faithfulness.

LORD, don't hold back your tender mercies from me.
   Let your unfailing love and faithfulness always protect me.
For troubles surround me—
   too many to count!
My sins pile up so high
   I can't see my way out.
They outnumber the hairs on my head.
   I have lost all courage.

Please, LORD, rescue me!
   Come quickly, LORD, and help me.
May those who try to destroy me
   be humiliated and put to shame.
May those who take delight in my trouble
   be turned back in disgrace.
Let them be horrified by their shame,
   for they said, "Aha! We've got him now!"

But may all who search for you
   be filled with joy and gladness in you.
May those who love your salvation
   repeatedly shout, "The LORD is great!"
As for me, since I am poor and needy,

let the Lord keep me in his thoughts.
You are my helper and my savior.
    O my God, do not delay.

PSALM 41

For the choir director: A psalm of David.

Oh, the joys of those who are kind to the poor!
    The Lord rescues them when they are in trouble.
The Lord protects them
    and keeps them alive.
He gives them prosperity in the land
    and rescues them from their enemies.
The Lord nurses them when they are sick
    and restores them to health.

"O Lord," I prayed, "have mercy on me.
    Heal me, for I have sinned against you."
But my enemies say nothing but evil about me.
    "How soon will he die and be forgotten?" they ask.
They visit me as if they were my friends,
    but all the while they gather gossip,
    and when they leave, they spread it everywhere.
All who hate me whisper about me,
    imagining the worst.
"He has some fatal disease," they say.
    "He will never get out of that bed!"
Even my best friend, the one I trusted completely,
    the one who shared my food, has turned against me.

Lord, have mercy on me.
    Make me well again, so I can pay them back!
I know you are pleased with me,
    for you have not let my enemies triumph over me.
You have preserved my life because I am innocent;
    you have brought me into your presence forever.

Praise the Lord, the God of Israel,
    who lives from everlasting to everlasting.
Amen and amen!

Book Two
(PSALMS 42–72)

PSALM 42–43
For the choir director: A psalm of the descendants of Korah.

As the deer longs for streams of water,
    so I long for you, O God.
I thirst for God, the living God.
    When can I go and stand before him?
Day and night I have only tears for food,
    while my enemies continually taunt me, saying,
    "Where is this God of yours?"

My heart is breaking
    as I remember how it used to be:
I walked among the crowds of worshipers,
    leading a great procession to the house of God,
singing for joy and giving thanks
    amid the sound of a great celebration!

Why am I discouraged?
    Why is my heart so sad?
I will put my hope in God!
    I will praise him again—
    my Savior and my God!

Now I am deeply discouraged,
    but I will remember you—
even from distant Mount Hermon, the source
        of the Jordan,
    from the land of Mount Mizar.
I hear the tumult of the raging seas
    as your waves and surging tides sweep over me.
But each day the LORD pours his unfailing love
        upon me,
    and through each night I sing his songs,
    praying to God who gives me life.

"O God my rock," I cry,
    "Why have you forgotten me?

Why must I wander around in grief,
　oppressed by my enemies?"
Their taunts break my bones.
　They scoff, "Where is this God of yours?"

Why am I discouraged?
　Why is my heart so sad?
I will put my hope in God!
　I will praise him again—
　my Savior and my God!

Declare me innocent, O God!
　Defend me against these ungodly people.
　Rescue me from these unjust liars.
For you are God, my only safe haven.
　Why have you tossed me aside?
Why must I wander around in grief,
　oppressed by my enemies?
Send out your light and your truth;
　let them guide me.
Let them lead me to your holy mountain,
　to the place where you live.
There I will go to the altar of God,
　to God—the source of all my joy.
I will praise you with my harp,
　O God, my God!

Why am I discouraged?
　Why is my heart so sad?
I will put my hope in God!
　I will praise him again—
　my Savior and my God!

PSALM 44
For the choir director: A psalm of the descendants of Korah.

O God, we have heard it with our own ears—
　our ancestors have told us
of all you did in their day,
　in days long ago:
You drove out the pagan nations by your power
　and gave all the land to our ancestors.
You crushed their enemies

and set our ancestors free.
They did not conquer the land with their swords;
    it was not their own strong arm that gave them victory.
It was your right hand and strong arm
    and the blinding light from your face that helped them,
    for you loved them.

You are my King and my God.
    You command victories for Israel.
Only by your power can we push back our enemies;
    only in your name can we trample our foes.
I do not trust in my bow;
    I do not count on my sword to save me.
You are the one who gives us victory over our enemies;
    you disgrace those who hate us.
O God, we give glory to you all day long
    and constantly praise your name.   *Interlude*

But now you have tossed us aside in dishonor.
    You no longer lead our armies to battle.
You make us retreat from our enemies
    and allow those who hate us to plunder our land.
You have butchered us like sheep
    and scattered us among the nations.
You sold your precious people for a pittance,
    making nothing on the sale.
You let our neighbors mock us.
    We are an object of scorn and derision to those around us.
You have made us the butt of their jokes;
    they shake their heads at us in scorn.
We can't escape the constant humiliation;
    shame is written across our faces.
All we hear are the taunts of our mockers.
    All we see are our vengeful enemies.

All this has happened though we have not forgotten you.
    We have not violated your covenant.
Our hearts have not deserted you.
    We have not strayed from your path.
Yet you have crushed us in the jackal's desert home.
    You have covered us with darkness and death.
If we had forgotten the name of our God
    or spread our hands in prayer to foreign gods,
God would surely have known it,

for he knows the secrets of every heart.
But for your sake we are killed every day;
    we are being slaughtered like sheep.

Wake up, O Lord! Why do you sleep?
    Get up! Do not reject us forever.
Why do you look the other way?
    Why do you ignore our suffering and oppression?
We collapse in the dust,
    lying face down in the dirt.
Rise up! Help us!
    Ransom us because of your unfailing love.

PSALM 45

For the choir director: A love song to be sung to the tune "Lilies." A psalm of the descendants of Korah.

Beautiful words stir my heart.
    I will recite a lovely poem about the king,
    for my tongue is like the pen of a skillful poet.

You are the most handsome of all.
    Gracious words stream from your lips.
    God himself has blessed you forever.
Put on your sword, O mighty warrior!
    You are so glorious, so majestic!
In your majesty, ride out to victory,
    defending truth, humility, and justice.
    Go forth to perform awe-inspiring deeds!
Your arrows are sharp, piercing your enemies' hearts.
    The nations fall beneath your feet.

Your throne, O God, endures forever and ever.
    You rule with a scepter of justice.
You love justice and hate evil.
    Therefore God, your God, has anointed you,
    pouring out the oil of joy on you more than on anyone else.
Myrrh, aloes, and cassia perfume your robes.
    In ivory palaces the music of strings entertains you.
Kings' daughters are among your noble women.
    At your right side stands the queen,
    wearing jewelry of finest gold from Ophir!

Listen to me, O royal daughter; take to heart what I say.
    Forget your people and your family far away.

For your royal husband delights in your beauty;
  honor him, for he is your lord.
The princess of Tyre will shower you with gifts.
  The wealthy will beg your favor.
The bride, a princess, looks glorious
  in her golden gown.
In her beautiful robes, she is led to the king,
  accompanied by her bridesmaids.
What a joyful and enthusiastic procession
  as they enter the king's palace!

Your sons will become kings like their father.
  You will make them rulers over many lands.
I will bring honor to your name in every generation.
  Therefore, the nations will praise you forever and ever.

PSALM 46

*For the choir director: A song of the descendants of Korah, to be sung
by soprano voices.*

God is our refuge and strength,
  always ready to help in times of trouble.
So we will not fear when earthquakes come
  and the mountains crumble into the sea.
Let the oceans roar and foam.
  Let the mountains tremble as the waters surge!   *Interlude*

A river brings joy to the city of our God,
  the sacred home of the Most High.
God dwells in that city; it cannot be destroyed.
  From the very break of day, God will protect it.
The nations are in chaos,
  and their kingdoms crumble!
God's voice thunders,
  and the earth melts!
The LORD of Heaven's Armies is here among us;
  the God of Israel is our fortress.   *Interlude*

Come, see the glorious works of the LORD:
  See how he brings destruction upon the world.
He causes wars to end throughout the earth.
  He breaks the bow and snaps the spear;
  he burns the shields with fire.

"Be still, and know that I am God!
    I will be honored by every nation.
    I will be honored throughout the world."

The LORD of Heaven's Armies is here among us;
    the God of Israel is our fortress.   *Interlude*

PSALM 47

For the choir director: A psalm of the descendants of Korah.

Come, everyone! Clap your hands!
    Shout to God with joyful praise!
For the LORD Most High is awesome.
    He is the great King of all the earth.
He subdues the nations before us,
    putting our enemies beneath our feet.
He chose the Promised Land as our inheritance,
    the proud possession of Jacob's descendants, whom
        he loves.   *Interlude*

God has ascended with a mighty shout.
    The LORD has ascended with trumpets blaring.
Sing praises to God, sing praises;
    sing praises to our King, sing praises!
For God is the King over all the earth.
    Praise him with a psalm.
God reigns above the nations,
    sitting on his holy throne.
The rulers of the world have gathered together
    with the people of the God of Abraham.
For all the kings of the earth belong to God.
    He is highly honored everywhere.

PSALM 48

A song. A psalm of the descendants of Korah.

How great is the LORD,
    how deserving of praise,
in the city of our God,
    which sits on his holy mountain!
It is high and magnificent;
    the whole earth rejoices to see it!

Mount Zion, the holy mountain,
  is the city of the great King!
God himself is in Jerusalem's towers,
  revealing himself as its defender.

The kings of the earth joined forces
  and advanced against the city.
But when they saw it, they were stunned;
  they were terrified and ran away.
They were gripped with terror
  and writhed in pain like a woman in labor.
You destroyed them like the mighty ships of Tarshish
  shattered by a powerful east wind.

We had heard of the city's glory,
  but now we have seen it ourselves—
  the city of the LORD of Heaven's Armies.
It is the city of our God;
  he will make it safe forever.   *Interlude*

O God, we meditate on your unfailing love
  as we worship in your Temple.
As your name deserves, O God,
  you will be praised to the ends of the earth.
  Your strong right hand is filled with victory.
Let the people on Mount Zion rejoice.
  Let all the towns of Judah be glad
  because of your justice.

Go, inspect the city of Jerusalem.
  Walk around and count the many towers.
Take note of the fortified walls,
  and tour all the citadels,
that you may describe them
  to future generations.
For that is what God is like.
  He is our God forever and ever,
  and he will guide us until we die.

PSALM 49

For the choir director: A psalm of the descendants of Korah.

Listen to this, all you people!
  Pay attention, everyone in the world!

High and low,
 rich and poor—listen!
For my words are wise,
 and my thoughts are filled with insight.
I listen carefully to many proverbs
 and solve riddles with inspiration from a harp.

Why should I fear when trouble comes,
 when enemies surround me?
They trust in their wealth
 and boast of great riches.
Yet they cannot redeem themselves from death
 by paying a ransom to God.
Redemption does not come so easily,
 for no one can ever pay enough
to live forever
 and never see the grave.

Those who are wise must finally die,
 just like the foolish and senseless,
 leaving all their wealth behind.
The grave is their eternal home,
 where they will stay forever.
They may name their estates after themselves,
 but their fame will not last.
 They will die, just like animals.
This is the fate of fools,
 though they are remembered as being wise.   *Interlude*

Like sheep, they are led to the grave,
 where death will be their shepherd.
In the morning the godly will rule over them.
 Their bodies will rot in the grave,
 far from their grand estates.
But as for me, God will redeem my life.
 He will snatch me from the power of the grave.   *Interlude*

So don't be dismayed when the wicked grow rich
 and their homes become ever more splendid.
For when they die, they take nothing with them.
 Their wealth will not follow them into the grave.
In this life they consider themselves fortunate
 and are applauded for their success.
But they will die like all before them

and never again see the light of day.
People who boast of their wealth don't understand;
    they will die, just like animals.

PSALM 50

A psalm of Asaph.

The LORD, the Mighty One, is God,
    and he has spoken;
he has summoned all humanity
    from where the sun rises to where it sets.
From Mount Zion, the perfection of beauty,
    God shines in glorious radiance.
Our God approaches,
    and he is not silent.
Fire devours everything in his way,
    and a great storm rages around him.
He calls on the heavens above and earth below
    to witness the judgment of his people.
"Bring my faithful people to me—
    those who made a covenant with me by giving sacrifices."
Then let the heavens proclaim his justice,
    for God himself will be the judge.   *Interlude*

"O my people, listen as I speak.
    Here are my charges against you, O Israel:
    I am God, your God!
I have no complaint about your sacrifices
    or the burnt offerings you constantly offer.
But I do not need the bulls from your barns
    or the goats from your pens.
For all the animals of the forest are mine,
    and I own the cattle on a thousand hills.
I know every bird on the mountains,
    and all the animals of the field are mine.
If I were hungry, I would not tell you,
    for all the world is mine and everything in it.
Do I eat the meat of bulls?
    Do I drink the blood of goats?
Make thankfulness your sacrifice to God,
    and keep the vows you made to the Most High.
Then call on me when you are in trouble,

and I will rescue you,
and you will give me glory."

But God says to the wicked:
"Why bother reciting my decrees
and pretending to obey my covenant?
For you refuse my discipline
and treat my words like trash.
When you see thieves, you approve of them,
and you spend your time with adulterers.
Your mouth is filled with wickedness,
and your tongue is full of lies.
You sit around and slander your brother—
your own mother's son.
While you did all this, I remained silent,
and you thought I didn't care.
But now I will rebuke you,
listing all my charges against you.
Repent, all of you who forget me,
or I will tear you apart,
and no one will help you.
But giving thanks is a sacrifice that truly honors me.
If you keep to my path,
I will reveal to you the salvation of God."

PSALM 51

For the choir director: A psalm of David, regarding the time Nathan the prophet came to him after David had committed adultery with Bathsheba.

Have mercy on me, O God,
because of your unfailing love.
Because of your great compassion,
blot out the stain of my sins.
Wash me clean from my guilt.
Purify me from my sin.
For I recognize my rebellion;
it haunts me day and night.
Against you, and you alone, have I sinned;
I have done what is evil in your sight.
You will be proved right in what you say,
and your judgment against me is just.
For I was born a sinner—
yes, from the moment my mother conceived me.

But you desire honesty from the womb,
    teaching me wisdom even there.

Purify me from my sins, and I will be clean;
    wash me, and I will be whiter than snow.
Oh, give me back my joy again;
    you have broken me—
    now let me rejoice.
Don't keep looking at my sins.
    Remove the stain of my guilt.
Create in me a clean heart, O God.
    Renew a loyal spirit within me.
Do not banish me from your presence,
    and don't take your Holy Spirit from me.

Restore to me the joy of your salvation,
    and make me willing to obey you.
Then I will teach your ways to rebels,
    and they will return to you.
Forgive me for shedding blood, O God who saves;
    then I will joyfully sing of your forgiveness.
Unseal my lips, O Lord,
    that my mouth may praise you.

You do not desire a sacrifice, or I would offer one.
    You do not want a burnt offering.
The sacrifice you desire is a broken spirit.
    You will not reject a broken and repentant heart, O God.
Look with favor on Zion and help her;
    rebuild the walls of Jerusalem.
Then you will be pleased with sacrifices offered in the right spirit—
    with burnt offerings and whole burnt offerings.
    Then bulls will again be sacrificed on your altar.

PSALM 52

*For the choir director: A psalm of David, regarding the time Doeg the Edomite said
to Saul, "David has gone to see Ahimelech."*

Why do you boast about your crimes, great warrior?
    Don't you realize God's justice continues forever?
All day long you plot destruction.
    Your tongue cuts like a sharp razor;
    you're an expert at telling lies.

You love evil more than good
 and lies more than truth.   *Interlude*

You love to destroy others with your words,
 you liar!
But God will strike you down once and for all.
 He will pull you from your home
 and uproot you from the land of the living. *Interlude*

The righteous will see it and be amazed.
 They will laugh and say,
"Look what happens to mighty warriors
 who do not trust in God.
They trust their wealth instead
 and grow more and more bold in their wickedness."

But I am like an olive tree, thriving in the house of God.
 I will always trust in God's unfailing love.
I will praise you forever, O God,
 for what you have done.
I will trust in your good name
 in the presence of your faithful people.

PSALM 53

For the choir director: A meditation; a psalm of David.

Only fools say in their hearts,
 "There is no God."
They are corrupt, and their actions are evil;
 not one of them does good!

God looks down from heaven
 on the entire human race;
he looks to see if anyone is truly wise,
 if anyone seeks God.
But no, all have turned away;
 all have become corrupt.
No one does good,
 not a single one!

Will those who do evil never learn?
 They eat up my people like bread
 and wouldn't think of praying to God.
Terror will grip them,

terror like they have never known before.
God will scatter the bones of your enemies.
You will put them to shame, for God has rejected them.

Who will come from Mount Zion to rescue Israel?
When God restores his people,
Jacob will shout with joy, and Israel will rejoice.

PSALM 54

For the choir director: A psalm of David, regarding the time the Ziphites came and said to Saul, "We know where David is hiding." To be accompanied by stringed instruments.

Come with great power, O God, and rescue me!
Defend me with your might.
Listen to my prayer, O God.
Pay attention to my plea.
For strangers are attacking me;
violent people are trying to kill me.
They care nothing for God.   *Interlude*

But God is my helper.
The Lord keeps me alive!
May the evil plans of my enemies be turned against them.
Do as you promised and put an end to them.

I will sacrifice a voluntary offering to you;
I will praise your name, O Lord,
for it is good.
For you have rescued me from my troubles
and helped me to triumph over my enemies.

PSALM 55

For the choir director: A psalm of David, to be accompanied by stringed instruments.

Listen to my prayer, O God.
Do not ignore my cry for help!
Please listen and answer me,
for I am overwhelmed by my troubles.
My enemies shout at me,
making loud and wicked threats.
They bring trouble on me
and angrily hunt me down.

My heart pounds in my chest.
    The terror of death assaults me.
Fear and trembling overwhelm me,
    and I can't stop shaking.
Oh, that I had wings like a dove;
    then I would fly away and rest!
I would fly far away
    to the quiet of the wilderness.   *Interlude*
How quickly I would escape—
    far from this wild storm of hatred.

Confuse them, Lord, and frustrate their plans,
    for I see violence and conflict in the city.
Its walls are patrolled day and night against invaders,
    but the real danger is wickedness within the city.
Everything is falling apart;
    threats and cheating are rampant in the streets.

It is not an enemy who taunts me—
    I could bear that.
It is not my foes who so arrogantly insult me—
    I could have hidden from them.
Instead, it is you—my equal,
    my companion and close friend.
What good fellowship we once enjoyed
    as we walked together to the house of God.

Let death stalk my enemies;
    let the grave swallow them alive,
    for evil makes its home within them.

But I will call on God,
    and the LORD will rescue me.
Morning, noon, and night
    I cry out in my distress,
    and the LORD hears my voice.
He ransoms me and keeps me safe
    from the battle waged against me,
    though many still oppose me.
God, who has ruled forever,
    will hear me and humble them.   *Interlude*
For my enemies refuse to change their ways;
    they do not fear God.

As for my companion, he betrayed his friends;
he broke his promises.
His words are as smooth as butter,
but in his heart is war.
His words are as soothing as lotion,
but underneath are daggers!

Give your burdens to the LORD,
and he will take care of you.
He will not permit the godly to slip and fall.

But you, O God, will send the wicked
down to the pit of destruction.
Murderers and liars will die young,
but I am trusting you to save me.

PSALM 56

For the choir director: A psalm of David, regarding the time the Philistines seized him in Gath. To be sung to the tune "Dove on Distant Oaks."

O God, have mercy on me,
for people are hounding me.
My foes attack me all day long.
I am constantly hounded by those who slander me,
and many are boldly attacking me.
But when I am afraid,
I will put my trust in you.
I praise God for what he has promised.
I trust in God, so why should I be afraid?
What can mere mortals do to me?

They are always twisting what I say;
they spend their days plotting to harm me.
They come together to spy on me—
watching my every step, eager to kill me.
Don't let them get away with their wickedness;
in your anger, O God, bring them down.

You keep track of all my sorrows.
You have collected all my tears in your bottle.
You have recorded each one in your book.

My enemies will retreat when I call to you for help.
This I know: God is on my side!

I praise God for what he has promised;
yes, I praise the LORD for what he has promised.
I trust in God, so why should I be afraid?
What can mere mortals do to me?

I will fulfill my vows to you, O God,
and will offer a sacrifice of thanks for your help.
For you have rescued me from death;
you have kept my feet from slipping.
So now I can walk in your presence, O God,
in your life-giving light.

PSALM 57

For the choir director: A psalm of David, regarding the time he fled from Saul and went into the cave. To be sung to the tune "Do Not Destroy!"

Have mercy on me, O God, have mercy!
I look to you for protection.
I will hide beneath the shadow of your wings
until the danger passes by.
I cry out to God Most High,
to God who will fulfill his purpose for me.
He will send help from heaven to rescue me,
disgracing those who hound me.   *Interlude*
My God will send forth his unfailing love and faithfulness.

I am surrounded by fierce lions
who greedily devour human prey—
whose teeth pierce like spears and arrows,
and whose tongues cut like swords.

Be exalted, O God, above the highest heavens!
May your glory shine over all the earth.

My enemies have set a trap for me.
I am weary from distress.
They have dug a deep pit in my path,
but they themselves have fallen into it.   *Interlude*

My heart is confident in you, O God;
my heart is confident.
No wonder I can sing your praises!
Wake up, my heart!
Wake up, O lyre and harp!
I will wake the dawn with my song.

I will thank you, Lord, among all the people.
    I will sing your praises among the nations.
For your unfailing love is as high as the heavens.
    Your faithfulness reaches to the clouds.

Be exalted, O God, above the highest heavens.
    May your glory shine over all the earth.

PSALM 58

For the choir director: A psalm of David, to be sung to the tune "Do Not Destroy!"

Justice—do you rulers know the meaning of the word?
    Do you judge the people fairly?
No! You plot injustice in your hearts.
    You spread violence throughout the land.
These wicked people are born sinners;
    even from birth they have lied and gone their own way.
They spit venom like deadly snakes;
    they are like cobras that refuse to listen,
ignoring the tunes of the snake charmers,
    no matter how skillfully they play.

Break off their fangs, O God!
    Smash the jaws of these lions, O LORD!
May they disappear like water into thirsty ground.
    Make their weapons useless in their hands.
May they be like snails that dissolve into slime,
    like a stillborn child who will never see the sun.
God will sweep them away, both young and old,
    faster than a pot heats over burning thorns.

The godly will rejoice when they see injustice avenged.
    They will wash their feet in the blood of the wicked.
Then at last everyone will say,
    "There truly is a reward for those who live for God;
    surely there is a God who judges justly here on earth."

PSALM 59

For the choir director: A psalm of David, regarding the time Saul sent soldiers to watch David's house in order to kill him. To be sung to the tune "Do Not Destroy!"

Rescue me from my enemies, O God.
    Protect me from those who have come to destroy me.

Rescue me from these criminals;
   save me from these murderers.
They have set an ambush for me.
   Fierce enemies are out there waiting, LORD,
   though I have not sinned or offended them.
I have done nothing wrong,
   yet they prepare to attack me.
   Wake up! See what is happening and help me!
O LORD God of Heaven's Armies, the God of Israel,
   wake up and punish those hostile nations.
   Show no mercy to wicked traitors.   *Interlude*

They come out at night,
   snarling like vicious dogs
   as they prowl the streets.
Listen to the filth that comes from their mouths;
   their words cut like swords.
   "After all, who can hear us?" they sneer.
But LORD, you laugh at them.
   You scoff at all the hostile nations.
You are my strength; I wait for you to rescue me,
   for you, O God, are my fortress.
In his unfailing love, my God will stand with me.
   He will let me look down in triumph on all my enemies.

Don't kill them, for my people soon forget such lessons;
   stagger them with your power, and bring them to
      their knees,
   O Lord our shield.
Because of the sinful things they say,
   because of the evil that is on their lips,
let them be captured by their pride,
   their curses, and their lies.
Destroy them in your anger!
   Wipe them out completely!
Then the whole world will know
   that God reigns in Israel.   *Interlude*

My enemies come out at night,
   snarling like vicious dogs
   as they prowl the streets.
They scavenge for food
   but go to sleep unsatisfied.

But as for me, I will sing about your power.
    Each morning I will sing with joy about your unfailing love.
For you have been my refuge,
    a place of safety when I am in distress.
O my Strength, to you I sing praises,
    for you, O God, are my refuge,
        the God who shows me unfailing love.

PSALM 60

*For the choir director: A psalm of David useful for teaching, regarding the time
David fought Aram-naharaim and Aram-zobah, and Joab returned and killed
12,000 Edomites in the Valley of Salt. To be sung to the tune "Lily of the Testimony."*

You have rejected us, O God, and broken our defenses.
    You have been angry with us; now restore us to your favor.
You have shaken our land and split it open.
    Seal the cracks, for the land trembles.
You have been very hard on us,
    making us drink wine that sent us reeling.
But you have raised a banner for those who fear you—
    a rallying point in the face of attack.   *Interlude*

Now rescue your beloved people.
    Answer and save us by your power.
God has promised this by his holiness:
"I will divide up Shechem with joy.
    I will measure out the valley of Succoth.
Gilead is mine,
    and Manasseh, too.
Ephraim, my helmet, will produce my warriors,
    and Judah, my scepter, will produce my kings.
But Moab, my washbasin, will become my servant,
    and I will wipe my feet on Edom
    and shout in triumph over Philistia."

Who will bring me into the fortified city?
    Who will bring me victory over Edom?
Have you rejected us, O God?
    Will you no longer march with our armies?
Oh, please help us against our enemies,
    for all human help is useless.
With God's help we will do mighty things,
    for he will trample down our foes.

PSALM 61

For the choir director: A psalm of David, to be accompanied by stringed instruments.

O God, listen to my cry!
    Hear my prayer!
From the ends of the earth,
    I cry to you for help
    when my heart is overwhelmed.
Lead me to the towering rock of safety,
    for you are my safe refuge,
    a fortress where my enemies cannot reach me.
Let me live forever in your sanctuary,
    safe beneath the shelter of your wings!   *Interlude*

For you have heard my vows, O God.
    You have given me an inheritance reserved for those who
        fear your name.
Add many years to the life of the king!
    May his years span the generations!
May he reign under God's protection forever.
    May your unfailing love and faithfulness watch over him.
Then I will sing praises to your name forever
    as I fulfill my vows each day.

PSALM 62

For Jeduthun, the choir director: A psalm of David.

I wait quietly before God,
    for my victory comes from him.
He alone is my rock and my salvation,
    my fortress where I will never be shaken.

So many enemies against one man—
    all of them trying to kill me.
To them I'm just a broken-down wall
    or a tottering fence.
They plan to topple me from my high position.
    They delight in telling lies about me.
They praise me to my face
    but curse me in their hearts.   *Interlude*

Let all that I am wait quietly before God,
    for my hope is in him.

He alone is my rock and my salvation,
　my fortress where I will not be shaken.
My victory and honor come from God alone.
　He is my refuge, a rock where no enemy can reach me.
O my people, trust in him at all times.
　Pour out your heart to him,
　for God is our refuge.　　　　　　　　　　*Interlude*

Common people are as worthless as a puff of wind,
　and the powerful are not what they appear to be.
If you weigh them on the scales,
　together they are lighter than a breath of air.

Don't make your living by extortion
　or put your hope in stealing.
And if your wealth increases,
　don't make it the center of your life.

God has spoken plainly,
　and I have heard it many times:
Power, O God, belongs to you;
　unfailing love, O Lord, is yours.
Surely you repay all people
　according to what they have done.

PSALM 63
A psalm of David, regarding a time when David was in the wilderness of Judah.

O God, you are my God;
　I earnestly search for you.
My soul thirsts for you;
　my whole body longs for you
in this parched and weary land
　where there is no water.
I have seen you in your sanctuary
　and gazed upon your power and glory.
Your unfailing love is better than life itself;
　how I praise you!
I will praise you as long as I live,
　lifting up my hands to you in prayer.
You satisfy me more than the richest feast.
　I will praise you with songs of joy.

I lie awake thinking of you,
 meditating on you through the night.
Because you are my helper,
 I sing for joy in the shadow of your wings.
I cling to you;
 your strong right hand holds me securely.

But those plotting to destroy me will come to ruin.
 They will go down into the depths of the earth.
They will die by the sword
 and become the food of jackals.
But the king will rejoice in God.
 All who swear to tell the truth will praise him,
 while liars will be silenced.

PSALM 64

For the choir director: A psalm of David.

O God, listen to my complaint.
 Protect my life from my enemies' threats.
Hide me from the plots of this evil mob,
 from this gang of wrongdoers.
They sharpen their tongues like swords
 and aim their bitter words like arrows.
They shoot from ambush at the innocent,
 attacking suddenly and fearlessly.
They encourage each other to do evil
 and plan how to set their traps in secret.
 "Who will ever notice?" they ask.
As they plot their crimes, they say,
 "We have devised the perfect plan!"
 Yes, the human heart and mind are cunning.

But God himself will shoot them with his arrows,
 suddenly striking them down.
Their own tongues will ruin them,
 and all who see them will shake their heads in scorn.
Then everyone will be afraid;
 they will proclaim the mighty acts of God
 and realize all the amazing things he does.
The godly will rejoice in the LORD
 and find shelter in him.
And those who do what is right
 will praise him.

PSALM 65

For the choir director: A song. A psalm of David.

What mighty praise, O God,
    belongs to you in Zion.
We will fulfill our vows to you,
    for you answer our prayers.
    All of us must come to you.
Though we are overwhelmed by our sins,
    you forgive them all.
What joy for those you choose to bring near,
    those who live in your holy courts.
What festivities await us
    inside your holy Temple.

You faithfully answer our prayers with awesome deeds,
    O God our savior.
You are the hope of everyone on earth,
    even those who sail on distant seas.
You formed the mountains by your power
    and armed yourself with mighty strength.
You quieted the raging oceans
    with their pounding waves
    and silenced the shouting of the nations.
Those who live at the ends of the earth
    stand in awe of your wonders.
From where the sun rises to where it sets,
    you inspire shouts of joy.

You take care of the earth and water it,
    making it rich and fertile.
The river of God has plenty of water;
    it provides a bountiful harvest of grain,
    for you have ordered it so.
You drench the plowed ground with rain,
    melting the clods and leveling the ridges.
You soften the earth with showers
    and bless its abundant crops.
You crown the year with a bountiful harvest;
    even the hard pathways overflow with abundance.
The grasslands of the wilderness become a lush pasture,
    and the hillsides blossom with joy.
The meadows are clothed with flocks of sheep,

and the valleys are carpeted with grain.
They all shout and sing for joy!

PSALM 66
For the choir director: A song. A psalm.

Shout joyful praises to God, all the earth!
   Sing about the glory of his name!
   Tell the world how glorious he is.
Say to God, "How awesome are your deeds!
   Your enemies cringe before your mighty power.
Everything on earth will worship you;
   they will sing your praises,
   shouting your name in glorious songs."   *Interlude*

Come and see what our God has done,
   what awesome miracles he performs for people!
He made a dry path through the Red Sea,
   and his people went across on foot.
   There we rejoiced in him.
For by his great power he rules forever.
   He watches every movement of the nations;
   let no rebel rise in defiance.   *Interlude*

Let the whole world bless our God
   and loudly sing his praises.
Our lives are in his hands,
   and he keeps our feet from stumbling.
You have tested us, O God;
   you have purified us like silver.
You captured us in your net
   and laid the burden of slavery on our backs.
Then you put a leader over us.
   We went through fire and flood,
   but you brought us to a place of great abundance.

Now I come to your Temple with burnt offerings
   to fulfill the vows I made to you—
yes, the sacred vows that I made
   when I was in deep trouble.
That is why I am sacrificing burnt offerings to you—
   the best of my rams as a pleasing aroma,
   and a sacrifice of bulls and male goats.   *Interlude*

Come and listen, all you who fear God,
    and I will tell you what he did for me.
For I cried out to him for help,
    praising him as I spoke.
If I had not confessed the sin in my heart,
    the Lord would not have listened.
But God did listen!
    He paid attention to my prayer.
Praise God, who did not ignore my prayer
    or withdraw his unfailing love from me.

PSALM 67
For the choir director: A song. A psalm, to be accompanied by stringed instruments.

May God be merciful and bless us.
    May his face smile with favor on us.   *Interlude*

May your ways be known throughout the earth,
    your saving power among people everywhere.
May the nations praise you, O God.
    Yes, may all the nations praise you.
Let the whole world sing for joy,
    because you govern the nations with justice
    and guide the people of the whole world.   *Interlude*

May the nations praise you, O God.
    Yes, may all the nations praise you.
Then the earth will yield its harvests,
    and God, our God, will richly bless us.
Yes, God will bless us,
    and people all over the world will fear him.

PSALM 68
For the choir director: A song. A psalm of David.

Rise up, O God, and scatter your enemies.
    Let those who hate God run for their lives.
Blow them away like smoke.
    Melt them like wax in a fire.
    Let the wicked perish in the presence of God.
But let the godly rejoice.
    Let them be glad in God's presence.
    Let them be filled with joy.

Sing praises to God and to his name!
　Sing loud praises to him who rides the clouds.
His name is the LORD—
　rejoice in his presence!

Father to the fatherless, defender of widows—
　this is God, whose dwelling is holy.
God places the lonely in families;
　he sets the prisoners free and gives them joy.
But he makes the rebellious live in a sun-scorched land.

O God, when you led your people out from Egypt,
　when you marched through the dry wasteland,　　　　*Interlude*
the earth trembled, and the heavens poured down rain
　before you, the God of Sinai,
　before God, the God of Israel.
You sent abundant rain, O God,
　to refresh the weary land.
There your people finally settled,
　and with a bountiful harvest, O God,
　you provided for your needy people.

The Lord gives the word,
　and a great army brings the good news.
Enemy kings and their armies flee,
　while the women of Israel divide the plunder.
Even those who lived among the sheepfolds found treasures—
　doves with wings of silver
　and feathers of gold.
The Almighty scattered the enemy kings
　like a blowing snowstorm on Mount Zalmon.

The mountains of Bashan are majestic,
　with many peaks stretching high into the sky.
Why do you look with envy, O rugged mountains,
　at Mount Zion, where God has chosen to live,
　where the LORD himself will live forever?

Surrounded by unnumbered thousands of chariots,
　the Lord came from Mount Sinai into his sanctuary.
When you ascended to the heights,
　you led a crowd of captives.
You received gifts from the people,
　even from those who rebelled against you.
　Now the LORD God will live among us there.

Praise the Lord; praise God our savior!
    For each day he carries us in his arms.   *Interlude*
Our God is a God who saves!
    The Sovereign LORD rescues us from death.

But God will smash the heads of his enemies,
    crushing the skulls of those who love their guilty ways.
The Lord says, "I will bring my enemies down from Bashan;
    I will bring them up from the depths of the sea.
You, my people, will wash your feet in their blood,
    and even your dogs will get their share!"

Your procession has come into view, O God—
    the procession of my God and King as he goes into the sanctuary.
Singers are in front, musicians behind;
    between them are young women playing tambourines.
Praise God, all you people of Israel;
    praise the LORD, the source of Israel's life.
Look, the little tribe of Benjamin leads the way.
    Then comes a great throng of rulers from Judah
    and all the rulers of Zebulun and Naphtali.

Summon your might, O God.
    Display your power, O God, as you have in the past.
The kings of the earth are bringing tribute
    to your Temple in Jerusalem.
Rebuke these enemy nations—
    these wild animals lurking in the reeds,
    this herd of bulls among the weaker calves.
Make them bring bars of silver in humble tribute.
    Scatter the nations that delight in war.
Let Egypt come with gifts of precious metals;
    let Ethiopia bring tribute to God.
Sing to God, you kingdoms of the earth.
    Sing praises to the Lord.   *Interlude*
Sing to the one who rides across the ancient heavens,
    his mighty voice thundering from the sky.
Tell everyone about God's power.
    His majesty shines down on Israel;
    his strength is mighty in the heavens.
God is awesome in his sanctuary.
    The God of Israel gives power and strength to his people.

Praise be to God!

PSALM 69

For the choir director: A psalm of David, to be sung to the tune "Lilies."

Save me, O God,
   for the floodwaters are up to my neck.
Deeper and deeper I sink into the mire;
   I can't find a foothold.
I am in deep water,
   and the floods overwhelm me.
I am exhausted from crying for help;
   my throat is parched.
My eyes are swollen with weeping,
   waiting for my God to help me.
Those who hate me without cause
   outnumber the hairs on my head.
Many enemies try to destroy me with lies,
   demanding that I give back what I didn't steal.

O God, you know how foolish I am;
   my sins cannot be hidden from you.
Don't let those who trust in you be ashamed because of me,
   O Sovereign LORD of Heaven's Armies.
Don't let me cause them to be humiliated,
   O God of Israel.
For I endure insults for your sake;
   humiliation is written all over my face.
Even my own brothers pretend they don't know me;
   they treat me like a stranger.

Passion for your house has consumed me,
   and the insults of those who insult you have fallen on me.
When I weep and fast,
   they scoff at me.
When I dress in burlap to show sorrow,
   they make fun of me.
I am the favorite topic of town gossip,
   and all the drunks sing about me.

But I keep praying to you, LORD,
   hoping this time you will show me favor.
In your unfailing love, O God,
   answer my prayer with your sure salvation.
Rescue me from the mud;
   don't let me sink any deeper!

Save me from those who hate me,
   and pull me from these deep waters.
Don't let the floods overwhelm me,
   or the deep waters swallow me,
   or the pit of death devour me.

Answer my prayers, O Lord,
   for your unfailing love is wonderful.
Take care of me,
   for your mercy is so plentiful.
Don't hide from your servant;
   answer me quickly, for I am in deep trouble!
Come and redeem me;
   free me from my enemies.

You know of my shame, scorn, and disgrace.
   You see all that my enemies are doing.
Their insults have broken my heart,
   and I am in despair.
If only one person would show some pity;
   if only one would turn and comfort me.
But instead, they give me poison for food;
   they offer me sour wine for my thirst.

Let the bountiful table set before them become a snare
   and their prosperity become a trap.
Let their eyes go blind so they cannot see,
   and make their bodies shake continually.
Pour out your fury on them;
   consume them with your burning anger.
Let their homes become desolate
   and their tents be deserted.
To the one you have punished, they add insult to injury;
   they add to the pain of those you have hurt.
Pile their sins up high,
   and don't let them go free.
Erase their names from the Book of Life;
   don't let them be counted among the righteous.

I am suffering and in pain.
   Rescue me, O God, by your saving power.

Then I will praise God's name with singing,
   and I will honor him with thanksgiving.

For this will please the LORD more than sacrificing cattle,
　　more than presenting a bull with its horns and hooves.
The humble will see their God at work and be glad.
　　Let all who seek God's help be encouraged.
For the LORD hears the cries of the needy;
　　he does not despise his imprisoned people.

Praise him, O heaven and earth,
　　the seas and all that move in them.
For God will save Jerusalem
　　and rebuild the towns of Judah.
His people will live there
　　and settle in their own land.
The descendants of those who obey him will inherit the land,
　　and those who love him will live there in safety.

PSALM 70

For the choir director: A psalm of David, asking God to remember him.

Please, God, rescue me!
　　Come quickly, LORD, and help me.
May those who try to kill me
　　be humiliated and put to shame.
May those who take delight in my trouble
　　be turned back in disgrace.
Let them be horrified by their shame,
　　for they said, "Aha! We've got him now!"
But may all who search for you
　　be filled with joy and gladness in you.
May those who love your salvation
　　repeatedly shout, "God is great!"
But as for me, I am poor and needy;
　　please hurry to my aid, O God.
You are my helper and my savior;
　　O LORD, do not delay.

PSALM 71

O LORD, I have come to you for protection;
　　don't let me be disgraced.
Save me and rescue me,
　　for you do what is right.

Turn your ear to listen to me,
   and set me free.
Be my rock of safety
   where I can always hide.
Give the order to save me,
   for you are my rock and my fortress.
My God, rescue me from the power of the wicked,
   from the clutches of cruel oppressors.
O Lord, you alone are my hope.
   I've trusted you, O LORD, from childhood.
Yes, you have been with me from birth;
   from my mother's womb you have cared for me.
   No wonder I am always praising you!

My life is an example to many,
   because you have been my strength and protection.
That is why I can never stop praising you;
   I declare your glory all day long.
And now, in my old age, don't set me aside.
   Don't abandon me when my strength is failing.
For my enemies are whispering against me.
   They are plotting together to kill me.
They say, "God has abandoned him.
   Let's go and get him,
   for no one will help him now."

O God, don't stay away.
   My God, please hurry to help me.
Bring disgrace and destruction on my accusers.
   Humiliate and shame those who want to harm me.
But I will keep on hoping for your help;
   I will praise you more and more.
I will tell everyone about your righteousness.
   All day long I will proclaim your saving power,
   though I am not skilled with words.
I will praise your mighty deeds, O Sovereign LORD.
   I will tell everyone that you alone are just.

O God, you have taught me from my earliest childhood,
   and I constantly tell others about the wonderful things
     you do.
Now that I am old and gray,
   do not abandon me, O God.

Let me proclaim your power to this new generation,
　　your mighty miracles to all who come after me.

Your righteousness, O God, reaches to the highest heavens.
　　You have done such wonderful things.
　　Who can compare with you, O God?
You have allowed me to suffer much hardship,
　　but you will restore me to life again
　　and lift me up from the depths of the earth.
You will restore me to even greater honor
　　and comfort me once again.

Then I will praise you with music on the harp,
　　because you are faithful to your promises, O my God.
I will sing praises to you with a lyre,
　　O Holy One of Israel.
I will shout for joy and sing your praises,
　　for you have ransomed me.
I will tell about your righteous deeds
　　all day long,
for everyone who tried to hurt me
　　has been shamed and humiliated.

PSALM 72

A psalm of Solomon.

Give your love of justice to the king, O God,
　　and righteousness to the king's son.
Help him judge your people in the right way;
　　let the poor always be treated fairly.
May the mountains yield prosperity for all,
　　and may the hills be fruitful.
Help him to defend the poor,
　　to rescue the children of the needy,
　　and to crush their oppressors.
May they fear you as long as the sun shines,
　　as long as the moon remains in the sky.
　　Yes, forever!

May the king's rule be refreshing like spring rain on freshly cut grass,
　　like the showers that water the earth.
May all the godly flourish during his reign.
　　May there be abundant prosperity until the moon is no more.

May he reign from sea to sea,
   and from the Euphrates River to the ends of the earth.
Desert nomads will bow before him;
   his enemies will fall before him in the dust.
The western kings of Tarshish and other distant lands
   will bring him tribute.
The eastern kings of Sheba and Seba
   will bring him gifts.
All kings will bow before him,
   and all nations will serve him.

He will rescue the poor when they cry to him;
   he will help the oppressed, who have no one to defend them.
He feels pity for the weak and the needy,
   and he will rescue them.
He will redeem them from oppression and violence,
   for their lives are precious to him.

Long live the king!
   May the gold of Sheba be given to him.
May the people always pray for him
   and bless him all day long.
May there be abundant grain throughout the land,
   flourishing even on the hilltops.
May the fruit trees flourish like the trees of Lebanon,
   and may the people thrive like grass in a field.
May the king's name endure forever;
   may it continue as long as the sun shines.
May all nations be blessed through him
   and bring him praise.

Praise the LORD God, the God of Israel,
   who alone does such wonderful things.
Praise his glorious name forever!
   Let the whole earth be filled with his glory.
Amen and amen!

(This ends the prayers of David son of Jesse.)

Book Three

(PSALMS 73-89)

PSALM 73
A psalm of Asaph.

Truly God is good to Israel,
  to those whose hearts are pure.
But as for me, I almost lost my footing.
  My feet were slipping, and I was almost gone.
For I envied the proud
  when I saw them prosper despite their wickedness.
They seem to live such painless lives;
  their bodies are so healthy and strong.
They don't have troubles like other people;
  they're not plagued with problems like everyone else.
They wear pride like a jeweled necklace
  and clothe themselves with cruelty.
These fat cats have everything
  their hearts could ever wish for!
They scoff and speak only evil;
  in their pride they seek to crush others.
They boast against the very heavens,
  and their words strut throughout the earth.
And so the people are dismayed and confused,
  drinking in all their words.
"What does God know?" they ask.
  "Does the Most High even know what's happening?"
Look at these wicked people—
  enjoying a life of ease while their riches multiply.

Did I keep my heart pure for nothing?
  Did I keep myself innocent for no reason?
I get nothing but trouble all day long;
  every morning brings me pain.

If I had really spoken this way to others,
  I would have been a traitor to your people.
So I tried to understand why the wicked prosper.
  But what a difficult task it is!

Then I went into your sanctuary, O God,
    and I finally understood the destiny of the wicked.
Truly, you put them on a slippery path
    and send them sliding over the cliff to destruction.
In an instant they are destroyed,
    completely swept away by terrors.
When you arise, O Lord,
    you will laugh at their silly ideas
    as a person laughs at dreams in the morning.

Then I realized that my heart was bitter,
    and I was all torn up inside.
I was so foolish and ignorant—
    I must have seemed like a senseless animal to you.
Yet I still belong to you;
    you hold my right hand.
You guide me with your counsel,
    leading me to a glorious destiny.
Whom have I in heaven but you?
    I desire you more than anything on earth.
My health may fail, and my spirit may grow weak,
    but God remains the strength of my heart;
    he is mine forever.

Those who desert him will perish,
    for you destroy those who abandon you.
But as for me, how good it is to be near God!
    I have made the Sovereign LORD my shelter,
    and I will tell everyone about the wonderful things you do.

PSALM 74
A psalm of Asaph.

O God, why have you rejected us so long?
    Why is your anger so intense against the sheep of your own pasture?
Remember that we are the people you chose long ago,
    the tribe you redeemed as your own special possession!
    And remember Jerusalem, your home here on earth.
Walk through the awful ruins of the city;
    see how the enemy has destroyed your sanctuary.

There your enemies shouted their victorious battle cries;
    there they set up their battle standards.

They swung their axes
   like woodcutters in a forest.
With axes and picks,
   they smashed the carved paneling.
They burned your sanctuary to the ground.
   They defiled the place that bears your name.
Then they thought, "Let's destroy everything!"
   So they burned down all the places where God was worshiped.

We no longer see your miraculous signs.
   All the prophets are gone,
   and no one can tell us when it will end.
How long, O God, will you allow our enemies to insult you?
   Will you let them dishonor your name forever?
Why do you hold back your strong right hand?
   Unleash your powerful fist and destroy them.

You, O God, are my king from ages past,
   bringing salvation to the earth.
You split the sea by your strength
   and smashed the heads of the sea monsters.
You crushed the heads of Leviathan
   and let the desert animals eat him.
You caused the springs and streams to gush forth,
   and you dried up rivers that never run dry.
Both day and night belong to you;
   you made the starlight and the sun.
You set the boundaries of the earth,
   and you made both summer and winter.

See how these enemies insult you, LORD.
   A foolish nation has dishonored your name.
Don't let these wild beasts destroy your turtledoves.
   Don't forget your suffering people forever.

Remember your covenant promises,
   for the land is full of darkness and violence!
Don't let the downtrodden be humiliated again.
   Instead, let the poor and needy praise your name.

Arise, O God, and defend your cause.
   Remember how these fools insult you all day long.
Don't overlook what your enemies have said
   or their growing uproar.

PSALM 75

For the choir director: A psalm of Asaph. A song to be sung to the tune "Do Not Destroy!"

We thank you, O God!
    We give thanks because you are near.
    People everywhere tell of your wonderful deeds.

God says, "At the time I have planned,
    I will bring justice against the wicked.
When the earth quakes and its people live in turmoil,
    I am the one who keeps its foundations firm.   *Interlude*

"I warned the proud, 'Stop your boasting!'
    I told the wicked, 'Don't raise your fists!
Don't raise your fists in defiance at the heavens
    or speak with such arrogance.'"
For no one on earth—from east or west,
    or even from the wilderness—
    should raise a defiant fist.
It is God alone who judges;
    he decides who will rise and who will fall.
For the Lord holds a cup in his hand
    that is full of foaming wine mixed with spices.
He pours out the wine in judgment,
    and all the wicked must drink it,
    draining it to the dregs.

But as for me, I will always proclaim what God has done;
    I will sing praises to the God of Jacob.
For God says, "I will break the strength of the
        wicked,
    but I will increase the power of the godly."

PSALM 76

For the choir director: A psalm of Asaph. A song to be accompanied by stringed instruments.

God is honored in Judah;
    his name is great in Israel.
Jerusalem is where he lives;
    Mount Zion is his home.
There he has broken the fiery arrows of the enemy,
    the shields and swords and weapons of war.   *Interlude*

You are glorious and more majestic
 than the everlasting mountains.
Our boldest enemies have been plundered.
 They lie before us in the sleep of death.
 No warrior could lift a hand against us.
At the blast of your breath, O God of Jacob,
 their horses and chariots lay still.

No wonder you are greatly feared!
 Who can stand before you when your anger explodes?
From heaven you sentenced your enemies;
 the earth trembled and stood silent before you.
You stand up to judge those who do evil, O God,
 and to rescue the oppressed of the earth.   *Interlude*
Human defiance only enhances your glory,
 for you use it as a weapon.

Make vows to the LORD your God, and keep them.
 Let everyone bring tribute to the Awesome One.
For he breaks the pride of princes,
 and the kings of the earth fear him.

PSALM 77
For Jeduthun, the choir director: A psalm of Asaph.

I cry out to God; yes, I shout.
 Oh, that God would listen to me!
When I was in deep trouble,
 I searched for the Lord.
All night long I prayed, with hands lifted toward heaven,
 but my soul was not comforted.
I think of God, and I moan,
 overwhelmed with longing for his help.   *Interlude*

You don't let me sleep.
 I am too distressed even to pray!
I think of the good old days,
 long since ended,
when my nights were filled with joyful songs.
 I search my soul and ponder the difference now.
Has the Lord rejected me forever?
 Will he never again be kind to me?
Is his unfailing love gone forever?
 Have his promises permanently failed?

Has God forgotten to be gracious?
　　Has he slammed the door on his compassion?　　　　*Interlude*

And I said, "This is my fate;
　　the Most High has turned his hand against me."
But then I recall all you have done, O LORD;
　　I remember your wonderful deeds of long ago.
They are constantly in my thoughts.
　　I cannot stop thinking about your mighty works.

O God, your ways are holy.
　　Is there any god as mighty as you?
You are the God of great wonders!
　　You demonstrate your awesome power among the nations.
By your strong arm, you redeemed your people,
　　the descendants of Jacob and Joseph.　　　　*Interlude*

When the Red Sea saw you, O God,
　　its waters looked and trembled!
　　The sea quaked to its very depths.
The clouds poured down rain;
　　the thunder rumbled in the sky.
　　Your arrows of lightning flashed.
Your thunder roared from the whirlwind;
　　the lightning lit up the world!
　　The earth trembled and shook.
Your road led through the sea,
　　your pathway through the mighty waters—
　　a pathway no one knew was there!
You led your people along that road like a flock of sheep,
　　with Moses and Aaron as their shepherds.

PSALM 78
A psalm of Asaph.

O my people, listen to my instructions.
　　Open your ears to what I am saying,
　　for I will speak to you in a parable.
I will teach you hidden lessons from our past—
　　stories we have heard and known,
　　stories our ancestors handed down to us.
We will not hide these truths from our children;
　　we will tell the next generation

about the glorious deeds of the LORD,
    about his power and his mighty wonders.
For he issued his laws to Jacob;
    he gave his instructions to Israel.
He commanded our ancestors
    to teach them to their children,
so the next generation might know them—
    even the children not yet born—
    and they in turn will teach their own children.
So each generation should set its hope anew on God,
    not forgetting his glorious miracles
    and obeying his commands.
Then they will not be like their ancestors—
    stubborn, rebellious, and unfaithful,
    refusing to give their hearts to God.

The warriors of Ephraim, though armed with bows,
    turned their backs and fled on the day of battle.
They did not keep God's covenant
    and refused to live by his instructions.
They forgot what he had done—
    the great wonders he had shown them,
the miracles he did for their ancestors
    on the plain of Zoan in the land of Egypt.
For he divided the sea and led them through,
    making the water stand up like walls!
In the daytime he led them by a cloud,
    and all night by a pillar of fire.
He split open the rocks in the wilderness
    to give them water, as from a gushing spring.
He made streams pour from the rock,
    making the waters flow down like a river!

Yet they kept on sinning against him,
    rebelling against the Most High in the desert.
They stubbornly tested God in their hearts,
    demanding the foods they craved.
They even spoke against God himself, saying,
    "God can't give us food in the wilderness.
Yes, he can strike a rock so water gushes out,
    but he can't give his people bread and meat."
When the LORD heard them, he was furious.
    The fire of his wrath burned against Jacob.

Yes, his anger rose against Israel,
for they did not believe God
  or trust him to care for them.
But he commanded the skies to open;
  he opened the doors of heaven.
He rained down manna for them to eat;
  he gave them bread from heaven.
They ate the food of angels!
  God gave them all they could hold.
He released the east wind in the heavens
  and guided the south wind by his mighty power.
He rained down meat as thick as dust—
  birds as plentiful as the sand on the seashore!
He caused the birds to fall within their camp
  and all around their tents.
The people ate their fill.
  He gave them what they craved.
But before they satisfied their craving,
  while the meat was yet in their mouths,
the anger of God rose against them,
  and he killed their strongest men.
  He struck down the finest of Israel's young men.

But in spite of this, the people kept sinning.
  Despite his wonders, they refused to trust him.
So he ended their lives in failure,
  their years in terror.
When God began killing them,
  they finally sought him.
  They repented and took God seriously.
Then they remembered that God was their rock,
  that God Most High was their redeemer.
But all they gave him was lip service;
  they lied to him with their tongues.
Their hearts were not loyal to him.
  They did not keep his covenant.
Yet he was merciful and forgave their sins
  and did not destroy them all.
Many times he held back his anger
  and did not unleash his fury!
For he remembered that they were merely mortal,
  gone like a breath of wind that never returns.

Oh, how often they rebelled against him in the wilderness
   and grieved his heart in that dry wasteland.
Again and again they tested God's patience
   and provoked the Holy One of Israel.
They did not remember his power
   and how he rescued them from their enemies.
They did not remember his miraculous signs in Egypt,
   his wonders on the plain of Zoan.
For he turned their rivers into blood,
   so no one could drink from the streams.
He sent vast swarms of flies to consume them
   and hordes of frogs to ruin them.
He gave their crops to caterpillars;
   their harvest was consumed by locusts.
He destroyed their grapevines with hail
   and shattered their sycamore-figs with sleet.
He abandoned their cattle to the hail,
   their livestock to bolts of lightning.
He loosed on them his fierce anger—
   all his fury, rage, and hostility.
He dispatched against them
   a band of destroying angels.
He turned his anger against them;
   he did not spare the Egyptians' lives
   but ravaged them with the plague.
He killed the oldest son in each Egyptian family,
   the flower of youth throughout the land of Egypt.
But he led his own people like a flock of sheep,
   guiding them safely through the wilderness.
He kept them safe so they were not afraid;
   but the sea covered their enemies.
He brought them to the border of his holy land,
   to this land of hills he had won for them.
He drove out the nations before them;
   he gave them their inheritance by lot.
   He settled the tribes of Israel into their homes.

But they kept testing and rebelling against God Most High.
   They did not obey his laws.
They turned back and were as faithless as their parents.
   They were as undependable as a crooked bow.
They angered God by building shrines to other gods;
   they made him jealous with their idols.

When God heard them, he was very angry,
  and he completely rejected Israel.
Then he abandoned his dwelling at Shiloh,
  the Tabernacle where he had lived among the people.
He allowed the Ark of his might to be captured;
  he surrendered his glory into enemy hands.
He gave his people over to be butchered by the sword,
  because he was so angry with his own people—his special
    possession.
Their young men were killed by fire;
  their young women died before singing their wedding songs.
Their priests were slaughtered,
  and their widows could not mourn their deaths.

Then the Lord rose up as though waking from sleep,
  like a warrior aroused from a drunken stupor.
He routed his enemies
  and sent them to eternal shame.
But he rejected Joseph's descendants;
  he did not choose the tribe of Ephraim.
He chose instead the tribe of Judah,
  and Mount Zion, which he loved.
There he built his sanctuary as high as the heavens,
  as solid and enduring as the earth.
He chose his servant David,
  calling him from the sheep pens.
He took David from tending the ewes and lambs
  and made him the shepherd of Jacob's descendants—
  God's own people, Israel.
He cared for them with a true heart
  and led them with skillful hands.

PSALM 79
A psalm of Asaph.

O God, pagan nations have conquered your land,
  your special possession.
They have defiled your holy Temple
  and made Jerusalem a heap of ruins.
They have left the bodies of your servants
  as food for the birds of heaven.
The flesh of your godly ones
  has become food for the wild animals.

Blood has flowed like water all around Jerusalem;
  no one is left to bury the dead.
We are mocked by our neighbors,
  an object of scorn and derision to those around us.

O Lord, how long will you be angry with us? Forever?
  How long will your jealousy burn like fire?
Pour out your wrath on the nations that refuse to acknowledge you—
  on kingdoms that do not call upon your name.
For they have devoured your people Israel,
  making the land a desolate wilderness.
Do not hold us guilty for the sins of our ancestors!
  Let your compassion quickly meet our needs,
  for we are on the brink of despair.

Help us, O God of our salvation!
  Help us for the glory of your name.
Save us and forgive our sins
  for the honor of your name.
Why should pagan nations be allowed to scoff,
  asking, "Where is their God?"
Show us your vengeance against the nations,
  for they have spilled the blood of your servants.
Listen to the moaning of the prisoners.
  Demonstrate your great power by saving those condemned to die.

O Lord, pay back our neighbors seven times
  for the scorn they have hurled at you.
Then we your people, the sheep of your pasture,
  will thank you forever and ever,
  praising your greatness from generation to generation.

PSALM 80

For the choir director: A psalm of Asaph, to be sung to the tune "Lilies of the Covenant."

Please listen, O Shepherd of Israel,
  you who lead Joseph's descendants like a flock.
O God, enthroned above the cherubim,
  display your radiant glory
  to Ephraim, Benjamin, and Manasseh.
Show us your mighty power.
  Come to rescue us!

Turn us again to yourself, O God.
   Make your face shine down upon us.
   Only then will we be saved.
O Lord God of Heaven's Armies,
   how long will you be angry with our prayers?
You have fed us with sorrow
   and made us drink tears by the bucketful.
You have made us the scorn of neighboring nations.
   Our enemies treat us as a joke.

Turn us again to yourself, O God of Heaven's Armies.
   Make your face shine down upon us.
   Only then will we be saved.
You brought us from Egypt like a grapevine;
   you drove away the pagan nations and transplanted us into your
      land.
You cleared the ground for us,
   and we took root and filled the land.
Our shade covered the mountains;
   our branches covered the mighty cedars.
We spread our branches west to the Mediterranean Sea;
   our shoots spread east to the Euphrates River.
But now, why have you broken down our walls
   so that all who pass by may steal our fruit?
The wild boar from the forest devours it,
   and the wild animals feed on it.

Come back, we beg you, O God of Heaven's Armies.
   Look down from heaven and see our plight.
Take care of this grapevine
   that you yourself have planted,
   this son you have raised for yourself.
For we are chopped up and burned by our enemies.
   May they perish at the sight of your frown.
Strengthen the man you love,
   the son of your choice.
Then we will never abandon you again.
   Revive us so we can call on your name once more.

Turn us again to yourself, O Lord God of Heaven's
      Armies.
   Make your face shine down upon us.
   Only then will we be saved.

PSALM 81

For the choir director: A psalm of Asaph, to be accompanied by a stringed instrument.

Sing praises to God, our strength.
　Sing to the God of Jacob.
Sing! Beat the tambourine.
　Play the sweet lyre and the harp.
Blow the ram's horn at new moon,
　and again at full moon to call a festival!
For this is required by the decrees of Israel;
　it is a regulation of the God of Jacob.
He made it a law for Israel
　when he attacked Egypt to set us free.

I heard an unknown voice say,
"Now I will take the load from your shoulders;
　I will free your hands from their heavy tasks.
You cried to me in trouble, and I saved you;
　I answered out of the thundercloud
　and tested your faith when there was no water
　　at Meribah.   *Interlude*

"Listen to me, O my people, while I give you stern warnings.
　O Israel, if you would only listen to me!
You must never have a foreign god;
　you must not bow down before a false god.
For it was I, the LORD your God,
　who rescued you from the land of Egypt.
　Open your mouth wide, and I will fill it with
　　good things.

"But no, my people wouldn't listen.
　Israel did not want me around.
So I let them follow their own stubborn desires,
　living according to their own ideas.
Oh, that my people would listen to me!
　Oh, that Israel would follow me, walking in my paths!
How quickly I would then subdue their enemies!
　How soon my hands would be upon their foes!
Those who hate the LORD would cringe before him;
　they would be doomed forever.
But I would feed you with the finest wheat.
　I would satisfy you with wild honey from the rock."

PSALM 82

A psalm of Asaph.

God presides over heaven's court;
　he pronounces judgment on the heavenly beings:
"How long will you hand down unjust decisions
　by favoring the wicked?　　　　　　　　　　　*Interlude*

"Give justice to the poor and the orphan;
　uphold the rights of the oppressed and the destitute.
Rescue the poor and helpless;
　deliver them from the grasp of evil people.
But these oppressors know nothing;
　they are so ignorant!
They wander about in darkness,
　while the whole world is shaken to the core.
I say, 'You are gods;
　you are all children of the Most High.
But you will die like mere mortals
　and fall like every other ruler.'"

Rise up, O God, and judge the earth,
　for all the nations belong to you.

PSALM 83

A song. A psalm of Asaph.

O God, do not be silent!
　Do not be deaf.
　Do not be quiet, O God.
Don't you hear the uproar of your enemies?
　Don't you see that your arrogant enemies are
　　rising up?
They devise crafty schemes against your people;
　they conspire against your precious ones.
"Come," they say, "let us wipe out Israel as a nation.
　We will destroy the very memory of its existence."
Yes, this was their unanimous decision.
　They signed a treaty as allies against you—
these Edomites and Ishmaelites;
　Moabites and Hagrites;
Gebalites, Ammonites, and Amalekites;
　and people from Philistia and Tyre.

Assyria has joined them, too,
     and is allied with the descendants of Lot.   *Interlude*

Do to them as you did to the Midianites
     and as you did to Sisera and Jabin at the Kishon River.
They were destroyed at Endor,
     and their decaying corpses fertilized the soil.
Let their mighty nobles die as Oreb and Zeeb did.
     Let all their princes die like Zebah and Zalmunna,
for they said, "Let us seize for our own use
     these pasturelands of God!"
O my God, scatter them like tumbleweed,
     like chaff before the wind!
As a fire burns a forest
     and as a flame sets mountains ablaze,
chase them with your fierce storm;
     terrify them with your tempest.
Utterly disgrace them
     until they submit to your name, O Lord.
Let them be ashamed and terrified forever.
     Let them die in disgrace.
Then they will learn that you alone are called the Lord,
     that you alone are the Most High,
          supreme over all the earth.

PSALM 84
*For the choir director: A psalm of the descendants of Korah, to be accompanied
by a stringed instrument.*

How lovely is your dwelling place,
     O Lord of Heaven's Armies.
I long, yes, I faint with longing
     to enter the courts of the Lord.
With my whole being, body and soul,
     I will shout joyfully to the living God.
Even the sparrow finds a home,
     and the swallow builds her nest and raises
          her young
at a place near your altar,
     O Lord of Heaven's Armies, my King and
          my God!
What joy for those who can live in your house,
     always singing your praises.   *Interlude*

What joy for those whose strength comes from the LORD,
who have set their minds on a pilgrimage to Jerusalem.
When they walk through the Valley of Weeping,
it will become a place of refreshing springs.
The autumn rains will clothe it with blessings.
They will continue to grow stronger,
and each of them will appear before God in Jerusalem.

O LORD God of Heaven's Armies, hear my prayer.
Listen, O God of Jacob. *Interlude*

O God, look with favor upon the king, our shield!
Show favor to the one you have anointed.

A single day in your courts
is better than a thousand anywhere else!
I would rather be a gatekeeper in the house of my God
than live the good life in the homes of the wicked.
For the LORD God is our sun and our shield.
He gives us grace and glory.
The LORD will withhold no good thing
from those who do what is right.
O LORD of Heaven's Armies,
what joy for those who trust in you.

PSALM 85

For the choir director: A psalm of the descendants of Korah.

LORD, you poured out blessings on your land!
You restored the fortunes of Israel.
You forgave the guilt of your people—
yes, you covered all their sins. *Interlude*
You held back your fury.
You kept back your blazing anger.

Now restore us again, O God of our salvation.
Put aside your anger against us once more.
Will you be angry with us always?
Will you prolong your wrath to all generations?
Won't you revive us again,
so your people can rejoice in you?
Show us your unfailing love, O LORD,
and grant us your salvation.

I listen carefully to what God the LORD is saying,
 for he speaks peace to his faithful people.
 But let them not return to their foolish ways.
Surely his salvation is near to those who fear him,
 so our land will be filled with his glory.

Unfailing love and truth have met together.
 Righteousness and peace have kissed!
Truth springs up from the earth,
 and righteousness smiles down from heaven.
Yes, the LORD pours down his blessings.
 Our land will yield its bountiful harvest.
Righteousness goes as a herald before him,
 preparing the way for his steps.

PSALM 86

A prayer of David.

Bend down, O LORD, and hear my prayer;
 answer me, for I need your help.
Protect me, for I am devoted to you.
 Save me, for I serve you and trust you.
 You are my God.
Be merciful to me, O Lord,
 for I am calling on you constantly.
Give me happiness, O Lord,
 for I give myself to you.
O Lord, you are so good, so ready to forgive,
 so full of unfailing love for all who ask for your help.
Listen closely to my prayer, O LORD;
 hear my urgent cry.
I will call to you whenever I'm in trouble,
 and you will answer me.

No pagan god is like you, O Lord.
 None can do what you do!
All the nations you made
 will come and bow before you, Lord;
 they will praise your holy name.
For you are great and perform wonderful deeds.
 You alone are God.

Teach me your ways, O LORD,
 that I may live according to your truth!

Grant me purity of heart,
  so that I may honor you.
With all my heart I will praise you, O Lord my God.
  I will give glory to your name forever,
for your love for me is very great.
  You have rescued me from the depths of death.

O God, insolent people rise up against me;
  a violent gang is trying to kill me.
  You mean nothing to them.
But you, O Lord,
  are a God of compassion and mercy,
slow to get angry
  and filled with unfailing love and faithfulness.
Look down and have mercy on me.
  Give your strength to your servant;
  save me, the son of your servant.
Send me a sign of your favor.
  Then those who hate me will be put to shame,
  for you, O Lord, help and comfort me.

PSALM 87

A song. A psalm of the descendants of Korah.

On the holy mountain
  stands the city founded by the Lord.
He loves the city of Jerusalem
  more than any other city in Israel.
O city of God,
  what glorious things are said of you!   *Interlude*

I will count Egypt and Babylon among those who
     know me—
  also Philistia and Tyre, and even distant Ethiopia.
  They have all become citizens of Jerusalem!
Regarding Jerusalem it will be said,
  "Everyone enjoys the rights of citizenship there."
  And the Most High will personally bless this city.
When the Lord registers the nations, he will say,
  "They have all become citizens of Jerusalem."   *Interlude*

The people will play flutes and sing,
  "The source of my life springs from Jerusalem!"

PSALM 88

For the choir director: A psalm of the descendants of Korah. A song to be sung to
the tune "The Suffering of Affliction." A psalm of Heman the Ezrahite.

O LORD, God of my salvation,
   I cry out to you by day.
   I come to you at night.
Now hear my prayer;
   listen to my cry.
For my life is full of troubles,
   and death draws near.
I am as good as dead,
   like a strong man with no strength left.
They have left me among the dead,
   and I lie like a corpse in a grave.
I am forgotten,
   cut off from your care.
You have thrown me into the lowest pit,
   into the darkest depths.
Your anger weighs me down;
   with wave after wave you have engulfed me.   *Interlude*

You have driven my friends away
   by making me repulsive to them.
I am in a trap with no way of escape.
   My eyes are blinded by my tears.
Each day I beg for your help, O LORD;
   I lift my hands to you for mercy.
Are your wonderful deeds of any use to the dead?
   Do the dead rise up and praise you?   *Interlude*

Can those in the grave declare your unfailing love?
   Can they proclaim your faithfulness in the place of destruction?
Can the darkness speak of your wonderful deeds?
   Can anyone in the land of forgetfulness talk about your
      righteousness?
O LORD, I cry out to you.
   I will keep on pleading day by day.
O LORD, why do you reject me?
   Why do you turn your face from me?

I have been sick and close to death since my youth.
   I stand helpless and desperate before your terrors.
Your fierce anger has overwhelmed me.

Your terrors have paralyzed me.
They swirl around me like floodwaters all day long.
They have engulfed me completely.
You have taken away my companions and loved ones.
Darkness is my closest friend.

PSALM 89
A psalm of Ethan the Ezrahite.

I will sing of the Lord's unfailing love forever!
Young and old will hear of your faithfulness.
Your unfailing love will last forever.
Your faithfulness is as enduring as the heavens.

The Lord said, "I have made a covenant with David,
my chosen servant.
I have sworn this oath to him:
'I will establish your descendants as kings forever;
they will sit on your throne from now until eternity.'"   *Interlude*
All heaven will praise your great wonders, Lord;
myriads of angels will praise you for your faithfulness.
For who in all of heaven can compare with the Lord?
What mightiest angel is anything like the Lord?
The highest angelic powers stand in awe of God.
He is far more awesome than all who surround his throne.
O Lord God of Heaven's Armies!
Where is there anyone as mighty as you, O Lord?
You are entirely faithful.

You rule the oceans.
You subdue their storm-tossed waves.
You crushed the great sea monster.
You scattered your enemies with your mighty arm.
The heavens are yours, and the earth is yours;
everything in the world is yours—you created it all.
You created north and south.
Mount Tabor and Mount Hermon praise your name.
Powerful is your arm!
Strong is your hand!
Your right hand is lifted high in glorious strength.
Righteousness and justice are the foundation of your throne.
Unfailing love and truth walk before you as attendants.
Happy are those who hear the joyful call to worship,

for they will walk in the light of your presence, LORD.
They rejoice all day long in your wonderful reputation.
  They exult in your righteousness.
You are their glorious strength.
  It pleases you to make us strong.
Yes, our protection comes from the LORD,
  and he, the Holy One of Israel, has given us our king.

Long ago you spoke in a vision to your faithful people.
You said, "I have raised up a warrior.
  I have selected him from the common people to be king.
I have found my servant David.
  I have anointed him with my holy oil.
I will steady him with my hand;
  with my powerful arm I will make him strong.
His enemies will not defeat him,
  nor will the wicked overpower him.
I will beat down his adversaries before him
  and destroy those who hate him.
My faithfulness and unfailing love will be with him,
  and by my authority he will grow in power.
I will extend his rule over the sea,
  his dominion over the rivers.
And he will call out to me, 'You are my Father,
  my God, and the Rock of my salvation.'
I will make him my firstborn son,
  the mightiest king on earth.
I will love him and be kind to him forever;
  my covenant with him will never end.
I will preserve an heir for him;
  his throne will be as endless as the days of heaven.
But if his descendants forsake my instructions
  and fail to obey my regulations,
if they do not obey my decrees
  and fail to keep my commands,
then I will punish their sin with the rod,
  and their disobedience with beating.
But I will never stop loving him
  nor fail to keep my promise to him.
No, I will not break my covenant;
  I will not take back a single word I said.
I have sworn an oath to David,

and in my holiness I cannot lie:
His dynasty will go on forever;
   his kingdom will endure as the sun.
It will be as eternal as the moon,
   my faithful witness in the sky!"   *Interlude*

But now you have rejected him and cast him off.
   You are angry with your anointed king.
You have renounced your covenant with him;
   you have thrown his crown in the dust.
You have broken down the walls protecting him
   and ruined every fort defending him.
Everyone who comes along has robbed him,
   and he has become a joke to his neighbors.
You have strengthened his enemies
   and made them all rejoice.
You have made his sword useless
   and refused to help him in battle.
You have ended his splendor
   and overturned his throne.
You have made him old before his time
   and publicly disgraced him.   *Interlude*

O Lord, how long will this go on?
   Will you hide yourself forever?
   How long will your anger burn like fire?
Remember how short my life is,
   how empty and futile this human existence!
No one can live forever; all will die.
   No one can escape the power of the grave.   *Interlude*

Lord, where is your unfailing love?
   You promised it to David with a faithful pledge.
Consider, Lord, how your servants are disgraced!
   I carry in my heart the insults of so many people.
Your enemies have mocked me, O Lord;
   they mock your anointed king wherever he goes.

Praise the Lord forever!
   Amen and amen!

Book Four

(PSALMS 90–106)

PSALM 90

A prayer of Moses, the man of God.

Lord, through all the generations
    you have been our home!
Before the mountains were born,
    before you gave birth to the earth and the world,
    from beginning to end, you are God.

You turn people back to dust, saying,
    "Return to dust, you mortals!"
For you, a thousand years are as a passing day,
    as brief as a few night hours.
You sweep people away like dreams that disappear.
    They are like grass that springs up in the morning.
In the morning it blooms and flourishes,
    but by evening it is dry and withered.
We wither beneath your anger;
    we are overwhelmed by your fury.
You spread out our sins before you—
    our secret sins—and you see them all.
We live our lives beneath your wrath,
    ending our years with a groan.

Seventy years are given to us!
    Some even live to eighty.
But even the best years are filled with pain and trouble;
    soon they disappear, and we fly away.
Who can comprehend the power of your anger?
    Your wrath is as awesome as the fear you deserve.
Teach us to realize the brevity of life,
    so that we may grow in wisdom.

O Lord, come back to us!
    How long will you delay?
    Take pity on your servants!
Satisfy us each morning with your unfailing love,
    so we may sing for joy to the end of our lives.

Give us gladness in proportion to our former misery!
    Replace the evil years with good.
Let us, your servants, see you work again;
    let our children see your glory.
And may the Lord our God show us his approval
    and make our efforts successful.
    Yes, make our efforts successful!

PSALM 91

Those who live in the shelter of the Most High
    will find rest in the shadow of the Almighty.
This I declare about the LORD:
He alone is my refuge, my place of safety;
    he is my God, and I trust him.
For he will rescue you from every trap
    and protect you from deadly disease.
He will cover you with his feathers.
    He will shelter you with his wings.
    His faithful promises are your armor and protection.
Do not be afraid of the terrors of the night,
    nor the arrow that flies in the day.
Do not dread the disease that stalks in darkness,
    nor the disaster that strikes at midday.
Though a thousand fall at your side,
    though ten thousand are dying around you,
    these evils will not touch you.
Just open your eyes,
    and see how the wicked are punished.

If you make the LORD your refuge,
    if you make the Most High your shelter,
no evil will conquer you;
    no plague will come near your home.
For he will order his angels
    to protect you wherever you go.
They will hold you up with their hands
    so you won't even hurt your foot on a stone.
You will trample upon lions and cobras;
    you will crush fierce lions and serpents under your feet!

The LORD says, "I will rescue those who love me.
    I will protect those who trust in my name.

When they call on me, I will answer;
  I will be with them in trouble.
  I will rescue and honor them.
I will reward them with a long life
  and give them my salvation."

PSALM 92

A psalm. A song to be sung on the Sabbath Day.

It is good to give thanks to the LORD,
  to sing praises to the Most High.
It is good to proclaim your unfailing love in the morning,
  your faithfulness in the evening,
accompanied by a ten-stringed instrument, a harp,
  and the melody of a lyre.

You thrill me, LORD, with all you have done for me!
  I sing for joy because of what you have done.
O LORD, what great works you do!
  And how deep are your thoughts.
Only a simpleton would not know,
  and only a fool would not understand this:
Though the wicked sprout like weeds
  and evildoers flourish,
  they will be destroyed forever.

But you, O LORD, will be exalted forever.
Your enemies, LORD, will surely perish;
  all evildoers will be scattered.
But you have made me as strong as a wild ox.
  You have anointed me with the finest oil.
My eyes have seen the downfall of my enemies;
  my ears have heard the defeat of my wicked opponents.
But the godly will flourish like palm trees
  and grow strong like the cedars of Lebanon.
For they are transplanted to the LORD's own house.
  They flourish in the courts of our God.
Even in old age they will still produce fruit;
  they will remain vital and green.
They will declare, "The LORD is just!
  He is my rock!
  There is no evil in him!"

PSALM 93

The LORD is king! He is robed in majesty.
Indeed, the LORD is robed in majesty and armed with strength.
The world stands firm
and cannot be shaken.

Your throne, O LORD, has stood from time immemorial.
You yourself are from the everlasting past.
The floods have risen up, O LORD.
The floods have roared like thunder;
the floods have lifted their pounding waves.
But mightier than the violent raging of the seas,
mightier than the breakers on the shore—
the LORD above is mightier than these!
Your royal laws cannot be changed.
Your reign, O LORD, is holy forever and ever.

PSALM 94

O LORD, the God of vengeance,
O God of vengeance, let your glorious justice shine forth!
Arise, O Judge of the earth.
Give the proud what they deserve.
How long, O LORD?
How long will the wicked be allowed to gloat?
How long will they speak with arrogance?
How long will these evil people boast?
They crush your people, LORD,
hurting those you claim as your own.
They kill widows and foreigners
and murder orphans.
"The LORD isn't looking," they say,
"and besides, the God of Israel doesn't care."

Think again, you fools!
When will you finally catch on?
Is he deaf—the one who made your ears?
Is he blind—the one who formed your eyes?
He punishes the nations—won't he also punish you?
He knows everything—doesn't he also know what you are doing?
The LORD knows people's thoughts;
he knows they are worthless!

Joyful are those you discipline, LORD,
  those you teach with your instructions.
You give them relief from troubled times
  until a pit is dug to capture the wicked.
The LORD will not reject his people;
  he will not abandon his special possession.
Judgment will again be founded on justice,
  and those with virtuous hearts will pursue it.

Who will protect me from the wicked?
  Who will stand up for me against evildoers?
Unless the LORD had helped me,
  I would soon have settled in the silence of the grave.
I cried out, "I am slipping!"
  but your unfailing love, O LORD, supported me.
When doubts filled my mind,
  your comfort gave me renewed hope and cheer.

Can unjust leaders claim that God is on their side—
  leaders whose decrees permit injustice?
They gang up against the righteous
  and condemn the innocent to death.
But the LORD is my fortress;
  my God is the mighty rock where I hide.
God will turn the sins of evil people back on them.
  He will destroy them for their sins.
  The LORD our God will destroy them.

PSALM 95

Come, let us sing to the LORD!
  Let us shout joyfully to the Rock of our salvation.
Let us come to him with thanksgiving.
  Let us sing psalms of praise to him.
For the LORD is a great God,
  a great King above all gods.
He holds in his hands the depths of the earth
  and the mightiest mountains.
The sea belongs to him, for he made it.
  His hands formed the dry land, too.

Come, let us worship and bow down.
  Let us kneel before the LORD our maker,
  for he is our God.

We are the people he watches over,
the flock under his care.

If only you would listen to his voice today!
The Lord says, "Don't harden your hearts as Israel did at Meribah,
as they did at Massah in the wilderness.
For there your ancestors tested and tried my patience,
even though they saw everything I did.
For forty years I was angry with them, and I said,
'They are a people whose hearts turn away from me.
They refuse to do what I tell them.'
So in my anger I took an oath:
'They will never enter my place of rest.'"

PSALM 96

Sing a new song to the Lord!
Let the whole earth sing to the Lord!
Sing to the Lord; praise his name.
Each day proclaim the good news that he saves.
Publish his glorious deeds among the nations.
Tell everyone about the amazing things he does.
Great is the Lord! He is most worthy of praise!
He is to be feared above all gods.
The gods of other nations are mere idols,
but the Lord made the heavens!
Honor and majesty surround him;
strength and beauty fill his sanctuary.

O nations of the world, recognize the Lord;
recognize that the Lord is glorious and strong.
Give to the Lord the glory he deserves!
Bring your offering and come into his courts.
Worship the Lord in all his holy splendor.
Let all the earth tremble before him.
Tell all the nations, "The Lord reigns!"
The world stands firm and cannot be shaken.
He will judge all peoples fairly.

Let the heavens be glad, and the earth rejoice!
Let the sea and everything in it shout his praise!
Let the fields and their crops burst out with joy!
Let the trees of the forest sing for joy

before the LORD, for he is coming!
    He is coming to judge the earth.
He will judge the world with justice,
    and the nations with his truth.

PSALM 97

The LORD is king!
    Let the earth rejoice!
    Let the farthest coastlands be glad.
Dark clouds surround him.
    Righteousness and justice are the foundation of his throne.
Fire spreads ahead of him
    and burns up all his foes.
His lightning flashes out across the world.
    The earth sees and trembles.
The mountains melt like wax before the LORD,
    before the Lord of all the earth.
The heavens proclaim his righteousness;
    every nation sees his glory.
Those who worship idols are disgraced—
    all who brag about their worthless gods—
    for every god must bow to him.
Jerusalem has heard and rejoiced,
    and all the towns of Judah are glad
    because of your justice, O LORD!
For you, O LORD, are supreme over all the earth;
    you are exalted far above all gods.

You who love the LORD, hate evil!
    He protects the lives of his godly people
    and rescues them from the power of the wicked.
Light shines on the godly,
    and joy on those whose hearts are right.
May all who are godly rejoice in the LORD
    and praise his holy name!

PSALM 98
A psalm.

Sing a new song to the LORD,
    for he has done wonderful deeds.

His right hand has won a mighty victory;
    his holy arm has shown his saving power!
The LORD has announced his victory
    and has revealed his righteousness to every nation!
He has remembered his promise to love and be faithful
      to Israel.
    The ends of the earth have seen the victory of our God.

Shout to the LORD, all the earth;
    break out in praise and sing for joy!
Sing your praise to the LORD with the harp,
    with the harp and melodious song,
with trumpets and the sound of the ram's horn.
    Make a joyful symphony before the LORD, the King!

Let the sea and everything in it shout his praise!
    Let the earth and all living things join in.
Let the rivers clap their hands in glee!
    Let the hills sing out their songs of joy
before the LORD,
    for he is coming to judge the earth.
He will judge the world with justice,
    and the nations with fairness.

PSALM 99

The LORD is king!
    Let the nations tremble!
He sits on his throne between the cherubim.
    Let the whole earth quake!
The LORD sits in majesty in Jerusalem,
    exalted above all the nations.
Let them praise your great and awesome name.
    Your name is holy!
Mighty King, lover of justice,
    you have established fairness.
You have acted with justice
    and righteousness throughout Israel.
Exalt the LORD our God!
    Bow low before his feet, for he is holy!

Moses and Aaron were among his priests;
    Samuel also called on his name.

They cried to the LORD for help,
    and he answered them.
He spoke to Israel from the pillar of cloud,
    and they followed the laws and decrees he gave them.
O LORD our God, you answered them.
    You were a forgiving God to them,
    but you punished them when they went wrong.

Exalt the LORD our God,
    and worship at his holy mountain in Jerusalem,
    for the LORD our God is holy!

PSALM 100

A psalm of thanksgiving.

Shout with joy to the LORD, all the earth!
    Worship the LORD with gladness.
    Come before him, singing with joy.
Acknowledge that the LORD is God!
    He made us, and we are his.
    We are his people, the sheep of his pasture.
Enter his gates with thanksgiving;
    go into his courts with praise.
    Give thanks to him and praise his name.
For the LORD is good.
    His unfailing love continues forever,
    and his faithfulness continues to each
        generation.

PSALM 101

A psalm of David.

I will sing of your love and justice, LORD.
    I will praise you with songs.
I will be careful to live a blameless life—
    when will you come to help me?
I will lead a life of integrity
    in my own home.
I will refuse to look at
    anything vile and vulgar.
I hate all who deal crookedly;
    I will have nothing to do with them.

I will reject perverse ideas
    and stay away from every evil.
I will not tolerate people who slander their neighbors.
    I will not endure conceit and pride.

I will search for faithful people
    to be my companions.
Only those who are above reproach
    will be allowed to serve me.
I will not allow deceivers to serve in my house,
    and liars will not stay in my presence.
My daily task will be to ferret out the wicked
    and free the city of the LORD from their grip.

PSALM 102

A prayer of one overwhelmed with trouble, pouring out problems before the LORD.

LORD, hear my prayer!
    Listen to my plea!
Don't turn away from me
    in my time of distress.
Bend down to listen,
    and answer me quickly when I call to you.
For my days disappear like smoke,
    and my bones burn like red-hot coals.
My heart is sick, withered like grass,
    and I have lost my appetite.
Because of my groaning,
    I am reduced to skin and bones.
I am like an owl in the desert,
    like a little owl in a far-off wilderness.
I lie awake,
    lonely as a solitary bird on the roof.
My enemies taunt me day after day.
    They mock and curse me.
I eat ashes for food.
    My tears run down into my drink
because of your anger and wrath.
    For you have picked me up and thrown me out.
My life passes as swiftly as the evening shadows.
    I am withering away like grass.

But you, O Lord, will sit on your throne forever.
  Your fame will endure to every generation.
You will arise and have mercy on Jerusalem—
  and now is the time to pity her,
  now is the time you promised to help.
For your people love every stone in her walls
  and cherish even the dust in her streets.
Then the nations will tremble before the Lord.
  The kings of the earth will tremble before his glory.
For the Lord will rebuild Jerusalem.
  He will appear in his glory.
He will listen to the prayers of the destitute.
  He will not reject their pleas.

Let this be recorded for future generations,
  so that a people not yet born will praise the Lord.
Tell them the Lord looked down
  from his heavenly sanctuary.
He looked down to earth from heaven
  to hear the groans of the prisoners,
  to release those condemned to die.
And so the Lord's fame will be celebrated
    in Zion,
  his praises in Jerusalem,
when multitudes gather together
  and kingdoms come to worship the Lord.

He broke my strength in midlife,
  cutting short my days.
But I cried to him, "O my God, who lives forever,
  don't take my life while I am so young!
Long ago you laid the foundation of the earth
  and made the heavens with your hands.
They will perish, but you remain forever;
  they will wear out like old clothing.
You will change them like a garment
  and discard them.
But you are always the same;
  you will live forever.
The children of your people
  will live in security.
Their children's children
  will thrive in your presence."

PSALM 103

A psalm of David.

Let all that I am praise the LORD;
  with my whole heart, I will praise his holy name.
Let all that I am praise the LORD;
  may I never forget the good things he does for me.
He forgives all my sins
  and heals all my diseases.
He redeems me from death
  and crowns me with love and tender mercies.
He fills my life with good things.
  My youth is renewed like the eagle's!

The LORD gives righteousness
  and justice to all who are treated unfairly.

He revealed his character to Moses
  and his deeds to the people of Israel.
The LORD is compassionate and merciful,
  slow to get angry and filled with unfailing love.
He will not constantly accuse us,
  nor remain angry forever.
He does not punish us for all our sins;
  he does not deal harshly with us, as we deserve.
For his unfailing love toward those who fear him
  is as great as the height of the heavens above the
    earth.
He has removed our sins as far from us
  as the east is from the west.
The LORD is like a father to his children,
  tender and compassionate to those who fear him.
For he knows how weak we are;
  he remembers we are only dust.
Our days on earth are like grass;
  like wildflowers, we bloom and die.
The wind blows, and we are gone—
  as though we had never been here.
But the love of the LORD remains forever
  with those who fear him.
His salvation extends to the children's children
  of those who are faithful to his covenant,
  of those who obey his commandments!

The Lord has made the heavens his throne;
    from there he rules over everything.

Praise the Lord, you angels,
    you mighty ones who carry out his plans,
    listening for each of his commands.
Yes, praise the Lord, you armies of angels
    who serve him and do his will!
Praise the Lord, everything he has created,
    everything in all his kingdom.

Let all that I am praise the Lord.

PSALM 104

Let all that I am praise the Lord.

O Lord my God, how great you are!
    You are robed with honor and majesty.
    You are dressed in a robe of light.
You stretch out the starry curtain of the heavens;
    you lay out the rafters of your home in the rain clouds.
You make the clouds your chariot;
    you ride upon the wings of the wind.
The winds are your messengers;
    flames of fire are your servants.

You placed the world on its foundation
    so it would never be moved.
You clothed the earth with floods of water,
    water that covered even the mountains.
At your command, the water fled;
    at the sound of your thunder, it hurried away.
Mountains rose and valleys sank
    to the levels you decreed.
Then you set a firm boundary for the seas,
    so they would never again cover the earth.

You make springs pour water into the ravines,
    so streams gush down from the mountains.
They provide water for all the animals,
    and the wild donkeys quench their thirst.
The birds nest beside the streams
    and sing among the branches of the trees.

You send rain on the mountains from your heavenly home,
 and you fill the earth with the fruit of your labor.
You cause grass to grow for the livestock
 and plants for people to use.
You allow them to produce food from the earth—
 wine to make them glad,
olive oil to soothe their skin,
 and bread to give them strength.
The trees of the LORD are well cared for—
 the cedars of Lebanon that he planted.
There the birds make their nests,
 and the storks make their homes in the cypresses.
High in the mountains live the wild goats,
 and the rocks form a refuge for the hyraxes.

You made the moon to mark the seasons,
 and the sun knows when to set.
You send the darkness, and it becomes night,
 when all the forest animals prowl about.
Then the young lions roar for their prey,
 stalking the food provided by God.
At dawn they slink back
 into their dens to rest.
Then people go off to their work,
 where they labor until evening.

O LORD, what a variety of things you have made!
 In wisdom you have made them all.
 The earth is full of your creatures.
Here is the ocean, vast and wide,
 teeming with life of every kind,
 both large and small.
See the ships sailing along,
 and Leviathan, which you made to play in the sea.

They all depend on you
 to give them food as they need it.
When you supply it, they gather it.
 You open your hand to feed them,
 and they are richly satisfied.
But if you turn away from them, they panic.
 When you take away their breath,
 they die and turn again to dust.

When you give them your breath, life is created,
and you renew the face of the earth.

May the glory of the LORD continue forever!
The LORD takes pleasure in all he has made!
The earth trembles at his glance;
the mountains smoke at his touch.

I will sing to the LORD as long as I live.
I will praise my God to my last breath!
May all my thoughts be pleasing to him,
for I rejoice in the LORD.
Let all sinners vanish from the face of the earth;
let the wicked disappear forever.

Let all that I am praise the LORD.

Praise the LORD!

PSALM 105

Give thanks to the LORD and proclaim his greatness.
Let the whole world know what he has done.
Sing to him; yes, sing his praises.
Tell everyone about his wonderful deeds.
Exult in his holy name;
rejoice, you who worship the LORD.
Search for the LORD and for his strength;
continually seek him.
Remember the wonders he has performed,
his miracles, and the rulings he has given,
you children of his servant Abraham,
you descendants of Jacob, his chosen ones.

He is the LORD our God.
His justice is seen throughout the land.
He always stands by his covenant—
the commitment he made to a thousand
generations.
This is the covenant he made with Abraham
and the oath he swore to Isaac.
He confirmed it to Jacob as a decree,
and to the people of Israel as a never-ending
covenant:

"I will give you the land of Canaan
    as your special possession."

He said this when they were few in number,
    a tiny group of strangers in Canaan.
They wandered from nation to nation,
    from one kingdom to another.
Yet he did not let anyone oppress them.
    He warned kings on their behalf:
"Do not touch my chosen people,
    and do not hurt my prophets."

He called for a famine on the land of Canaan,
    cutting off its food supply.
Then he sent someone to Egypt ahead of them—
    Joseph, who was sold as a slave.
They bruised his feet with fetters
    and placed his neck in an iron collar.
Until the time came to fulfill his dreams,
    the LORD tested Joseph's character.
Then Pharaoh sent for him and set him free;
    the ruler of the nation opened his prison door.
Joseph was put in charge of all the king's household;
    he became ruler over all the king's possessions.
He could instruct the king's aides as he pleased
    and teach the king's advisers.

Then Israel arrived in Egypt;
    Jacob lived as a foreigner in the land of Ham.
And the LORD multiplied the people of Israel
    until they became too mighty for their enemies.
Then he turned the Egyptians against the Israelites,
    and they plotted against the LORD's servants.

But the LORD sent his servant Moses,
    along with Aaron, whom he had chosen.
They performed miraculous signs among the
        Egyptians,
    and wonders in the land of Ham.
The LORD blanketed Egypt in darkness,
    for they had defied his commands to let his
        people go.
He turned their water into blood,
    poisoning all the fish.

Then frogs overran the land
   and even invaded the king's bedrooms.
When the LORD spoke, flies descended on the Egyptians,
   and gnats swarmed across Egypt.
He sent them hail instead of rain,
   and lightning flashed over the land.
He ruined their grapevines and fig trees
   and shattered all the trees.
He spoke, and hordes of locusts came—
   young locusts beyond number.
They ate up everything green in the land,
   destroying all the crops in their fields.
Then he killed the oldest son in each Egyptian home,
   the pride and joy of each family.

The LORD brought his people out of Egypt, loaded with silver
     and gold;
   and not one among the tribes of Israel even stumbled.
Egypt was glad when they were gone,
   for they feared them greatly.
The LORD spread a cloud above them as a covering
   and gave them a great fire to light the darkness.
They asked for meat, and he sent them quail;
   he satisfied their hunger with manna—bread from heaven.
He split open a rock, and water gushed out
   to form a river through the dry wasteland.
For he remembered his sacred promise
   to his servant Abraham.
So he brought his people out of Egypt with joy,
   his chosen ones with rejoicing.
He gave his people the lands of pagan nations,
   and they harvested crops that others had planted.
All this happened so they would follow his decrees
   and obey his instructions.

Praise the LORD!

PSALM 106

Praise the LORD!

Give thanks to the LORD, for he is good!
   His faithful love endures forever.

Who can list the glorious miracles of the LORD?
    Who can ever praise him enough?
There is joy for those who deal justly with others
    and always do what is right.

Remember me, LORD, when you show favor to your
       people;
    come near and rescue me.
Let me share in the prosperity of your chosen ones.
    Let me rejoice in the joy of your people;
    let me praise you with those who are your heritage.

Like our ancestors, we have sinned.
    We have done wrong! We have acted wickedly!
Our ancestors in Egypt
    were not impressed by the LORD's miraculous deeds.
They soon forgot his many acts of kindness to them.
    Instead, they rebelled against him at the Red Sea.
Even so, he saved them—
    to defend the honor of his name
    and to demonstrate his mighty power.
He commanded the Red Sea to dry up.
    He led Israel across the sea as if it were a desert.
So he rescued them from their enemies
    and redeemed them from their foes.
Then the water returned and covered their enemies;
    not one of them survived.
Then his people believed his promises.
    Then they sang his praise.

Yet how quickly they forgot what he had done!
    They wouldn't wait for his counsel!
In the wilderness their desires ran wild,
    testing God's patience in that dry wasteland.
So he gave them what they asked for,
    but he sent a plague along with it.
The people in the camp were jealous of Moses
    and envious of Aaron, the LORD's holy priest.
Because of this, the earth opened up;
    it swallowed Dathan
    and buried Abiram and the other rebels.
Fire fell upon their followers;
    a flame consumed the wicked.

The people made a calf at Mount Sinai;
  they bowed before an image made of gold.
They traded their glorious God
  for a statue of a grass-eating bull.
They forgot God, their savior,
  who had done such great things in Egypt—
such wonderful things in the land of Ham,
  such awesome deeds at the Red Sea.
So he declared he would destroy them.
  But Moses, his chosen one, stepped between the LORD
    and the people.
  He begged him to turn from his anger and not destroy
    them.

The people refused to enter the pleasant land,
  for they wouldn't believe his promise to care for them.
Instead, they grumbled in their tents
  and refused to obey the LORD.
Therefore, he solemnly swore
  that he would kill them in the wilderness,
that he would scatter their descendants among the
    nations,
  exiling them to distant lands.

Then our ancestors joined in the worship of Baal at Peor;
  they even ate sacrifices offered to the dead!
They angered the LORD with all these things,
  so a plague broke out among them.
But Phinehas had the courage to intervene,
  and the plague was stopped.
So he has been regarded as a righteous man
  ever since that time.

At Meribah, too, they angered the LORD,
  causing Moses serious trouble.
They made Moses angry,
  and he spoke foolishly.

Israel failed to destroy the nations in the land,
  as the LORD had commanded them.
Instead, they mingled among the pagans
  and adopted their evil customs.
They worshiped their idols,
  which led to their downfall.

They even sacrificed their sons
   and their daughters to the demons.
They shed innocent blood,
   the blood of their sons and daughters.
By sacrificing them to the idols of Canaan,
   they polluted the land with murder.
They defiled themselves by their evil deeds,
   and their love of idols was adultery in the
      LORD's sight.

That is why the LORD's anger burned against
     his people,
   and he abhorred his own special possession.
He handed them over to pagan nations,
   and they were ruled by those who hated them.
Their enemies crushed them
   and brought them under their cruel power.
Again and again he rescued them,
   but they chose to rebel against him,
   and they were finally destroyed by their sin.
Even so, he pitied them in their distress
   and listened to their cries.
He remembered his covenant with them
   and relented because of his unfailing love.
He even caused their captors
   to treat them with kindness.

Save us, O LORD our God!
   Gather us back from among the nations,
so we can thank your holy name
   and rejoice and praise you.

Praise the LORD, the God of Israel,
   who lives from everlasting to everlasting!
Let all the people say, "Amen!"

Praise the LORD!

Book Five

(PSALMS 107–150)

PSALM 107

Give thanks to the LORD, for he is good!
　His faithful love endures forever.
Has the LORD redeemed you? Then speak out!
　Tell others he has redeemed you from your enemies.
For he has gathered the exiles from many lands,
　from east and west,
　from north and south.

Some wandered in the wilderness,
　lost and homeless.
Hungry and thirsty,
　they nearly died.
"LORD, help!" they cried in their trouble,
　and he rescued them from their distress.
He led them straight to safety,
　to a city where they could live.
Let them praise the LORD for his great love
　and for the wonderful things he has done for them.
For he satisfies the thirsty
　and fills the hungry with good things.

Some sat in darkness and deepest gloom,
　imprisoned in iron chains of misery.
They rebelled against the words of God,
　scorning the counsel of the Most High.
That is why he broke them with hard labor;
　they fell, and no one was there to help them.
"LORD, help!" they cried in their trouble,
　and he saved them from their distress.
He led them from the darkness and deepest gloom;
　he snapped their chains.
Let them praise the LORD for his great love
　and for the wonderful things he has done for them.
For he broke down their prison gates of bronze;
　he cut apart their bars of iron.

Some were fools; they rebelled
    and suffered for their sins.
They couldn't stand the thought of food,
    and they were knocking on death's door.
"Lord, help!" they cried in their trouble,
    and he saved them from their distress.
He sent out his word and healed them,
    snatching them from the door of death.
Let them praise the Lord for his great love
    and for the wonderful things he has done for them.
Let them offer sacrifices of thanksgiving
    and sing joyfully about his glorious acts.

Some went off to sea in ships,
    plying the trade routes of the world.
They, too, observed the Lord's power in action,
    his impressive works on the deepest seas.
He spoke, and the winds rose,
    stirring up the waves.
Their ships were tossed to the heavens
    and plunged again to the depths;
    the sailors cringed in terror.
They reeled and staggered like drunkards
    and were at their wits' end.
"Lord, help!" they cried in their trouble,
    and he saved them from their distress.
He calmed the storm to a whisper
    and stilled the waves.
What a blessing was that stillness
    as he brought them safely into harbor!
Let them praise the Lord for his great love
    and for the wonderful things he has done for them.
Let them exalt him publicly before the congregation
    and before the leaders of the nation.

He changes rivers into deserts,
    and springs of water into dry, thirsty land.
He turns the fruitful land into salty wastelands,
    because of the wickedness of those who live there.
But he also turns deserts into pools of water,
    the dry land into springs of water.
He brings the hungry to settle there
    and to build their cities.

They sow their fields, plant their vineyards,
    and harvest their bumper crops.
How he blesses them!
    They raise large families there,
    and their herds of livestock increase.

When they decrease in number and become impoverished
    through oppression, trouble, and sorrow,
the LORD pours contempt on their princes,
    causing them to wander in trackless wastelands.
But he rescues the poor from trouble
    and increases their families like flocks of sheep.
The godly will see these things and be glad,
    while the wicked are struck silent.
Those who are wise will take all this to heart;
    they will see in our history the faithful love of the LORD.

PSALM 108

A song. A psalm of David.

My heart is confident in you, O God;
    no wonder I can sing your praises with all my heart!
Wake up, lyre and harp!
    I will wake the dawn with my song.
I will thank you, LORD, among all the people.
    I will sing your praises among the nations.
For your unfailing love is higher than the heavens.
    Your faithfulness reaches to the clouds.
Be exalted, O God, above the highest heavens.
    May your glory shine over all the earth.

Now rescue your beloved people.
    Answer and save us by your power.
God has promised this by his holiness:
"I will divide up Shechem with joy.
    I will measure out the valley of Succoth.
Gilead is mine,
    and Manasseh, too.
Ephraim, my helmet, will produce my warriors,
    and Judah, my scepter, will produce my kings.
But Moab, my washbasin, will become my servant,
    and I will wipe my feet on Edom
    and shout in triumph over Philistia."

Who will bring me into the fortified city?
  Who will bring me victory over Edom?
Have you rejected us, O God?
  Will you no longer march with our armies?
Oh, please help us against our enemies,
  for all human help is useless.
With God's help we will do mighty things,
  for he will trample down our foes.

PSALM 109
For the choir director: A psalm of David.

O God, whom I praise,
  don't stand silent and aloof
while the wicked slander me
  and tell lies about me.
They surround me with hateful words
  and fight against me for no reason.
I love them, but they try to destroy me with accusations
  even as I am praying for them!
They repay evil for good,
  and hatred for my love.

They say, "Get an evil person to turn against him.
  Send an accuser to bring him to trial.
When his case comes up for judgment,
  let him be pronounced guilty.
  Count his prayers as sins.
Let his years be few;
  let someone else take his position.
May his children become fatherless,
  and his wife a widow.
May his children wander as beggars
  and be driven from their ruined homes.
May creditors seize his entire estate,
  and strangers take all he has earned.
Let no one be kind to him;
  let no one pity his fatherless children.
May all his offspring die.
  May his family name be blotted out in the next generation.
May the LORD never forget the sins of his fathers;
  may his mother's sins never be erased from the record.

May the LORD always remember these sins,
    and may his name disappear from human memory.
For he refused all kindness to others;
    he persecuted the poor and needy,
    and he hounded the brokenhearted to death.
He loved to curse others;
    now you curse him.
He never blessed others;
    now don't you bless him.
Cursing is as natural to him as his clothing,
    or the water he drinks,
    or the rich food he eats.
Now may his curses return and cling to him like
        clothing;
    may they be tied around him like a belt."

May those curses become the LORD's punishment
    for my accusers who speak evil of me.
But deal well with me, O Sovereign LORD,
    for the sake of your own reputation!
Rescue me
    because you are so faithful and good.
For I am poor and needy,
    and my heart is full of pain.
I am fading like a shadow at dusk;
    I am brushed off like a locust.
My knees are weak from fasting,
    and I am skin and bones.
I am a joke to people everywhere;
    when they see me, they shake their heads in scorn.

Help me, O LORD my God!
    Save me because of your unfailing love.
Let them see that this is your doing,
    that you yourself have done it, LORD.
Then let them curse me if they like,
    but you will bless me!
When they attack me, they will be disgraced!
    But I, your servant, will go right on rejoicing!
May my accusers be clothed with disgrace;
    may their humiliation cover them like a cloak.
But I will give repeated thanks to the LORD,
    praising him to everyone.

For he stands beside the needy,
   ready to save them from those who condemn them.

PSALM 110

A psalm of David.

The LORD said to my Lord,
   "Sit in the place of honor at my right hand
until I humble your enemies,
   making them a footstool under your feet."

The LORD will extend your powerful kingdom from Jerusalem;
   you will rule over your enemies.
When you go to war,
   your people will serve you willingly.
You are arrayed in holy garments,
   and your strength will be renewed each day like the morning dew.

The LORD has taken an oath and will not break his vow:
   "You are a priest forever in the order of Melchizedek."

The Lord stands at your right hand to protect you.
   He will strike down many kings when his anger erupts.
He will punish the nations
   and fill their lands with corpses;
   he will shatter heads over the whole earth.
But he himself will be refreshed from brooks along the way.
   He will be victorious.

PSALM 111

Praise the LORD!

I will thank the LORD with all my heart
   as I meet with his godly people.
How amazing are the deeds of the LORD!
   All who delight in him should ponder them.
Everything he does reveals his glory and majesty.
   His righteousness never fails.
He causes us to remember his wonderful works.
   How gracious and merciful is our LORD!
He gives food to those who fear him;
   he always remembers his covenant.

He has shown his great power to his people
 by giving them the lands of other nations.
All he does is just and good,
 and all his commandments are trustworthy.
They are forever true,
 to be obeyed faithfully and with integrity.
He has paid a full ransom for his people.
 He has guaranteed his covenant with them forever.
 What a holy, awe-inspiring name he has!
Fear of the Lord is the foundation of true wisdom.
 All who obey his commandments will grow in
  wisdom.

Praise him forever!

PSALM 112

Praise the Lord!

How joyful are those who fear the Lord
 and delight in obeying his commands.
Their children will be successful everywhere;
 an entire generation of godly people will be
  blessed.
They themselves will be wealthy,
 and their good deeds will last forever.
Light shines in the darkness for the godly.
 They are generous, compassionate, and righteous.
Good comes to those who lend money generously
 and conduct their business fairly.
Such people will not be overcome by evil.
 Those who are righteous will be long remembered.
They do not fear bad news;
 they confidently trust the Lord to care for them.
They are confident and fearless
 and can face their foes triumphantly.
They share freely and give generously to those in need.
 Their good deeds will be remembered forever.
 They will have influence and honor.
The wicked will see this and be infuriated.
 They will grind their teeth in anger;
 they will slink away, their hopes thwarted.

PSALM 113

Praise the Lord!

Yes, give praise, O servants of the Lord.
    Praise the name of the Lord!
Blessed be the name of the Lord
    now and forever.
Everywhere—from east to west—
    praise the name of the Lord.
For the Lord is high above the nations;
    his glory is higher than the heavens.

Who can be compared with the Lord our God,
    who is enthroned on high?
He stoops to look down
    on heaven and on earth.
He lifts the poor from the dust
    and the needy from the garbage dump.
He sets them among princes,
    even the princes of his own people!
He gives the childless woman a family,
    making her a happy mother.

Praise the Lord!

PSALM 114

When the Israelites escaped from Egypt—
    when the family of Jacob left that foreign land—
the land of Judah became God's sanctuary,
    and Israel became his kingdom.

The Red Sea saw them coming and hurried out of their way!
    The water of the Jordan River turned away.
The mountains skipped like rams,
    the hills like lambs!
What's wrong, Red Sea, that made you hurry out of their way?
    What happened, Jordan River, that you turned away?
Why, mountains, did you skip like rams?
    Why, hills, like lambs?

Tremble, O earth, at the presence of the Lord,
    at the presence of the God of Jacob.
He turned the rock into a pool of water;
    yes, a spring of water flowed from solid rock.

PSALM 115

Not to us, O LORD, not to us,
  but to your name goes all the glory
  for your unfailing love and faithfulness.
Why let the nations say,
  "Where is their God?"
Our God is in the heavens,
  and he does as he wishes.
Their idols are merely things of silver and gold,
  shaped by human hands.
They have mouths but cannot speak,
  and eyes but cannot see.
They have ears but cannot hear,
  and noses but cannot smell.
They have hands but cannot feel,
  and feet but cannot walk,
  and throats but cannot make a sound.
And those who make idols are just like them,
  as are all who trust in them.

O Israel, trust the LORD!
  He is your helper and your shield.
O priests, descendants of Aaron, trust the LORD!
  He is your helper and your shield.
All you who fear the LORD, trust the LORD!
  He is your helper and your shield.

The LORD remembers us and will bless us.
  He will bless the people of Israel
  and bless the priests, the descendants of Aaron.
He will bless those who fear the LORD,
  both great and lowly.

May the LORD richly bless
  both you and your children.
May you be blessed by the LORD,
  who made heaven and earth.
The heavens belong to the LORD,
  but he has given the earth to all humanity.
The dead cannot sing praises to the LORD,
  for they have gone into the silence of the grave.
But we can praise the LORD
  both now and forever!

Praise the LORD!

PSALM 116

I love the LORD because he hears my voice
  and my prayer for mercy.
Because he bends down to listen,
  I will pray as long as I have breath!
Death wrapped its ropes around me;
  the terrors of the grave overtook me.
  I saw only trouble and sorrow.
Then I called on the name of the LORD:
  "Please, LORD, save me!"
How kind the LORD is! How good he is!
  So merciful, this God of ours!
The LORD protects those of childlike faith;
  I was facing death, and he saved me.
Let my soul be at rest again,
  for the LORD has been good to me.
He has saved me from death,
  my eyes from tears,
  my feet from stumbling.
And so I walk in the LORD's presence
  as I live here on earth!
I believed in you, so I said,
  "I am deeply troubled, LORD."
In my anxiety I cried out to you,
  "These people are all liars!"
What can I offer the LORD
  for all he has done for me?
I will lift up the cup of salvation
  and praise the LORD's name for saving me.
I will keep my promises to the LORD
  in the presence of all his people.

The LORD cares deeply
  when his loved ones die.
O LORD, I am your servant;
  yes, I am your servant, born into your
    household;
  you have freed me from my chains.
I will offer you a sacrifice of thanksgiving
  and call on the name of the LORD.
I will fulfill my vows to the LORD
  in the presence of all his people—

in the house of the LORD
in the heart of Jerusalem.

Praise the LORD!

PSALM 117

Praise the LORD, all you nations.
Praise him, all you people of the earth.
For his unfailing love for us is powerful;
the LORD's faithfulness endures forever.

Praise the LORD!

PSALM 118

Give thanks to the LORD, for he is good!
His faithful love endures forever.

Let all Israel repeat:
"His faithful love endures forever."
Let Aaron's descendants, the priests, repeat:
"His faithful love endures forever."
Let all who fear the LORD repeat:
"His faithful love endures forever."

In my distress I prayed to the LORD,
and the LORD answered me and set me free.
The LORD is for me, so I will have no fear.
What can mere people do to me?
Yes, the LORD is for me; he will help me.
I will look in triumph at those who hate me.
It is better to take refuge in the LORD
than to trust in people.
It is better to take refuge in the LORD
than to trust in princes.

Though hostile nations surrounded me,
I destroyed them all with the authority of the LORD.
Yes, they surrounded and attacked me,
but I destroyed them all with the authority of the LORD.
They swarmed around me like bees;
they blazed against me like a crackling fire.
But I destroyed them all with the authority of the LORD.

My enemies did their best to kill me,
    but the LORD rescued me.
The LORD is my strength and my song;
    he has given me victory.
Songs of joy and victory are sung in the camp of the godly.
    The strong right arm of the LORD has done glorious things!
The strong right arm of the LORD is raised in triumph.
    The strong right arm of the LORD has done glorious things!
I will not die; instead, I will live
    to tell what the LORD has done.
The LORD has punished me severely,
    but he did not let me die.

Open for me the gates where the righteous enter,
    and I will go in and thank the LORD.
These gates lead to the presence of the LORD,
    and the godly enter there.
I thank you for answering my prayer
    and giving me victory!

The stone that the builders rejected
    has now become the cornerstone.
This is the LORD's doing,
    and it is wonderful to see.
This is the day the LORD has made.
    We will rejoice and be glad in it.
Please, LORD, please save us.
    Please, LORD, please give us success.
Bless the one who comes in the name of the LORD.
    We bless you from the house of the LORD.
The LORD is God, shining upon us.
    Take the sacrifice and bind it with cords on the altar.
You are my God, and I will praise you!
    You are my God, and I will exalt you!

Give thanks to the LORD, for he is good!
    His faithful love endures forever.

PSALM 119

Aleph

Joyful are people of integrity,
    who follow the instructions of the LORD.

Joyful are those who obey his laws
    and search for him with all their hearts.
They do not compromise with evil,
    and they walk only in his paths.
You have charged us
    to keep your commandments carefully.
Oh, that my actions would consistently
    reflect your decrees!
Then I will not be ashamed
    when I compare my life with your commands.
As I learn your righteous regulations,
    I will thank you by living as I should!
I will obey your decrees.
    Please don't give up on me!

Beth

How can a young person stay pure?
    By obeying your word.
I have tried hard to find you—
    don't let me wander from your commands.
I have hidden your word in my heart,
    that I might not sin against you.
I praise you, O LORD;
    teach me your decrees.
I have recited aloud
    all the regulations you have given us.
I have rejoiced in your laws
    as much as in riches.
I will study your commandments
    and reflect on your ways.
I will delight in your decrees
    and not forget your word.

Gimel

Be good to your servant,
    that I may live and obey your word.
Open my eyes to see
    the wonderful truths in your instructions.
I am only a foreigner in the land.
    Don't hide your commands from me!
I am always overwhelmed
    with a desire for your regulations.

You rebuke the arrogant;
   those who wander from your commands are cursed.
Don't let them scorn and insult me,
   for I have obeyed your laws.
Even princes sit and speak against me,
   but I will meditate on your decrees.
Your laws please me;
   they give me wise advice.

Daleth

I lie in the dust;
   revive me by your word.
I told you my plans, and you answered.
   Now teach me your decrees.
Help me understand the meaning of your commandments,
   and I will meditate on your wonderful deeds.
I weep with sorrow;
   encourage me by your word.
Keep me from lying to myself;
   give me the privilege of knowing your instructions.
I have chosen to be faithful;
   I have determined to live by your regulations.
I cling to your laws.
   LORD, don't let me be put to shame!
I will pursue your commands,
   for you expand my understanding.

He

Teach me your decrees, O LORD;
   I will keep them to the end.
Give me understanding and I will obey your instructions;
   I will put them into practice with all my heart.
Make me walk along the path of your commands,
   for that is where my happiness is found.
Give me an eagerness for your laws
   rather than a love for money!
Turn my eyes from worthless things,
   and give me life through your word.
Reassure me of your promise,
   made to those who fear you.
Help me abandon my shameful ways;
   for your regulations are good.

I long to obey your commandments!
    Renew my life with your goodness.

Waw

LORD, give me your unfailing love,
    the salvation that you promised me.
Then I can answer those who taunt me,
    for I trust in your word.
Do not snatch your word of truth from me,
    for your regulations are my only hope.
I will keep on obeying your instructions
    forever and ever.
I will walk in freedom,
    for I have devoted myself to your commandments.
I will speak to kings about your laws,
    and I will not be ashamed.
How I delight in your commands!
    How I love them!
I honor and love your commands.
    I meditate on your decrees.

Zayin

Remember your promise to me;
    it is my only hope.
Your promise revives me;
    it comforts me in all my troubles.
The proud hold me in utter contempt,
    but I do not turn away from your instructions.
I meditate on your age-old regulations;
    O LORD, they comfort me.
I become furious with the wicked,
    because they reject your instructions.
Your decrees have been the theme of my songs
    wherever I have lived.
I reflect at night on who you are, O LORD;
    therefore, I obey your instructions.
This is how I spend my life:
    obeying your commandments.

Heth

LORD, you are mine!
    I promise to obey your words!

With all my heart I want your blessings.
  Be merciful as you promised.
I pondered the direction of my life,
  and I turned to follow your laws.
I will hurry, without delay,
  to obey your commands.
Evil people try to drag me into sin,
  but I am firmly anchored to your instructions.
I rise at midnight to thank you
  for your just regulations.
I am a friend to anyone who fears you—
  anyone who obeys your commandments.
O Lord, your unfailing love fills the earth;
  teach me your decrees.

Teth

You have done many good things for me, Lord,
  just as you promised.
I believe in your commands;
  now teach me good judgment and knowledge.
I used to wander off until you disciplined me;
  but now I closely follow your word.
You are good and do only good;
  teach me your decrees.
Arrogant people smear me with lies,
  but in truth I obey your commandments with all my heart.
Their hearts are dull and stupid,
  but I delight in your instructions.
My suffering was good for me,
  for it taught me to pay attention to your decrees.
Your instructions are more valuable to me
  than millions in gold and silver.

Yodh

You made me; you created me.
  Now give me the sense to follow your commands.
May all who fear you find in me a cause for joy,
  for I have put my hope in your word.
I know, O Lord, that your regulations are fair;
  you disciplined me because I needed it.
Now let your unfailing love comfort me,
  just as you promised me, your servant.

Surround me with your tender mercies so I may live,
    for your instructions are my delight.
Bring disgrace upon the arrogant people who lied about me;
    meanwhile, I will concentrate on your commandments.
Let me be united with all who fear you,
    with those who know your laws.
May I be blameless in keeping your decrees;
    then I will never be ashamed.

Kaph

I am worn out waiting for your rescue,
    but I have put my hope in your word.
My eyes are straining to see your promises come true.
    When will you comfort me?
I am shriveled like a wineskin in the smoke,
    but I have not forgotten to obey your decrees.
How long must I wait?
    When will you punish those who persecute me?
These arrogant people who hate your instructions
    have dug deep pits to trap me.
All your commands are trustworthy.
    Protect me from those who hunt me down without cause.
They almost finished me off,
    but I refused to abandon your commandments.
In your unfailing love, spare my life;
    then I can continue to obey your laws.

Lamedh

Your eternal word, O LORD,
    stands firm in heaven.
Your faithfulness extends to every generation,
    as enduring as the earth you created.
Your regulations remain true to this day,
    for everything serves your plans.
If your instructions hadn't sustained me with joy,
    I would have died in my misery.
I will never forget your commandments,
    for by them you give me life.
I am yours; rescue me!
    For I have worked hard at obeying your commandments.
Though the wicked hide along the way to kill me,
    I will quietly keep my mind on your laws.

Even perfection has its limits,
    but your commands have no limit.

Mem

Oh, how I love your instructions!
    I think about them all day long.
Your commands make me wiser than my enemies,
    for they are my constant guide.
Yes, I have more insight than my teachers,
    for I am always thinking of your laws.
I am even wiser than my elders,
    for I have kept your commandments.
I have refused to walk on any evil path,
    so that I may remain obedient to your word.
I haven't turned away from your regulations,
    for you have taught me well.
How sweet your words taste to me;
    they are sweeter than honey.
Your commandments give me understanding;
    no wonder I hate every false way of life.

Nun

Your word is a lamp to guide my feet
    and a light for my path.
I've promised it once, and I'll promise it again:
    I will obey your righteous regulations.
I have suffered much, O Lord;
    restore my life again as you promised.
Lord, accept my offering of praise,
    and teach me your regulations.
My life constantly hangs in the balance,
    but I will not stop obeying your instructions.
The wicked have set their traps for me,
    but I will not turn from your commandments.
Your laws are my treasure;
    they are my heart's delight.
I am determined to keep your decrees
    to the very end.

Samekh

I hate those with divided loyalties,
    but I love your instructions.

You are my refuge and my shield;
> your word is my source of hope.

Get out of my life, you evil-minded people,
> for I intend to obey the commands of my God.

LORD, sustain me as you promised, that I may live!
> Do not let my hope be crushed.

Sustain me, and I will be rescued;
> then I will meditate continually on your decrees.

But you have rejected all who stray from your decrees.
> They are only fooling themselves.

You skim off the wicked of the earth like scum;
> no wonder I love to obey your laws!

I tremble in fear of you;
> I stand in awe of your regulations.

Ayin

Don't leave me to the mercy of my enemies,
> for I have done what is just and right.

Please guarantee a blessing for me.
> Don't let the arrogant oppress me!

My eyes strain to see your rescue,
> to see the truth of your promise fulfilled.

I am your servant; deal with me in unfailing love,
> and teach me your decrees.

Give discernment to me, your servant;
> then I will understand your laws.

LORD, it is time for you to act,
> for these evil people have violated your instructions.

Truly, I love your commands
> more than gold, even the finest gold.

Each of your commandments is right.
> That is why I hate every false way.

Pe

Your laws are wonderful.
> No wonder I obey them!

The teaching of your word gives light,
> so even the simple can understand.

I pant with expectation,
> longing for your commands.

Come and show me your mercy,
> as you do for all who love your name.

Guide my steps by your word,
   so I will not be overcome by evil.
Ransom me from the oppression of evil people;
   then I can obey your commandments.
Look upon me with love;
   teach me your decrees.
Rivers of tears gush from my eyes
   because people disobey your instructions.

Tsadhe

O LORD, you are righteous,
   and your regulations are fair.
Your laws are perfect
   and completely trustworthy.
I am overwhelmed with indignation,
   for my enemies have disregarded your words.
Your promises have been thoroughly tested;
   that is why I love them so much.
I am insignificant and despised,
   but I don't forget your commandments.
Your justice is eternal,
   and your instructions are perfectly true.
As pressure and stress bear down on me,
   I find joy in your commands.
Your laws are always right;
   help me to understand them so I may live.

Qoph

I pray with all my heart; answer me, LORD!
   I will obey your decrees.
I cry out to you; rescue me,
   that I may obey your laws.
I rise early, before the sun is up;
   I cry out for help and put my hope in your words.
I stay awake through the night,
   thinking about your promise.
In your faithful love, O LORD, hear my cry;
   let me be revived by following your regulations.
Lawless people are coming to attack me;
   they live far from your instructions.
But you are near, O LORD,
   and all your commands are true.

I have known from my earliest days
   that your laws will last forever.

Resh

Look upon my suffering and rescue me,
   for I have not forgotten your instructions.
Argue my case; take my side!
   Protect my life as you promised.
The wicked are far from rescue,
   for they do not bother with your decrees.
LORD, how great is your mercy;
   let me be revived by following your regulations.
Many persecute and trouble me,
   yet I have not swerved from your laws.
Seeing these traitors makes me sick at heart,
   because they care nothing for your word.
See how I love your commandments, LORD.
   Give back my life because of your unfailing love.
The very essence of your words is truth;
   all your just regulations will stand forever.

Shin

Powerful people harass me without cause,
   but my heart trembles only at your word.
I rejoice in your word
   like one who discovers a great treasure.
I hate and abhor all falsehood,
   but I love your instructions.
I will praise you seven times a day
   because all your regulations are just.
Those who love your instructions have great peace
   and do not stumble.
I long for your rescue, LORD,
   so I have obeyed your commands.
I have obeyed your laws,
   for I love them very much.
Yes, I obey your commandments and laws
   because you know everything I do.

Taw

O LORD, listen to my cry;
   give me the discerning mind you promised.

Listen to my prayer;
    rescue me as you promised.
Let praise flow from my lips,
    for you have taught me your decrees.
Let my tongue sing about your word,
    for all your commands are right.
Give me a helping hand,
    for I have chosen to follow your commandments.
O Lord, I have longed for your rescue,
    and your instructions are my delight.
Let me live so I can praise you,
    and may your regulations help me.
I have wandered away like a lost sheep;
    come and find me,
    for I have not forgotten your commands.

PSALM 120

A song for pilgrims ascending to Jerusalem.

I took my troubles to the Lord;
    I cried out to him, and he answered my prayer.
Rescue me, O Lord, from liars
    and from all deceitful people.
O deceptive tongue, what will God do to you?
    How will he increase your punishment?
You will be pierced with sharp arrows
    and burned with glowing coals.

How I suffer in far-off Meshech.
    It pains me to live in distant Kedar.
I am tired of living
    among people who hate peace.
I search for peace;
    but when I speak of peace, they want war!

PSALM 121

A song for pilgrims ascending to Jerusalem.

I look up to the mountains—
    does my help come from there?
My help comes from the Lord,
    who made heaven and earth!

He will not let you stumble;
  the one who watches over you will not
    slumber.
Indeed, he who watches over Israel
  never slumbers or sleeps.

The LORD himself watches over you!
  The LORD stands beside you as your protective
    shade.
The sun will not harm you by day,
  nor the moon at night.

The LORD keeps you from all harm
  and watches over your life.
The LORD keeps watch over you as you come and go,
  both now and forever.

PSALM 122

A song for pilgrims ascending to Jerusalem. A psalm of David.

I was glad when they said to me,
  "Let us go to the house of the LORD."
And now here we are,
  standing inside your gates, O Jerusalem.
Jerusalem is a well-built city;
  its seamless walls cannot be breached.
All the tribes of Israel—the LORD's people—
  make their pilgrimage here.
They come to give thanks to the name of the LORD,
  as the law requires of Israel.
Here stand the thrones where judgment is
      given,
  the thrones of the dynasty of David.

Pray for peace in Jerusalem.
  May all who love this city prosper.
O Jerusalem, may there be peace within your
      walls
  and prosperity in your palaces.
For the sake of my family and friends, I will say,
  "May you have peace."
For the sake of the house of the LORD our God,
  I will seek what is best for you, O Jerusalem.

PSALM 123

A song for pilgrims ascending to Jerusalem.

I lift my eyes to you,
  O God, enthroned in heaven.
We keep looking to the LORD our God for his mercy,
  just as servants keep their eyes on their master,
  as a slave girl watches her mistress for the slightest signal.
Have mercy on us, LORD, have mercy,
  for we have had our fill of contempt.
We have had more than our fill of the scoffing of the proud
  and the contempt of the arrogant.

PSALM 124

A song for pilgrims ascending to Jerusalem. A psalm of David.

What if the LORD had not been on our side?
  Let all Israel repeat:
What if the LORD had not been on our side
  when people attacked us?
They would have swallowed us alive
  in their burning anger.
The waters would have engulfed us;
  a torrent would have overwhelmed us.
Yes, the raging waters of their fury
  would have overwhelmed our very lives.

Praise the LORD,
  who did not let their teeth tear us apart!
We escaped like a bird from a hunter's trap.
  The trap is broken, and we are free!
Our help is from the LORD,
  who made heaven and earth.

PSALM 125

A song for pilgrims ascending to Jerusalem.

Those who trust in the LORD are as secure as Mount Zion;
  they will not be defeated but will endure forever.
Just as the mountains surround Jerusalem,
  so the LORD surrounds his people, both now and forever.
The wicked will not rule the land of the godly,

for then the godly might be tempted to do wrong.
O LORD, do good to those who are good,
    whose hearts are in tune with you.
But banish those who turn to crooked ways, O LORD.
    Take them away with those who do evil.

May Israel have peace!

PSALM 126

A song for pilgrims ascending to Jerusalem.

When the LORD brought back his exiles to Jerusalem,
    it was like a dream!
We were filled with laughter,
    and we sang for joy.
And the other nations said,
    "What amazing things the LORD has done for them."
Yes, the LORD has done amazing things for us!
    What joy!

Restore our fortunes, LORD,
    as streams renew the desert.
Those who plant in tears
    will harvest with shouts of joy.
They weep as they go to plant their seed,
    but they sing as they return with the harvest.

PSALM 127

A song for pilgrims ascending to Jerusalem. A psalm of Solomon.

Unless the LORD builds a house,
    the work of the builders is wasted.
Unless the LORD protects a city,
    guarding it with sentries will do no good.
It is useless for you to work so hard
    from early morning until late at night,
anxiously working for food to eat;
    for God gives rest to his loved ones.

Children are a gift from the LORD;
    they are a reward from him.
Children born to a young man
    are like arrows in a warrior's hands.

How joyful is the man whose quiver is full of them!
   He will not be put to shame when he confronts his accusers
      at the city gates.

PSALM 128

A song for pilgrims ascending to Jerusalem.

How joyful are those who fear the LORD—
   all who follow his ways!
You will enjoy the fruit of your labor.
   How joyful and prosperous you will be!
Your wife will be like a fruitful grapevine,
   flourishing within your home.
Your children will be like vigorous young olive trees
   as they sit around your table.
That is the LORD's blessing
   for those who fear him.

May the LORD continually bless you from Zion.
   May you see Jerusalem prosper as long as you live.
May you live to enjoy your grandchildren.
   May Israel have peace!

PSALM 129

A song for pilgrims ascending to Jerusalem.

From my earliest youth my enemies have persecuted me.
   Let all Israel repeat this:
From my earliest youth my enemies have persecuted me,
   but they have never defeated me.
My back is covered with cuts,
   as if a farmer had plowed long furrows.
But the LORD is good;
   he has cut me free from the ropes of the ungodly.

May all who hate Jerusalem
   be turned back in shameful defeat.
May they be as useless as grass on a rooftop,
   turning yellow when only half grown,
ignored by the harvester,
   despised by the binder.
And may those who pass by

refuse to give them this blessing:
"The LORD bless you;
  we bless you in the LORD's name."

PSALM 130

A song for pilgrims ascending to Jerusalem.

From the depths of despair, O LORD,
  I call for your help.
Hear my cry, O Lord.
  Pay attention to my prayer.

LORD, if you kept a record of our sins,
  who, O Lord, could ever survive?
But you offer forgiveness,
  that we might learn to fear you.

I am counting on the LORD;
  yes, I am counting on him.
  I have put my hope in his word.
I long for the Lord
  more than sentries long for the dawn,
  yes, more than sentries long for the dawn.

O Israel, hope in the LORD;
  for with the LORD there is unfailing love.
  His redemption overflows.
He himself will redeem Israel
  from every kind of sin.

PSALM 131

A song for pilgrims ascending to Jerusalem. A psalm of David.

LORD, my heart is not proud;
  my eyes are not haughty.
I don't concern myself with matters too great
  or too awesome for me to grasp.
Instead, I have calmed and quieted myself,
  like a weaned child who no longer cries for its mother's milk.
  Yes, like a weaned child is my soul within me.

O Israel, put your hope in the LORD—
  now and always.

PSALM 132

A song for pilgrims ascending to Jerusalem.

LORD, remember David
    and all that he suffered.
He made a solemn promise to the LORD.
    He vowed to the Mighty One of Israel,
"I will not go home;
    I will not let myself rest.
I will not let my eyes sleep
    nor close my eyelids in slumber
until I find a place to build a house for the LORD,
    a sanctuary for the Mighty One of Israel."

We heard that the Ark was in Ephrathah;
    then we found it in the distant countryside of Jaar.
Let us go to the sanctuary of the LORD;
    let us worship at the footstool of his throne.
Arise, O LORD, and enter your resting place,
    along with the Ark, the symbol of your power.
May your priests be clothed in godliness;
    may your loyal servants sing for joy.
For the sake of your servant David,
    do not reject the king you have anointed.
The LORD swore an oath to David
    with a promise he will never take back:
"I will place one of your descendants
    on your throne.
If your descendants obey the terms of my covenant
    and the laws that I teach them,
then your royal line
    will continue forever and ever."

For the LORD has chosen Jerusalem;
    he has desired it for his home.
"This is my resting place forever," he said.
    "I will live here, for this is the home I desired.
I will bless this city and make it prosperous;
    I will satisfy its poor with food.
I will clothe its priests with godliness;
    its faithful servants will sing for joy.
Here I will increase the power of David;
    my anointed one will be a light for my people.

I will clothe his enemies with shame,
  but he will be a glorious king."

PSALM 133

A song for pilgrims ascending to Jerusalem. A psalm of David.

How wonderful and pleasant it is
  when brothers live together in harmony!
For harmony is as precious as the anointing oil
    that was poured over Aaron's head,
    that ran down his beard
    and onto the border of his robe.
Harmony is as refreshing as the dew from
      Mount Hermon
    that falls on the mountains of Zion.
And there the LORD has pronounced his blessing,
  even life everlasting.

PSALM 134

A song for pilgrims ascending to Jerusalem.

Oh, praise the LORD, all you servants of the LORD,
  you who serve at night in the house of the LORD.
Lift your hands toward the sanctuary,
  and praise the LORD.

May the LORD, who made heaven and earth,
  bless you from Jerusalem.

PSALM 135

Praise the LORD!

Praise the name of the LORD!
  Praise him, you who serve the LORD,
you who serve in the house of the LORD,
  in the courts of the house of our God.

Praise the LORD, for the LORD is good;
  celebrate his lovely name with music.
For the LORD has chosen Jacob for himself,
  Israel for his own special treasure.

I know the greatness of the LORD—
    that our Lord is greater than any other god.
The LORD does whatever pleases him
    throughout all heaven and earth,
    and on the seas and in their depths.
He causes the clouds to rise over the whole earth.
    He sends the lightning with the rain
    and releases the wind from his storehouses.

He destroyed the firstborn in each Egyptian home,
    both people and animals.
He performed miraculous signs and wonders in Egypt
    against Pharaoh and all his people.
He struck down great nations
    and slaughtered mighty kings—
Sihon king of the Amorites,
    Og king of Bashan,
    and all the kings of Canaan.
He gave their land as an inheritance,
    a special possession to his people Israel.

Your name, O LORD, endures forever;
    your fame, O LORD, is known to every generation.
For the LORD will give justice to his people
    and have compassion on his servants.

The idols of the nations are merely things of silver
      and gold,
    shaped by human hands.
They have mouths but cannot speak,
    and eyes but cannot see.
They have ears but cannot hear,
    and mouths but cannot breathe.
And those who make idols are just like them,
    as are all who trust in them.

O Israel, praise the LORD!
    O priests—descendants of Aaron—praise the LORD!
O Levites, praise the LORD!
    All you who fear the LORD, praise the LORD!
The LORD be praised from Zion,
    for he lives here in Jerusalem.

Praise the LORD!

PSALM 136

Give thanks to the LORD, for he is good!
His faithful love endures forever.
Give thanks to the God of gods.
His faithful love endures forever.
Give thanks to the Lord of lords.
His faithful love endures forever.

Give thanks to him who alone does mighty miracles.
His faithful love endures forever.
Give thanks to him who made the heavens so skillfully.
His faithful love endures forever.
Give thanks to him who placed the earth among the waters.
His faithful love endures forever.
Give thanks to him who made the heavenly lights—
His faithful love endures forever.
the sun to rule the day,
His faithful love endures forever.
and the moon and stars to rule the night.
His faithful love endures forever.

Give thanks to him who killed the firstborn of Egypt.
His faithful love endures forever.
He brought Israel out of Egypt.
His faithful love endures forever.
He acted with a strong hand and powerful arm.
His faithful love endures forever.
Give thanks to him who parted the Red Sea.
His faithful love endures forever.
He led Israel safely through,
His faithful love endures forever.
but he hurled Pharaoh and his army into the Red Sea.
His faithful love endures forever.
Give thanks to him who led his people through the
    wilderness.
His faithful love endures forever.

Give thanks to him who struck down mighty kings.
His faithful love endures forever.
He killed powerful kings—
His faithful love endures forever.
Sihon king of the Amorites,
His faithful love endures forever.

and Og king of Bashan.
> *His faithful love endures forever.*

God gave the land of these kings as an inheritance—
> *His faithful love endures forever.*

a special possession to his servant Israel.
> *His faithful love endures forever.*

He remembered us in our weakness.
> *His faithful love endures forever.*

He saved us from our enemies.
> *His faithful love endures forever.*

He gives food to every living thing.
> *His faithful love endures forever.*

Give thanks to the God of heaven.
> *His faithful love endures forever.*

PSALM 137

Beside the rivers of Babylon, we sat and wept
as we thought of Jerusalem.
We put away our harps,
hanging them on the branches of poplar trees.
For our captors demanded a song from us.
Our tormentors insisted on a joyful hymn:
"Sing us one of those songs of Jerusalem!"
But how can we sing the songs of the LORD
while in a pagan land?

If I forget you, O Jerusalem,
let my right hand forget how to play the harp.
May my tongue stick to the roof of my mouth
if I fail to remember you,
if I don't make Jerusalem my greatest joy.

O LORD, remember what the Edomites did
on the day the armies of Babylon captured Jerusalem.
"Destroy it!" they yelled.
"Level it to the ground!"
O Babylon, you will be destroyed.
Happy is the one who pays you back
for what you have done to us.
Happy is the one who takes your babies
and smashes them against the rocks!

PSALM 138

A psalm of David.

I give you thanks, O Lord, with all my heart;
   I will sing your praises before the gods.
I bow before your holy Temple as I worship.
   I praise your name for your unfailing love and
      faithfulness;
for your promises are backed
   by all the honor of your name.
As soon as I pray, you answer me;
   you encourage me by giving me strength.

Every king in all the earth will thank you, Lord,
   for all of them will hear your words.
Yes, they will sing about the Lord's ways,
   for the glory of the Lord is very great.
Though the Lord is great, he cares for the
      humble,
   but he keeps his distance from the proud.

Though I am surrounded by troubles,
   you will protect me from the anger of my enemies.
You reach out your hand,
   and the power of your right hand saves me.
The Lord will work out his plans for my life—
   for your faithful love, O Lord, endures forever.
   Don't abandon me, for you made me.

PSALM 139

For the choir director: A psalm of David.

O Lord, you have examined my heart
   and know everything about me.
You know when I sit down or stand up.
   You know my thoughts even when I'm far away.
You see me when I travel
   and when I rest at home.
   You know everything I do.
You know what I am going to say
   even before I say it, Lord.
You go before me and follow me.
   You place your hand of blessing on my head.

Such knowledge is too wonderful for me,
  too great for me to understand!

I can never escape from your Spirit!
  I can never get away from your presence!
If I go up to heaven, you are there;
  if I go down to the grave, you are there.
If I ride the wings of the morning,
  if I dwell by the farthest oceans,
even there your hand will guide me,
  and your strength will support me.
I could ask the darkness to hide me
  and the light around me to become night—
  but even in darkness I cannot hide from you.
To you the night shines as bright as day.
  Darkness and light are the same to you.

You made all the delicate, inner parts of my body
  and knit me together in my mother's womb.
Thank you for making me so wonderfully complex!
  Your workmanship is marvelous—how well I know it.
You watched me as I was being formed in utter seclusion,
  as I was woven together in the dark of the womb.
You saw me before I was born.
  Every day of my life was recorded in your book.
Every moment was laid out
  before a single day had passed.

How precious are your thoughts about me, O God.
  They cannot be numbered!
I can't even count them;
  they outnumber the grains of sand!
And when I wake up,
  you are still with me!

O God, if only you would destroy the wicked!
  Get out of my life, you murderers!
They blaspheme you;
  your enemies misuse your name.
O Lord, shouldn't I hate those who hate you?
  Shouldn't I despise those who oppose you?
Yes, I hate them with total hatred,
  for your enemies are my enemies.

Search me, O God, and know my heart;
>   test me and know my anxious thoughts.
Point out anything in me that offends you,
>   and lead me along the path of everlasting life.

PSALM 140

For the choir director: A psalm of David.

O LORD, rescue me from evil people.
>   Protect me from those who are violent,
those who plot evil in their hearts
>   and stir up trouble all day long.
Their tongues sting like a snake;
>   the venom of a viper drips from their lips.   *Interlude*

O LORD, keep me out of the hands of the
>   wicked.
>   Protect me from those who are violent,
>   for they are plotting against me.
The proud have set a trap to catch me;
>   they have stretched out a net;
>   they have placed traps all along the way.   *Interlude*

I said to the LORD, "You are my God!"
>   Listen, O LORD, to my cries for mercy!
O Sovereign LORD, the strong one who rescued me,
>   you protected me on the day of battle.
LORD, do not let evil people have their way.
>   Do not let their evil schemes succeed,
>   or they will become proud.   *Interlude*

Let my enemies be destroyed
>   by the very evil they have planned for me.
Let burning coals fall down on their heads.
>   Let them be thrown into the fire
>   or into watery pits from which they can't escape.
Don't let liars prosper here in our land.
>   Cause great disasters to fall on the violent.

But I know the LORD will help those they
>   persecute;
>   he will give justice to the poor.
Surely righteous people are praising your name;
>   the godly will live in your presence.

PSALM 141

A psalm of David.

O Lord, I am calling to you. Please hurry!
　　Listen when I cry to you for help!
Accept my prayer as incense offered to you,
　　and my upraised hands as an evening offering.

Take control of what I say, O Lord,
　　and guard my lips.
Don't let me drift toward evil
　　or take part in acts of wickedness.
Don't let me share in the delicacies
　　of those who do wrong.

Let the godly strike me!
　　It will be a kindness!
If they correct me, it is soothing medicine.
　　Don't let me refuse it.

But I pray constantly
　　against the wicked and their deeds.
When their leaders are thrown down from a cliff,
　　the wicked will listen to my words and find them true.
Like rocks brought up by a plow,
　　the bones of the wicked will lie scattered without burial.

I look to you for help, O Sovereign Lord.
　　You are my refuge; don't let them kill me.
Keep me from the traps they have set for me,
　　from the snares of those who do wrong.
Let the wicked fall into their own nets,
　　but let me escape.

PSALM 142

A psalm of David, regarding his experience in the cave. A prayer.

I cry out to the Lord;
　　I plead for the Lord's mercy.
I pour out my complaints before him
　　and tell him all my troubles.
When I am overwhelmed,
　　you alone know the way I should turn.
Wherever I go,

my enemies have set traps for me.
I look for someone to come and help me,
    but no one gives me a passing thought!
No one will help me;
    no one cares a bit what happens to me.
Then I pray to you, O LORD.
    I say, "You are my place of refuge.
    You are all I really want in life.
Hear my cry,
    for I am very low.
Rescue me from my persecutors,
    for they are too strong for me.
Bring me out of prison
    so I can thank you.
The godly will crowd around me,
    for you are good to me."

PSALM 143
A psalm of David.

Hear my prayer, O LORD;
    listen to my plea!
    Answer me because you are faithful and righteous.
Don't put your servant on trial,
    for no one is innocent before you.
My enemy has chased me.
    He has knocked me to the ground
    and forces me to live in darkness like those in the grave.
I am losing all hope;
    I am paralyzed with fear.
I remember the days of old.
    I ponder all your great works
    and think about what you have done.
I lift my hands to you in prayer.
    I thirst for you as parched land thirsts for rain.   *Interlude*

Come quickly, LORD, and answer me,
    for my depression deepens.
Don't turn away from me,
    or I will die.
Let me hear of your unfailing love each morning,
    for I am trusting you.

Show me where to walk,
    for I give myself to you.
Rescue me from my enemies, LORD;
    I run to you to hide me.
Teach me to do your will,
    for you are my God.
May your gracious Spirit lead me forward
    on a firm footing.
For the glory of your name, O LORD, preserve my life.
    Because of your faithfulness, bring me out of this distress.
In your unfailing love, silence all my enemies
    and destroy all my foes,
    for I am your servant.

PSALM 144

A psalm of David.

Praise the LORD, who is my rock.
    He trains my hands for war
    and gives my fingers skill for battle.
He is my loving ally and my fortress,
    my tower of safety, my rescuer.
He is my shield, and I take refuge in him.
    He makes the nations submit to me.

O LORD, what are human beings that you should notice them,
    mere mortals that you should think about them?
For they are like a breath of air;
    their days are like a passing shadow.

Open the heavens, LORD, and come down.
    Touch the mountains so they billow smoke.
Hurl your lightning bolts and scatter your enemies!
    Shoot your arrows and confuse them!
Reach down from heaven and rescue me;
    rescue me from deep waters,
    from the power of my enemies.
Their mouths are full of lies;
    they swear to tell the truth, but they lie instead.

I will sing a new song to you, O God!
    I will sing your praises with a ten-stringed harp.
For you grant victory to kings!

You rescued your servant David from the fatal sword.
Save me!
  Rescue me from the power of my enemies.
Their mouths are full of lies;
  they swear to tell the truth, but they lie instead.

May our sons flourish in their youth
  like well-nurtured plants.
May our daughters be like graceful pillars,
  carved to beautify a palace.
May our barns be filled
  with crops of every kind.
May the flocks in our fields multiply by the thousands,
  even tens of thousands,
  and may our oxen be loaded down with produce.
May there be no enemy breaking through our walls,
  no going into captivity,
  no cries of alarm in our town squares.
Yes, joyful are those who live like this!
  Joyful indeed are those whose God is the LORD.

PSALM 145
A psalm of praise of David.

I will exalt you, my God and King,
  and praise your name forever and ever.
I will praise you every day;
  yes, I will praise you forever.
Great is the LORD! He is most worthy of praise!
  No one can measure his greatness.

Let each generation tell its children of your mighty acts;
  let them proclaim your power.
I will meditate on your majestic, glorious splendor
  and your wonderful miracles.
Your awe-inspiring deeds will be on every tongue;
  I will proclaim your greatness.
Everyone will share the story of your wonderful
      goodness;
  they will sing with joy about your righteousness.

The LORD is merciful and compassionate,
  slow to get angry and filled with unfailing love.

The LORD is good to everyone.
    He showers compassion on all his creation.
All of your works will thank you, LORD,
    and your faithful followers will praise you.
They will speak of the glory of your kingdom;
    they will give examples of your power.
They will tell about your mighty deeds
    and about the majesty and glory of your reign.
For your kingdom is an everlasting kingdom.
    You rule throughout all generations.

The LORD always keeps his promises;
    he is gracious in all he does.
The LORD helps the fallen
    and lifts those bent beneath their loads.
The eyes of all look to you in hope;
    you give them their food as they need it.
When you open your hand,
    you satisfy the hunger and thirst of every living thing.
The LORD is righteous in everything he does;
    he is filled with kindness.
The LORD is close to all who call on him,
    yes, to all who call on him in truth.
He grants the desires of those who fear him;
    he hears their cries for help and rescues them.
The LORD protects all those who love him,
    but he destroys the wicked.

I will praise the LORD,
    and may everyone on earth bless his holy name
    forever and ever.

PSALM 146

Praise the LORD!

Let all that I am praise the LORD.
    I will praise the LORD as long as I live.
    I will sing praises to my God with my dying breath.

Don't put your confidence in powerful people;
    there is no help for you there.
When they breathe their last, they return to the earth,
    and all their plans die with them.

But joyful are those who have the God of Israel as their helper,
    whose hope is in the LORD their God.
He made heaven and earth,
    the sea, and everything in them.
    He keeps every promise forever.
He gives justice to the oppressed
    and food to the hungry.
The LORD frees the prisoners.
    The LORD opens the eyes of the blind.
The LORD lifts up those who are weighed down.
    The LORD loves the godly.
The LORD protects the foreigners among us.
    He cares for the orphans and widows,
    but he frustrates the plans of the wicked.

The LORD will reign forever.
    He will be your God, O Jerusalem, throughout the
      generations.

Praise the LORD!

PSALM 147

Praise the LORD!

How good to sing praises to our God!
    How delightful and how fitting!
The LORD is rebuilding Jerusalem
    and bringing the exiles back to Israel.
He heals the brokenhearted
    and bandages their wounds.
He counts the stars
    and calls them all by name.
How great is our Lord! His power is absolute!
    His understanding is beyond comprehension!
The LORD supports the humble,
    but he brings the wicked down into the dust.

Sing out your thanks to the LORD;
    sing praises to our God with a harp.
He covers the heavens with clouds,
    provides rain for the earth,
    and makes the grass grow in mountain pastures.

He gives food to the wild animals
and feeds the young ravens when they cry.
He takes no pleasure in the strength of a horse
or in human might.
No, the LORD's delight is in those who fear him,
those who put their hope in his unfailing love.

Glorify the LORD, O Jerusalem!
Praise your God, O Zion!
For he has strengthened the bars of your gates
and blessed your children within your walls.
He sends peace across your nation
and satisfies your hunger with the finest wheat.
He sends his orders to the world—
how swiftly his word flies!
He sends the snow like white wool;
he scatters frost upon the ground like ashes.
He hurls the hail like stones.
Who can stand against his freezing cold?
Then, at his command, it all melts.
He sends his winds, and the ice thaws.
He has revealed his words to Jacob,
his decrees and regulations to Israel.
He has not done this for any other nation;
they do not know his regulations.

Praise the LORD!

PSALM 148

Praise the LORD!

Praise the LORD from the heavens!
Praise him from the skies!
Praise him, all his angels!
Praise him, all the armies of heaven!
Praise him, sun and moon!
Praise him, all you twinkling stars!
Praise him, skies above!
Praise him, vapors high above the clouds!
Let every created thing give praise to the LORD,
for he issued his command, and they came
into being.

He set them in place forever and ever.
　　His decree will never be revoked.

Praise the LORD from the earth,
　　you creatures of the ocean depths,
fire and hail, snow and clouds,
　　wind and weather that obey him,
mountains and all hills,
　　fruit trees and all cedars,
wild animals and all livestock,
　　small scurrying animals and birds,
kings of the earth and all people,
　　rulers and judges of the earth,
young men and young women,
　　old men and children.

Let them all praise the name of the LORD.
　　For his name is very great;
　　his glory towers over the earth and heaven!
He has made his people strong,
　　honoring his faithful ones—
　　the people of Israel who are close to him.

Praise the LORD!

PSALM 149

Praise the LORD!

Sing to the LORD a new song.
　　Sing his praises in the assembly of the faithful.

O Israel, rejoice in your Maker.
　　O people of Jerusalem, exult in your King.
Praise his name with dancing,
　　accompanied by tambourine and harp.
For the LORD delights in his people;
　　he crowns the humble with victory.
Let the faithful rejoice that he honors them.
　　Let them sing for joy as they lie on their beds.

Let the praises of God be in their mouths,
　　and a sharp sword in their hands—
to execute vengeance on the nations
　　and punishment on the peoples,

to bind their kings with shackles
and their leaders with iron chains,
to execute the judgment written against them.
This is the glorious privilege of his faithful ones.

Praise the LORD!

PSALM 150

Praise the LORD!

Praise God in his sanctuary;
praise him in his mighty heaven!
Praise him for his mighty works;
praise his unequaled greatness!
Praise him with a blast of the ram's horn;
praise him with the lyre and harp!
Praise him with the tambourine and dancing;
praise him with strings and flutes!
Praise him with a clash of cymbals;
praise him with loud clanging cymbals.
Let everything that breathes sing praises to the LORD!

Praise the LORD!

IMMERSED IN LAMENTATIONS

IN 587 BC, the city of Jerusalem was attacked and overrun by the Babylonians. The great Temple of Solomon was utterly destroyed, and most of the population was either killed or taken captive. A few poor stragglers were left behind in the rubble. It was an event that shook the people of God to their core, because their suffering and loss was immense. But the disaster also raised larger questions about God's relationship to his people and the future of their story together. If God's people are now scattered and God's chosen place of worship has been demolished, how can his work in the world go forward?

The book of Lamentations speaks to the experience of God's people while still in the midst of deep suffering (in contrast to many laments in Psalms that conclude with words of hope or thanksgiving). The five poems are set in what's left of the city of Jerusalem after its destruction. (Tradition identifies the prophet Jeremiah as the author of these poems, though the book itself does not identify who wrote them.) God's enemies have triumphed over God's people, who are now suffering atrocities and deprivations that can barely be described. All of this raises serious questions about God himself. Where is the God revealed in Psalms as "our refuge and strength, always ready to help in times of trouble"?

The subject matter is so difficult to handle that the poems in Lamentations are among the most tightly arranged in the Bible. It's as if only an orderly structure can hold the sorrow, doubt, and despair together long enough to be offered to God as a desperate prayer. Most of these poems are acrostics, meaning that their stanzas begin with the twenty-two consecutive letters of the Hebrew alphabet. The stanzas have three lines each, and in the third poem each individual line begins with the same letter, the pattern tightening to the extreme. But after that, the pattern doesn't hold together. The fourth poem has two-line stanzas, with the acrostic sequence followed only in the first line of each stanza. And the final poem consists of twenty-two single lines from which the acrostic pattern disappears completely, as if the power of the poet to speak order into the situation fades in the face of its enormity and the only remaining response is silence.

But deep in the heart of Lamentations, the seed of something new is planted, something that speaks of hope and renewal, even in the face of utter loss. The five songs are all laments that unrelentingly recount the details of the disaster. But right in the center of the central song, we find words of hope—an as-yet-unseen faithfulness and an as-yet-unknown compassion. No one is abandoned forever, it says, for God will show his mercy and unfailing love.

We need these hard words of pain and unimaginable suffering in our Bible—words that we choke on and can barely speak, words that drift off into silence. This confirms that the Scriptures confront the most difficult realities we know. But we are also offered words of a deeper hope, an enduring faith by which we ultimately throw ourselves completely on God himself. In this broken world, we have not yet seen these words come to their complete fruition, but we are looking for the coming of something new, something as yet unknown—the restoration of all things.

LAMENTATIONS

✢

Jerusalem, once so full of people,
    is now deserted.
She who was once great among the nations
    now sits alone like a widow.
Once the queen of all the earth,
    she is now a slave.

She sobs through the night;
    tears stream down her cheeks.
Among all her lovers,
    there is no one left to comfort her.
All her friends have betrayed her
    and become her enemies.

Judah has been led away into captivity,
    oppressed with cruel slavery.
She lives among foreign nations
    and has no place of rest.
Her enemies have chased her down,
    and she has nowhere to turn.

The roads to Jerusalem are in mourning,
    for crowds no longer come to celebrate the festivals.
The city gates are silent,
    her priests groan,
her young women are crying—
    how bitter is her fate!

Her oppressors have become her masters,
    and her enemies prosper,
for the LORD has punished Jerusalem
    for her many sins.
Her children have been captured
    and taken away to distant lands.

All the majesty of beautiful Jerusalem
　　has been stripped away.
Her princes are like starving deer
　　searching for pasture.
They are too weak to run
　　from the pursuing enemy.

In the midst of her sadness and wandering,
　　Jerusalem remembers her ancient splendor.
But now she has fallen to her enemy,
　　and there is no one to help her.
Her enemy struck her down
　　and laughed as she fell.

Jerusalem has sinned greatly,
　　so she has been tossed away like a filthy rag.
All who once honored her now despise her,
　　for they have seen her stripped naked and humiliated.
All she can do is groan
　　and hide her face.

She defiled herself with immorality
　　and gave no thought to her future.
Now she lies in the gutter
　　with no one to lift her out.
"Lord, see my misery," she cries.
　　"The enemy has triumphed."

The enemy has plundered her completely,
　　taking every precious thing she owns.
She has seen foreigners violate her sacred Temple,
　　the place the Lord had forbidden them to enter.

Her people groan as they search for bread.
　　They have sold their treasures for food to stay alive.
"O Lord, look," she mourns,
　　"and see how I am despised.

"Does it mean nothing to you, all you who pass by?
　　Look around and see if there is any suffering like mine,
which the Lord brought on me
　　when he erupted in fierce anger.

"He has sent fire from heaven that burns in my bones.
　　He has placed a trap in my path and turned me back.

He has left me devastated,
  racked with sickness all day long.

"He wove my sins into ropes
  to hitch me to a yoke of captivity.
The Lord sapped my strength and turned me over to my enemies;
  I am helpless in their hands.

"The Lord has treated my mighty men
  with contempt.
At his command a great army has come
  to crush my young warriors.
The Lord has trampled his beloved city
  like grapes are trampled in a winepress.

"For all these things I weep;
  tears flow down my cheeks.
No one is here to comfort me;
  any who might encourage me are far away.
My children have no future,
  for the enemy has conquered us."

Jerusalem reaches out for help,
  but no one comforts her.
Regarding his people Israel,
  the LORD has said,
"Let their neighbors be their enemies!
  Let them be thrown away like a filthy rag!"

"The LORD is right," Jerusalem says,
  "for I rebelled against him.
Listen, people everywhere;
  look upon my anguish and despair,
for my sons and daughters
  have been taken captive to distant lands.

"I begged my allies for help,
  but they betrayed me.
My priests and leaders
  starved to death in the city,
even as they searched for food
  to save their lives.

"LORD, see my anguish!
  My heart is broken

and my soul despairs,
    for I have rebelled against you.
In the streets the sword kills,
    and at home there is only death.

"Others heard my groans,
    but no one turned to comfort me.
When my enemies heard about my troubles,
    they were happy to see what you had done.
Oh, bring the day you promised,
    when they will suffer as I have suffered.

"Look at all their evil deeds, LORD.
    Punish them,
as you have punished me
    for all my sins.
My groans are many,
    and I am sick at heart."

✢

The Lord in his anger
    has cast a dark shadow over beautiful Jerusalem.
The fairest of Israel's cities lies in the dust,
    thrown down from the heights of heaven.
In his day of great anger,
    the Lord has shown no mercy even to his Temple.

Without mercy the Lord has destroyed
    every home in Israel.
In his anger he has broken down
    the fortress walls of beautiful Jerusalem.
He has brought them to the ground,
    dishonoring the kingdom and its rulers.

All the strength of Israel
    vanishes beneath his fierce anger.
The Lord has withdrawn his protection
    as the enemy attacks.
He consumes the whole land of Israel
    like a raging fire.

He bends his bow against his people,
    as though he were their enemy.
His strength is used against them

to kill their finest youth.
His fury is poured out like fire
　on beautiful Jerusalem.

Yes, the Lord has vanquished Israel
　like an enemy.
He has destroyed her palaces
　and demolished her fortresses.
He has brought unending sorrow and tears
　upon beautiful Jerusalem.

He has broken down his Temple
　as though it were merely a garden shelter.
The LORD has blotted out all memory
　of the holy festivals and Sabbath days.
Kings and priests fall together
　before his fierce anger.

The Lord has rejected his own altar;
　he despises his own sanctuary.
He has given Jerusalem's palaces
　to her enemies.
They shout in the LORD's Temple
　as though it were a day of celebration.

The LORD was determined
　to destroy the walls of beautiful Jerusalem.
He made careful plans for their destruction,
　then did what he had planned.
Therefore, the ramparts and walls
　have fallen down before him.

Jerusalem's gates have sunk into the ground.
　He has smashed their locks and bars.
Her kings and princes have been exiled to distant lands;
　her law has ceased to exist.
Her prophets receive
　no more visions from the LORD.

The leaders of beautiful Jerusalem
　sit on the ground in silence.
They are clothed in burlap
　and throw dust on their heads.
The young women of Jerusalem
　hang their heads in shame.

I have cried until the tears no longer come;
  my heart is broken.
My spirit is poured out in agony
  as I see the desperate plight of my people.
Little children and tiny babies
  are fainting and dying in the streets.

They cry out to their mothers,
  "We need food and drink!"
Their lives ebb away in the streets
  like the life of a warrior wounded in battle.
They gasp for life
  as they collapse in their mothers' arms.

What can I say about you?
  Who has ever seen such sorrow?
O daughter of Jerusalem,
  to what can I compare your anguish?
O virgin daughter of Zion,
  how can I comfort you?
For your wound is as deep as the sea.
  Who can heal you?

Your prophets have said
  so many foolish things, false to the core.
They did not save you from exile
  by pointing out your sins.
Instead, they painted false pictures,
  filling you with false hope.

All who pass by jeer at you.
  They scoff and insult beautiful Jerusalem, saying,
"Is this the city called 'Most Beautiful in All the World'
  and 'Joy of All the Earth'?"

All your enemies mock you.
  They scoff and snarl and say,
"We have destroyed her at last!
  We have long waited for this day,
  and it is finally here!"

But it is the LORD who did just as he planned.
  He has fulfilled the promises of disaster
  he made long ago.
He has destroyed Jerusalem without mercy.

He has caused her enemies to gloat over her
and has given them power over her.

Cry aloud before the Lord,
O walls of beautiful Jerusalem!
Let your tears flow like a river
day and night.
Give yourselves no rest;
give your eyes no relief.

Rise during the night and cry out.
Pour out your hearts like water to the Lord.
Lift up your hands to him in prayer,
pleading for your children,
for in every street
they are faint with hunger.

"O Lord, think about this!
Should you treat your own people this way?
Should mothers eat their own children,
those they once bounced on their knees?
Should priests and prophets be killed
within the Lord's Temple?

"See them lying in the streets—
young and old,
boys and girls,
killed by the swords of the enemy.
You have killed them in your anger,
slaughtering them without mercy.

"You have invited terrors from all around,
as though you were calling them to a day of feasting.
In the day of the Lord's anger,
no one has escaped or survived.
The enemy has killed all the children
whom I carried and raised."

✝

I am the one who has seen the afflictions
that come from the rod of the Lord's anger.
He has led me into darkness,
shutting out all light.

He has turned his hand against me
   again and again, all day long.

He has made my skin and flesh grow old.
   He has broken my bones.
He has besieged and surrounded me
   with anguish and distress.
He has buried me in a dark place,
   like those long dead.

He has walled me in, and I cannot escape.
   He has bound me in heavy chains.
And though I cry and shout,
   he has shut out my prayers.
He has blocked my way with a high stone wall;
   he has made my road crooked.

He has hidden like a bear or a lion,
   waiting to attack me.
He has dragged me off the path and torn me in pieces,
   leaving me helpless and devastated.
He has drawn his bow
   and made me the target for his arrows.

He shot his arrows
   deep into my heart.
My own people laugh at me.
   All day long they sing their mocking songs.
He has filled me with bitterness
   and given me a bitter cup of sorrow to drink.

He has made me chew on gravel.
   He has rolled me in the dust.
Peace has been stripped away,
   and I have forgotten what prosperity is.
I cry out, "My splendor is gone!
   Everything I had hoped for from the LORD is lost!"

The thought of my suffering and homelessness
   is bitter beyond words.
I will never forget this awful time,
   as I grieve over my loss.
Yet I still dare to hope
   when I remember this:

The faithful love of the LORD never ends!
His mercies never cease.
Great is his faithfulness;
his mercies begin afresh each morning.
I say to myself, "The LORD is my inheritance;
therefore, I will hope in him!"

The LORD is good to those who depend on him,
to those who search for him.
So it is good to wait quietly
for salvation from the LORD.
And it is good for people to submit at an early age
to the yoke of his discipline:

Let them sit alone in silence
beneath the LORD's demands.
Let them lie face down in the dust,
for there may be hope at last.
Let them turn the other cheek to those who strike them
and accept the insults of their enemies.

For no one is abandoned
by the Lord forever.
Though he brings grief, he also shows compassion
because of the greatness of his unfailing love.
For he does not enjoy hurting people
or causing them sorrow.

If people crush underfoot
all the prisoners of the land,
if they deprive others of their rights
in defiance of the Most High,
if they twist justice in the courts—
doesn't the Lord see all these things?

Who can command things to happen
without the Lord's permission?
Does not the Most High
send both calamity and good?
Then why should we, mere humans, complain
when we are punished for our sins?

Instead, let us test and examine our ways.
Let us turn back to the LORD.
Let us lift our hearts and hands

to God in heaven and say,
"We have sinned and rebelled,
    and you have not forgiven us.

"You have engulfed us with your anger, chased us down,
    and slaughtered us without mercy.
You have hidden yourself in a cloud
    so our prayers cannot reach you.
You have discarded us as refuse and garbage
    among the nations.

"All our enemies
    have spoken out against us.
We are filled with fear,
    for we are trapped, devastated, and ruined."
Tears stream from my eyes
    because of the destruction of my people!

My tears flow endlessly;
    they will not stop
until the LORD looks down
    from heaven and sees.
My heart is breaking
    over the fate of all the women of Jerusalem.

My enemies, whom I have never harmed,
    hunted me down like a bird.
They threw me into a pit
    and dropped stones on me.
The water rose over my head,
    and I cried out, "This is the end!"

But I called on your name, LORD,
    from deep within the pit.
You heard me when I cried, "Listen to my pleading!
    Hear my cry for help!"
Yes, you came when I called;
    you told me, "Do not fear."

Lord, you have come to my defense;
    you have redeemed my life.
You have seen the wrong they have done to me, LORD.
    Be my judge, and prove me right.
You have seen the vengeful plots
    my enemies have laid against me.

Lord, you have heard the vile names they call me.
  You know all about the plans they have made.
My enemies whisper and mutter
  as they plot against me all day long.
Look at them! Whether they sit or stand,
  I am the object of their mocking songs.

Pay them back, Lord,
  for all the evil they have done.
Give them hard and stubborn hearts,
  and then let your curse fall on them!
Chase them down in your anger,
  destroying them beneath the Lord's heavens.

✛

How the gold has lost its luster!
  Even the finest gold has become dull.
The sacred gemstones
  lie scattered in the streets!

See how the precious children of Jerusalem,
  worth their weight in fine gold,
are now treated like pots of clay
  made by a common potter.

Even the jackals feed their young,
  but not my people Israel.
They ignore their children's cries,
  like ostriches in the desert.

The parched tongues of their little ones
  stick to the roofs of their mouths in thirst.
The children cry for bread,
  but no one has any to give them.

The people who once ate the richest foods
  now beg in the streets for anything they can get.
Those who once wore the finest clothes
  now search the garbage dumps for food.

The guilt of my people
  is greater than that of Sodom,
where utter disaster struck in a moment
  and no hand offered help.

Our princes once glowed with health—
  brighter than snow, whiter than milk.
Their faces were as ruddy as rubies,
  their appearance like fine jewels.

But now their faces are blacker than soot.
  No one recognizes them in the streets.
Their skin sticks to their bones;
  it is as dry and hard as wood.

Those killed by the sword are better off
  than those who die of hunger.
Starving, they waste away
  for lack of food from the fields.

Tenderhearted women
  have cooked their own children.
They have eaten them
  to survive the siege.

But now the anger of the LORD is satisfied.
  His fierce anger has been poured out.
He started a fire in Jerusalem
  that burned the city to its foundations.

Not a king in all the earth—
  no one in all the world—
would have believed that an enemy
  could march through the gates of Jerusalem.

Yet it happened because of the sins of her prophets
  and the sins of her priests,
who defiled the city
  by shedding innocent blood.

They wandered blindly
  through the streets,
so defiled by blood
  that no one dared touch them.

"Get away!" the people shouted at them.
  "You're defiled! Don't touch us!"
So they fled to distant lands
  and wandered among foreign nations,
  but none would let them stay.

The LORD himself has scattered them,
    and he no longer helps them.
People show no respect for the priests
    and no longer honor the leaders.

We looked in vain for our allies
    to come and save us,
but we were looking to nations
    that could not help us.

We couldn't go into the streets
    without danger to our lives.
Our end was near; our days were numbered.
    We were doomed!

Our enemies were swifter than eagles in flight.
    If we fled to the mountains, they found us.
If we hid in the wilderness,
    they were waiting for us there.

Our king—the LORD's anointed, the very life of our nation—
    was caught in their snares.
We had thought that his shadow
    would protect us against any nation on earth!

Are you rejoicing in the land of Uz,
    O people of Edom?
But you, too, must drink from the cup of the LORD's anger.
    You, too, will be stripped naked in your drunkenness.

O beautiful Jerusalem, your punishment will end;
    you will soon return from exile.
But Edom, your punishment is just beginning;
    soon your many sins will be exposed.

+

LORD, remember what has happened to us.
    See how we have been disgraced!
Our inheritance has been turned over to strangers,
    our homes to foreigners.
We are orphaned and fatherless.
    Our mothers are widowed.
We have to pay for water to drink,
    and even firewood is expensive.

Those who pursue us are at our heels;
    we are exhausted but are given no rest.
We submitted to Egypt and Assyria
    to get enough food to survive.
Our ancestors sinned, but they have died—
    and we are suffering the punishment they deserved!

Slaves have now become our masters;
    there is no one left to rescue us.
We hunt for food at the risk of our lives,
    for violence rules the countryside.
The famine has blackened our skin
    as though baked in an oven.
Our enemies rape the women in Jerusalem
    and the young girls in all the towns of Judah.
Our princes are being hanged by their thumbs,
    and our elders are treated with contempt.
Young men are led away to work at millstones,
    and boys stagger under heavy loads of wood.
The elders no longer sit in the city gates;
    the young men no longer dance and sing.
Joy has left our hearts;
    our dancing has turned to mourning.
The garlands have fallen from our heads.
    Weep for us because we have sinned.
Our hearts are sick and weary,
    and our eyes grow dim with tears.
For Jerusalem is empty and desolate,
    a place haunted by jackals.

But LORD, you remain the same forever!
    Your throne continues from generation to generation.
Why do you continue to forget us?
    Why have you abandoned us for so long?
Restore us, O LORD, and bring us back to you again!
    Give us back the joys we once had!
Or have you utterly rejected us?
    Are you angry with us still?

IMMERSED IN SONG OF SONGS

WHEN WE FALL IN LOVE, we desperately want to express what we feel. In such times, we often look to songs and poems written by others to help us say what we would like to say. Almost all cultures have a treasury of love songs that people draw upon to declare their love to one another.

The cultures of the Middle East, including that of ancient Israel, are no exception. A collection of these love songs has been preserved for us in the Song of Songs. It contains song lyrics that, like the psalms, have been preserved from earlier times to help people celebrate their devotion to and delight in another person.

A traditional heading to the book identifies Solomon as the writer of these songs, and at one point they describe the splendor of his wedding. For this reason, the book is sometimes called the Song of Solomon. (The author is not otherwise identified in the poems themselves.) But read as a whole, the collection follows the courtship and marriage of a young man and woman. It presents a series of romantic conversations between them, punctuated by observations from the "young women of Jerusalem," presumably the bride's friends.

It's important to appreciate that in traditional Hebrew culture, as in many other world cultures, brides and grooms are often portrayed (and sometimes even dressed) as queens and kings. So it may actually be this practice that is reflected in such lyrics as, "Come out to see King Solomon, young women of Jerusalem. He wears the crown his mother gave him on his wedding day, his most joyous day."

This allusion to the wedding couple as a king and queen in a garden reminds us of the first couple of the Bible, Adam and Eve. We recall that humans are God's appointed rulers of creation, and God himself delights in the goodness of physical, sensual love. Our joy is a reflection of God's own joy in his creatures.

Using richly evocative symbolism drawn from the natural world, these songs portray the beauties of the human body and the splendors of human love as glorious aspects of God's creation. No book in the Bible uses the imagery of poetry more densely and elaborately than the Song of Songs. And this celebration of love gives us a sense that even as we await God's renewal of all things in his new garden, some aspects of our present life already anticipate the joys that are to come.

SONG OF SONGS

✛

This is Solomon's song of songs, more wonderful than any other.

Kiss me and kiss me again,
   for your love is sweeter than wine.
How pleasing is your fragrance;
   your name is like the spreading fragrance of scented oils.
   No wonder all the young women love you!
Take me with you; come, let's run!
   The king has brought me into his bedroom.

How happy we are for you, O king.
   We praise your love even more than wine.

How right they are to adore you.

I am dark but beautiful,
   O women of Jerusalem—
dark as the tents of Kedar,
   dark as the curtains of Solomon's tents.
Don't stare at me because I am dark—
   the sun has darkened my skin.
My brothers were angry with me;
   they forced me to care for their vineyards,
   so I couldn't care for myself—my own vineyard.

Tell me, my love, where are you leading your flock today?
   Where will you rest your sheep at noon?
For why should I wander like a prostitute
   among your friends and their flocks?

If you don't know, O most beautiful woman,
   follow the trail of my flock,
   and graze your young goats by the shepherds' tents.

You are as exciting, my darling,
    as a mare among Pharaoh's stallions.
How lovely are your cheeks;
    your earrings set them afire!
How lovely is your neck,
    enhanced by a string of jewels.
We will make for you earrings of gold
    and beads of silver.

The king is lying on his couch,
    enchanted by the fragrance of my perfume.
My lover is like a sachet of myrrh
    lying between my breasts.
He is like a bouquet of sweet henna blossoms
    from the vineyards of En-gedi.

How beautiful you are, my darling,
    how beautiful!
    Your eyes are like doves.

You are so handsome, my love,
    pleasing beyond words!
The soft grass is our bed;
    fragrant cedar branches are the beams of our
        house,
    and pleasant smelling firs are the rafters.

+

I am the spring crocus blooming on the Sharon
        Plain,
    the lily of the valley.

Like a lily among thistles
    is my darling among young women.

Like the finest apple tree in the orchard
    is my lover among other young men.
I sit in his delightful shade
    and taste his delicious fruit.
He escorts me to the banquet hall;
    it's obvious how much he loves me.

Strengthen me with raisin cakes,
   refresh me with apples,
     for I am weak with love.
His left arm is under my head,
   and his right arm embraces me.

Promise me, O women of Jerusalem,
   by the gazelles and wild deer,
     not to awaken love until the time is right.

+

Ah, I hear my lover coming!
   He is leaping over the mountains,
     bounding over the hills.
My lover is like a swift gazelle
   or a young stag.
Look, there he is behind the wall,
   looking through the window,
     peering into the room.

My lover said to me,
   "Rise up, my darling!
   Come away with me, my fair one!
Look, the winter is past,
   and the rains are over and gone.
The flowers are springing up,
   the season of singing birds has come,
     and the cooing of turtledoves fills the air.
The fig trees are forming young fruit,
   and the fragrant grapevines are blossoming.
Rise up, my darling!
   Come away with me, my fair one!"

My dove is hiding behind the rocks,
   behind an outcrop on the cliff.
Let me see your face;
   let me hear your voice.
For your voice is pleasant,
   and your face is lovely.

Catch all the foxes,
   those little foxes,

before they ruin the vineyard of love,
   for the grapevines are blossoming!

My lover is mine, and I am his.
   He browses among the lilies.
Before the dawn breezes blow
   and the night shadows flee,
return to me, my love, like a gazelle
   or a young stag on the rugged mountains.

+

One night as I lay in bed, I yearned for my lover.
   I yearned for him, but he did not come.
So I said to myself, "I will get up and roam the city,
   searching in all its streets and squares.
I will search for the one I love."
   So I searched everywhere but did not find him.
The watchmen stopped me as they made their rounds,
   and I asked, "Have you seen the one I love?"
Then scarcely had I left them
   when I found my love!
I caught and held him tightly,
   then I brought him to my mother's house,
   into my mother's bed, where I had been conceived.

Promise me, O women of Jerusalem,
   by the gazelles and wild deer,
   not to awaken love until the time is right.

+

Who is this sweeping in from the wilderness
   like a cloud of smoke?
Who is it, fragrant with myrrh and frankincense
   and every kind of spice?
Look, it is Solomon's carriage,
   surrounded by sixty heroic men,
   the best of Israel's soldiers.
They are all skilled swordsmen,
   experienced warriors.
Each wears a sword on his thigh,
   ready to defend the king against an attack in the night.

King Solomon's carriage is built
  of wood imported from Lebanon.
Its posts are silver,
  its canopy gold;
  its cushions are purple.
It was decorated with love
  by the young women of Jerusalem.

Come out to see King Solomon,
  young women of Jerusalem.
He wears the crown his mother gave him on his wedding day,
  his most joyous day.

          +

You are beautiful, my darling,
  beautiful beyond words.
Your eyes are like doves
  behind your veil.
Your hair falls in waves,
  like a flock of goats winding down the slopes of Gilead.
Your teeth are as white as sheep,
  recently shorn and freshly washed.
Your smile is flawless,
  each tooth matched with its twin.
Your lips are like scarlet ribbon;
  your mouth is inviting.
Your cheeks are like rosy pomegranates
  behind your veil.
Your neck is as beautiful as the tower of David,
  jeweled with the shields of a thousand heroes.
Your breasts are like two fawns,
  twin fawns of a gazelle grazing among the lilies.
Before the dawn breezes blow
  and the night shadows flee,
I will hurry to the mountain of myrrh
  and to the hill of frankincense.
You are altogether beautiful, my darling,
  beautiful in every way.

Come with me from Lebanon, my bride,
  come with me from Lebanon.

Come down from Mount Amana,
   from the peaks of Senir and Hermon,
where the lions have their dens
   and leopards live among the hills.

You have captured my heart,
   my treasure, my bride.
You hold it hostage with one glance of your eyes,
   with a single jewel of your necklace.
Your love delights me,
   my treasure, my bride.
Your love is better than wine,
   your perfume more fragrant than spices.
Your lips are as sweet as nectar, my bride.
   Honey and milk are under your tongue.
Your clothes are scented
   like the cedars of Lebanon.

You are my private garden, my treasure, my bride,
   a secluded spring, a hidden fountain.
Your thighs shelter a paradise of pomegranates
   with rare spices—
henna with nard,
   nard and saffron,
   fragrant calamus and cinnamon,
with all the trees of frankincense, myrrh,
     and aloes,
   and every other lovely spice.
You are a garden fountain,
   a well of fresh water
   streaming down from Lebanon's mountains.

Awake, north wind!
   Rise up, south wind!
Blow on my garden
   and spread its fragrance all around.
Come into your garden, my love;
   taste its finest fruits.

+

I have entered my garden, my treasure, my bride!
   I gather myrrh with my spices

and eat honeycomb with my honey.
   I drink wine with my milk.

Oh, lover and beloved, eat and drink!
   Yes, drink deeply of your love!

I slept, but my heart was awake,
   when I heard my lover knocking and calling:
"Open to me, my treasure, my darling,
   my dove, my perfect one.
My head is drenched with dew,
   my hair with the dampness of the night."

But I responded,
"I have taken off my robe.
   Should I get dressed again?
I have washed my feet.
   Should I get them soiled?"

My lover tried to unlatch the door,
   and my heart thrilled within me.
I jumped up to open the door for my love,
   and my hands dripped with perfume.
My fingers dripped with lovely myrrh
   as I pulled back the bolt.
I opened to my lover,
   but he was gone!
   My heart sank.
I searched for him
   but could not find him anywhere.
I called to him,
   but there was no reply.
The night watchmen found me
   as they made their rounds.
They beat and bruised me
   and stripped off my veil,
   those watchmen on the walls.

Make this promise, O women of Jerusalem—
   If you find my lover,
   tell him I am weak with love.

✛

Why is your lover better than all others,
    O woman of rare beauty?
What makes your lover so special
    that we must promise this?

My lover is dark and dazzling,
    better than ten thousand others!
His head is finest gold,
    his wavy hair is black as a raven.
His eyes sparkle like doves
    beside springs of water;
they are set like jewels
    washed in milk.
His cheeks are like gardens of spices
    giving off fragrance.
His lips are like lilies,
    perfumed with myrrh.
His arms are like rounded bars of gold,
    set with beryl.
His body is like bright ivory,
    glowing with lapis lazuli.
His legs are like marble pillars
    set in sockets of finest gold.
His posture is stately,
    like the noble cedars of Lebanon.
His mouth is sweetness itself;
    he is desirable in every way.
Such, O women of Jerusalem,
    is my lover, my friend.

+

Where has your lover gone,
    O woman of rare beauty?
Which way did he turn
    so we can help you find him?

My lover has gone down to his garden,
    to his spice beds,
to browse in the gardens
    and gather the lilies.

I am my lover's, and my lover is mine.
  He browses among the lilies.

You are beautiful, my darling,
  like the lovely city of Tirzah.
Yes, as beautiful as Jerusalem,
  as majestic as an army with billowing banners.
Turn your eyes away,
  for they overpower me.
Your hair falls in waves,
    like a flock of goats winding down the slopes
      of Gilead.
Your teeth are as white as sheep
  that are freshly washed.
Your smile is flawless,
  each tooth matched with its twin.
Your cheeks are like rosy pomegranates
  behind your veil.

Even among sixty queens
  and eighty concubines
  and countless young women,
I would still choose my dove, my perfect one—
  the favorite of her mother,
  dearly loved by the one who bore her.
The young women see her and praise her;
  even queens and royal concubines sing her praises:
"Who is this, arising like the dawn,
  as fair as the moon,
as bright as the sun,
  as majestic as an army with billowing banners?"

I went down to the grove of walnut trees
  and out to the valley to see the new spring growth,
to see whether the grapevines had budded
  or the pomegranates were in bloom.
Before I realized it,
    my strong desires had taken me to the chariot of
      a noble man.

Return, return to us, O maid of Shulam.
  Come back, come back, that we may see you again.

Why do you stare at this young woman of Shulam,
  as she moves so gracefully between two lines of dancers?

How beautiful are your sandaled feet,
  O queenly maiden.
Your rounded thighs are like jewels,
  the work of a skilled craftsman.
Your navel is perfectly formed
  like a goblet filled with mixed wine.
Between your thighs lies a mound of wheat
  bordered with lilies.
Your breasts are like two fawns,
  twin fawns of a gazelle.
Your neck is as beautiful as an ivory tower.
Your eyes are like the sparkling pools in Heshbon
  by the gate of Bath-rabbim.
Your nose is as fine as the tower of Lebanon
  overlooking Damascus.
Your head is as majestic as Mount Carmel,
  and the sheen of your hair radiates royalty.
  The king is held captive by its tresses.
Oh, how beautiful you are!
  How pleasing, my love, how full of delights!
You are slender like a palm tree,
  and your breasts are like its clusters of fruit.
I said, "I will climb the palm tree
  and take hold of its fruit."
May your breasts be like grape clusters,
  and the fragrance of your breath like apples.
May your kisses be as exciting as the best wine—

Yes, wine that goes down smoothly for my lover,
  flowing gently over lips and teeth.
I am my lover's,
  and he claims me as his own.
Come, my love, let us go out to the fields
  and spend the night among the wildflowers.
Let us get up early and go to the vineyards
  to see if the grapevines have budded,
if the blossoms have opened,
  and if the pomegranates have bloomed.
  There I will give you my love.

There the mandrakes give off their fragrance,
   and the finest fruits are at our door,
new delights as well as old,
   which I have saved for you, my lover.

+

Oh, I wish you were my brother,
   who nursed at my mother's breasts.
Then I could kiss you no matter who was watching,
   and no one would criticize me.
I would bring you to my childhood home,
   and there you would teach me.
I would give you spiced wine to drink,
   my sweet pomegranate wine.
Your left arm would be under my head,
   and your right arm would embrace me.

Promise me, O women of Jerusalem,
   not to awaken love until the time is right.

+

Who is this sweeping in from the desert,
   leaning on her lover?

I aroused you under the apple tree,
   where your mother gave you birth,
   where in great pain she delivered you.
Place me like a seal over your heart,
   like a seal on your arm.
For love is as strong as death,
   its jealousy as enduring as the grave.
Love flashes like fire,
   the brightest kind of flame.
Many waters cannot quench love,
   nor can rivers drown it.
If a man tried to buy love
   with all his wealth,
   his offer would be utterly scorned.

We have a little sister
   too young to have breasts.

What will we do for our sister
   if someone asks to marry her?
If she is a virgin, like a wall,
   we will protect her with a silver tower.
But if she is promiscuous, like a swinging door,
   we will block her door with a cedar bar.

I was a virgin, like a wall;
   now my breasts are like towers.
When my lover looks at me,
   he is delighted with what he sees.

Solomon has a vineyard at Baal-hamon,
   which he leases out to tenant farmers.
Each of them pays a thousand pieces of silver
   for harvesting its fruit.
But my vineyard is mine to give,
   and Solomon need not pay a thousand pieces of silver.
But I will give two hundred pieces
   to those who care for its vines.

O my darling, lingering in the gardens,
   your companions are fortunate to hear your voice.
   Let me hear it, too!

Come away, my love! Be like a gazelle
   or a young stag on the mountains of spices.

IMMERSED IN PROVERBS

THE CREATOR INTENDS for us to flourish in our life on this earth. There is a way of wisdom, rooted in deep respect and reverence for God himself, that leads us to this good life. One particular literary tradition in Israel was centered on exploring and teaching this path. Today we find it reflected in the Bible's wisdom books.

The first example of this tradition is found in the book of Proverbs. Proverbs does not take the form of a narrative, but its wisdom teachings are an integral part of the story of the Bible. In this book, the ancient Israelites collected wise sayings (or proverbs) to help them follow the right course in life. These proverbs are not absolute promises about what will happen in all situations. Rather, they are short, memorable sayings that offer practical advice for good living.

It's a universal phenomenon for cultures to produce maxims that express their perspectives on how life is to be lived wisely. For example: "Don't put all your eggs in one basket"; "measure twice, cut once"; "a journey of a thousand miles begins with a single step." Israel's proverbs offer such practical wisdom but also have the incomparable advantage of being informed by the nation's experiences in its covenant relationship with God.

The proverbs in the Bible display the basic literary device found in all Hebrew poetry: parallelism. Hebrew proverbs are usually expressed in poetic couplets—two-line compositions in which the second line echoes, contrasts, or elaborates on the first. Here are a few examples:

Just as the rich rule the poor,
  so the borrower is servant to the lender.

Sensible children bring joy to their father;
  foolish children despise their mother.

Stay away from fools,
  for you won't find knowledge on their lips.

Such proverbs are not like lyric poetry—that is, they probably weren't originally sung like the poems in Israel's songbooks. But nevertheless, the brevity, repetition, and imagery of the proverbs (for example, "As a door swings back and forth on its hinges, so the lazy person turns over in bed") make them just as memorable as words set to music.

The biblical book of Proverbs contains six collections of such sayings. They have been gathered from named figures, including Solomon, Agur, and Lemuel, as well as from unnamed figures known simply as "the wise." To introduce these collections, the book offers a series of exhortations in poetic form, though in stanzas longer than couplets. These poems praise the benefits of learning from the sages of the past by feasting on the banquet of their wisdom. The book ends with an acrostic poem (following the letters of the Hebrew alphabet) about "a virtuous and capable wife." This may be seen as an idealized application of the book's overall teaching to offer an example of how the way of wisdom might be lived out.

The collected proverbs presented throughout the book share a common vision of life. There are two paths that can be followed: that of the "fool" (or the "wicked") and that of the "wise" (or the "righteous"). The proverbs appeal to experience and common sense to make the case that, everything else being equal, the wise prosper in this life (enjoying financial success, health, good relationships, and a good reputation through diligence and hard work) while the foolish take shortcuts (get-rich-quick schemes, shady friendships, and cutting corners) and end up missing out.

The other wisdom books in the First Testament—Ecclesiastes and Job—will add important qualifications to this view. But the place to begin the journey is with the down-to-earth advice offered in the book of Proverbs. It offers a solid presentation of wisdom that is rooted in a right relationship with God and seeks to follow the way that leads to the best possible kind of life.

PROVERBS

✛

These are the proverbs of Solomon, David's son, king of Israel.

Their purpose is to teach people wisdom and discipline,
    to help them understand the insights of the wise.
Their purpose is to teach people to live disciplined and successful
      lives,
    to help them do what is right, just, and fair.
These proverbs will give insight to the simple,
    knowledge and discernment to the young.

Let the wise listen to these proverbs and become even wiser.
    Let those with understanding receive guidance
by exploring the meaning in these proverbs and parables,
    the words of the wise and their riddles.

Fear of the LORD is the foundation of true knowledge,
    but fools despise wisdom and discipline.

✛ ✛ ✛

My child, listen when your father corrects you.
    Don't neglect your mother's instruction.
What you learn from them will crown you with grace
    and be a chain of honor around your neck.

My child, if sinners entice you,
    turn your back on them!
They may say, "Come and join us.
    Let's hide and kill someone!
    Just for fun, let's ambush the innocent!
Let's swallow them alive, like the grave;
    let's swallow them whole, like those who go down to the pit
      of death.
Think of the great things we'll get!

We'll fill our houses with all the stuff we take.
Come, throw in your lot with us;
   we'll all share the loot."

My child, don't go along with them!
   Stay far away from their paths.
They rush to commit evil deeds.
   They hurry to commit murder.
If a bird sees a trap being set,
   it knows to stay away.
But these people set an ambush for themselves;
   they are trying to get themselves killed.
Such is the fate of all who are greedy for money;
   it robs them of life.

+

Wisdom shouts in the streets.
   She cries out in the public square.
She calls to the crowds along the main street,
   to those gathered in front of the city gate:
"How long, you simpletons,
   will you insist on being simpleminded?
How long will you mockers relish your mocking?
   How long will you fools hate knowledge?
Come and listen to my counsel.
I'll share my heart with you
   and make you wise.

"I called you so often, but you wouldn't come.
   I reached out to you, but you paid no attention.
You ignored my advice
   and rejected the correction I offered.
So I will laugh when you are in trouble!
   I will mock you when disaster overtakes you—
when calamity overtakes you like a storm,
   when disaster engulfs you like a cyclone,
   and anguish and distress overwhelm you.

"When they cry for help, I will not answer.
   Though they anxiously search for me, they will not find me.
For they hated knowledge
   and chose not to fear the LORD.

They rejected my advice
    and paid no attention when I corrected them.
Therefore, they must eat the bitter fruit of living their own way,
    choking on their own schemes.
For simpletons turn away from me—to death.
    Fools are destroyed by their own complacency.
But all who listen to me will live in peace,
    untroubled by fear of harm."

+

My child, listen to what I say,
    and treasure my commands.
Tune your ears to wisdom,
    and concentrate on understanding.
Cry out for insight,
    and ask for understanding.
Search for them as you would for silver;
    seek them like hidden treasures.
Then you will understand what it means to fear the LORD,
    and you will gain knowledge of God.
For the LORD grants wisdom!
    From his mouth come knowledge and understanding.
He grants a treasure of common sense to the honest.
    He is a shield to those who walk with integrity.
He guards the paths of the just
    and protects those who are faithful to him.

Then you will understand what is right, just, and fair,
    and you will find the right way to go.
For wisdom will enter your heart,
    and knowledge will fill you with joy.
Wise choices will watch over you.
    Understanding will keep you safe.

Wisdom will save you from evil people,
    from those whose words are twisted.
These men turn from the right way
    to walk down dark paths.
They take pleasure in doing wrong,
    and they enjoy the twisted ways of evil.
Their actions are crooked,
    and their ways are wrong.

Wisdom will save you from the immoral woman,
   from the seductive words of the promiscuous woman.
She has abandoned her husband
   and ignores the covenant she made before God.
Entering her house leads to death;
   it is the road to the grave.
The man who visits her is doomed.
   He will never reach the paths of life.

So follow the steps of the good,
   and stay on the paths of the righteous.
For only the godly will live in the land,
   and those with integrity will remain in it.
But the wicked will be removed from the land,
   and the treacherous will be uprooted.

+

My child, never forget the things I have taught you.
   Store my commands in your heart.
If you do this, you will live many years,
   and your life will be satisfying.
Never let loyalty and kindness leave you!
   Tie them around your neck as a reminder.
   Write them deep within your heart.
Then you will find favor with both God and people,
   and you will earn a good reputation.

Trust in the LORD with all your heart;
   do not depend on your own understanding.
Seek his will in all you do,
   and he will show you which path to take.

Don't be impressed with your own wisdom.
   Instead, fear the LORD and turn away from evil.
Then you will have healing for your body
   and strength for your bones.

Honor the LORD with your wealth
   and with the best part of everything you produce.
Then he will fill your barns with grain,
   and your vats will overflow with good wine.

My child, don't reject the LORD's discipline,
   and don't be upset when he corrects you.

For the LORD corrects those he loves,
    just as a father corrects a child in whom he delights.

Joyful is the person who finds wisdom,
    the one who gains understanding.
For wisdom is more profitable than silver,
    and her wages are better than gold.
Wisdom is more precious than rubies;
    nothing you desire can compare with her.
She offers you long life in her right hand,
    and riches and honor in her left.
She will guide you down delightful paths;
    all her ways are satisfying.
Wisdom is a tree of life to those who embrace her;
    happy are those who hold her tightly.

By wisdom the LORD founded the earth;
    by understanding he created the heavens.
By his knowledge the deep fountains of the earth burst forth,
    and the dew settles beneath the night sky.

My child, don't lose sight of common sense and
      discernment.
    Hang on to them,
for they will refresh your soul.
    They are like jewels on a necklace.
They keep you safe on your way,
    and your feet will not stumble.
You can go to bed without fear;
    you will lie down and sleep soundly.
You need not be afraid of sudden disaster
    or the destruction that comes upon the wicked,
for the LORD is your security.
    He will keep your foot from being caught in a trap.

Do not withhold good from those who deserve it
    when it's in your power to help them.
If you can help your neighbor now, don't say,
    "Come back tomorrow, and then I'll help you."

Don't plot harm against your neighbor,
    for those who live nearby trust you.
Don't pick a fight without reason,
    when no one has done you harm.

Don't envy violent people
  or copy their ways.
Such wicked people are detestable to the LORD,
  but he offers his friendship to the godly.

The LORD curses the house of the wicked,
  but he blesses the home of the upright.

The LORD mocks the mockers
  but is gracious to the humble.

The wise inherit honor,
  but fools are put to shame!

✦

My children, listen when your father corrects you.
  Pay attention and learn good judgment,
for I am giving you good guidance.
  Don't turn away from my instructions.
For I, too, was once my father's son,
  tenderly loved as my mother's only child.

My father taught me,
"Take my words to heart.
  Follow my commands, and you will live.
Get wisdom; develop good judgment.
  Don't forget my words or turn away from them.
Don't turn your back on wisdom, for she will protect you.
  Love her, and she will guard you.
Getting wisdom is the wisest thing you can do!
  And whatever else you do, develop good judgment.
If you prize wisdom, she will make you great.
  Embrace her, and she will honor you.
She will place a lovely wreath on your head;
  she will present you with a beautiful crown."

My child, listen to me and do as I say,
  and you will have a long, good life.
I will teach you wisdom's ways
  and lead you in straight paths.
When you walk, you won't be held back;
  when you run, you won't stumble.
Take hold of my instructions; don't let them go.
  Guard them, for they are the key to life.

Don't do as the wicked do,
    and don't follow the path of evildoers.
Don't even think about it; don't go that way.
    Turn away and keep moving.
For evil people can't sleep until they've done their evil deed
        for the day.
    They can't rest until they've caused someone to stumble.
They eat the food of wickedness
    and drink the wine of violence!

The way of the righteous is like the first gleam of dawn,
    which shines ever brighter until the full light of day.
But the way of the wicked is like total darkness.
    They have no idea what they are stumbling over.

My child, pay attention to what I say.
    Listen carefully to my words.
Don't lose sight of them.
    Let them penetrate deep into your heart,
for they bring life to those who find them,
    and healing to their whole body.

Guard your heart above all else,
    for it determines the course of your life.

Avoid all perverse talk;
    stay away from corrupt speech.

Look straight ahead,
    and fix your eyes on what lies before you.
Mark out a straight path for your feet;
    stay on the safe path.
Don't get sidetracked;
    keep your feet from following evil.

+

My son, pay attention to my wisdom;
    listen carefully to my wise counsel.
Then you will show discernment,
    and your lips will express what you've learned.
For the lips of an immoral woman are as sweet as honey,
    and her mouth is smoother than oil.
But in the end she is as bitter as poison,

as dangerous as a double-edged sword.
Her feet go down to death;
  her steps lead straight to the grave.
For she cares nothing about the path to life.
  She staggers down a crooked trail and doesn't realize it.

So now, my sons, listen to me.
  Never stray from what I am about to say:
Stay away from her!
  Don't go near the door of her house!
If you do, you will lose your honor
  and will lose to merciless people all you have achieved.
Strangers will consume your wealth,
  and someone else will enjoy the fruit of your labor.
In the end you will groan in anguish
  when disease consumes your body.
You will say, "How I hated discipline!
  If only I had not ignored all the warnings!
Oh, why didn't I listen to my teachers?
  Why didn't I pay attention to my instructors?
I have come to the brink of utter ruin,
  and now I must face public disgrace."

Drink water from your own well—
  share your love only with your wife.
Why spill the water of your springs in the streets,
  having sex with just anyone?
You should reserve it for yourselves.
  Never share it with strangers.

Let your wife be a fountain of blessing for you.
  Rejoice in the wife of your youth.
She is a loving deer, a graceful doe.
  Let her breasts satisfy you always.
  May you always be captivated by her love.
Why be captivated, my son, by an immoral woman,
  or fondle the breasts of a promiscuous woman?

For the LORD sees clearly what a man does,
  examining every path he takes.
An evil man is held captive by his own sins;
  they are ropes that catch and hold him.
He will die for lack of self-control;
  he will be lost because of his great foolishness.

+

My child, if you have put up security for a friend's debt
    or agreed to guarantee the debt of a stranger—
if you have trapped yourself by your agreement
    and are caught by what you said—
follow my advice and save yourself,
    for you have placed yourself at your friend's mercy.
Now swallow your pride;
    go and beg to have your name erased.
Don't put it off; do it now!
    Don't rest until you do.
Save yourself like a gazelle escaping from a hunter,
    like a bird fleeing from a net.

Take a lesson from the ants, you lazybones.
    Learn from their ways and become wise!
Though they have no prince
    or governor or ruler to make them work,
they labor hard all summer,
    gathering food for the winter.
But you, lazybones, how long will you sleep?
    When will you wake up?
A little extra sleep, a little more slumber,
    a little folding of the hands to rest—
then poverty will pounce on you like a bandit;
    scarcity will attack you like an armed robber.

What are worthless and wicked people like?
    They are constant liars,
signaling their deceit with a wink of the eye,
    a nudge of the foot, or the wiggle of fingers.
Their perverted hearts plot evil,
    and they constantly stir up trouble.
But they will be destroyed suddenly,
    broken in an instant beyond all hope of healing.

There are six things the LORD hates—
    no, seven things he detests:
haughty eyes,
    a lying tongue,
    hands that kill the innocent,
a heart that plots evil,

feet that race to do wrong,
a false witness who pours out lies,
    a person who sows discord in a family.

+

My son, obey your father's commands,
    and don't neglect your mother's instruction.
Keep their words always in your heart.
    Tie them around your neck.
When you walk, their counsel will lead you.
    When you sleep, they will protect you.
    When you wake up, they will advise you.
For their command is a lamp
    and their instruction a light;
their corrective discipline
    is the way to life.
It will keep you from the immoral woman,
    from the smooth tongue of a promiscuous woman.
Don't lust for her beauty.
    Don't let her coy glances seduce you.
For a prostitute will bring you to poverty,
    but sleeping with another man's wife will cost you your life.
Can a man scoop a flame into his lap
    and not have his clothes catch on fire?
Can he walk on hot coals
    and not blister his feet?
So it is with the man who sleeps with another man's wife.
    He who embraces her will not go unpunished.

Excuses might be found for a thief
    who steals because he is starving.
But if he is caught, he must pay back seven times what
        he stole,
    even if he has to sell everything in his house.
But the man who commits adultery is an utter fool,
    for he destroys himself.
He will be wounded and disgraced.
    His shame will never be erased.
For the woman's jealous husband will be furious,
    and he will show no mercy when he takes revenge.
He will accept no compensation,
    nor be satisfied with a payoff of any size.

+

Follow my advice, my son;
　　always treasure my commands.
Obey my commands and live!
　　Guard my instructions as you guard your own eyes.
Tie them on your fingers as a reminder.
　　Write them deep within your heart.

Love wisdom like a sister;
　　make insight a beloved member of your family.
Let them protect you from an affair with an immoral woman,
　　from listening to the flattery of a promiscuous woman.

While I was at the window of my house,
　　looking through the curtain,
I saw some naive young men,
　　and one in particular who lacked common sense.
He was crossing the street near the house of an immoral
　　　　woman,
　　strolling down the path by her house.
It was at twilight, in the evening,
　　as deep darkness fell.
The woman approached him,
　　seductively dressed and sly of heart.
She was the brash, rebellious type,
　　never content to stay at home.
She is often in the streets and markets,
　　soliciting at every corner.
She threw her arms around him and kissed him,
　　and with a brazen look she said,
"I've just made my peace offerings
　　and fulfilled my vows.
You're the one I was looking for!
　　I came out to find you, and here you are!
My bed is spread with beautiful blankets,
　　with colored sheets of Egyptian linen.
I've perfumed my bed
　　with myrrh, aloes, and cinnamon.
Come, let's drink our fill of love until morning.
　　Let's enjoy each other's caresses,
for my husband is not home.
　　He's away on a long trip.

He has taken a wallet full of money with him
and won't return until later this month."

So she seduced him with her pretty speech
and enticed him with her flattery.
He followed her at once,
like an ox going to the slaughter.
He was like a stag caught in a trap,
awaiting the arrow that would pierce its heart.
He was like a bird flying into a snare,
little knowing it would cost him his life.

So listen to me, my sons,
and pay attention to my words.
Don't let your hearts stray away toward her.
Don't wander down her wayward path.
For she has been the ruin of many;
many men have been her victims.
Her house is the road to the grave.
Her bedroom is the den of death.

+

Listen as Wisdom calls out!
Hear as understanding raises her voice!
On the hilltop along the road,
she takes her stand at the crossroads.
By the gates at the entrance to the town,
on the road leading in, she cries aloud,
"I call to you, to all of you!
I raise my voice to all people.
You simple people, use good judgment.
You foolish people, show some understanding.
Listen to me! For I have important things to tell you.
Everything I say is right,
for I speak the truth
and detest every kind of deception.
My advice is wholesome.
There is nothing devious or crooked in it.
My words are plain to anyone with understanding,
clear to those with knowledge.
Choose my instruction rather than silver,
and knowledge rather than pure gold.

For wisdom is far more valuable than rubies.
　　Nothing you desire can compare with it.

"I, Wisdom, live together with good judgment.
　　I know where to discover knowledge and discernment.
All who fear the LORD will hate evil.
　　Therefore, I hate pride and arrogance,
　　corruption and perverse speech.
Common sense and success belong to me.
　　Insight and strength are mine.
Because of me, kings reign,
　　and rulers make just decrees.
Rulers lead with my help,
　　and nobles make righteous judgments.

"I love all who love me.
　　Those who search will surely find me.
I have riches and honor,
　　as well as enduring wealth and justice.
My gifts are better than gold, even the purest gold,
　　my wages better than sterling silver!
I walk in righteousness,
　　in paths of justice.
Those who love me inherit wealth.
　　I will fill their treasuries.

"The LORD formed me from the beginning,
　　before he created anything else.
I was appointed in ages past,
　　at the very first, before the earth began.
I was born before the oceans were created,
　　before the springs bubbled forth their waters.
Before the mountains were formed,
　　before the hills, I was born—
before he had made the earth and fields
　　and the first handfuls of soil.
I was there when he established the heavens,
　　when he drew the horizon on the oceans.
I was there when he set the clouds above,
　　when he established springs deep in the earth.
I was there when he set the limits of the seas,
　　so they would not spread beyond their boundaries.
And when he marked off the earth's foundations,

I was the architect at his side.
I was his constant delight,
   rejoicing always in his presence.
And how happy I was with the world he created;
   how I rejoiced with the human family!

"And so, my children, listen to me,
   for all who follow my ways are joyful.
Listen to my instruction and be wise.
   Don't ignore it.
Joyful are those who listen to me,
   watching for me daily at my gates,
   waiting for me outside my home!
For whoever finds me finds life
   and receives favor from the LORD.
But those who miss me injure themselves.
   All who hate me love death."

✢

Wisdom has built her house;
   she has carved its seven columns.
She has prepared a great banquet,
   mixed the wines, and set the table.
She has sent her servants to invite everyone to come.
   She calls out from the heights overlooking the city.
"Come in with me," she urges the simple.
   To those who lack good judgment, she says,
"Come, eat my food,
   and drink the wine I have mixed.
Leave your simple ways behind, and begin to live;
   learn to use good judgment."

Anyone who rebukes a mocker will get an insult in return.
   Anyone who corrects the wicked will get hurt.
So don't bother correcting mockers;
   they will only hate you.
But correct the wise,
   and they will love you.
Instruct the wise,
   and they will be even wiser.
Teach the righteous,
   and they will learn even more.

Fear of the LORD is the foundation of wisdom.
>Knowledge of the Holy One results in good
>>judgment.

Wisdom will multiply your days
>and add years to your life.
If you become wise, you will be the one to benefit.
>If you scorn wisdom, you will be the one to suffer.

The woman named Folly is brash.
>She is ignorant and doesn't know it.
She sits in her doorway
>on the heights overlooking the city.
She calls out to men going by
>who are minding their own business.
"Come in with me," she urges the simple.
>To those who lack good judgment, she says,
"Stolen water is refreshing;
>food eaten in secret tastes the best!"
But little do they know that the dead are there.
>Her guests are in the depths of the grave.

+ + +

The proverbs of Solomon:

A wise child brings joy to a father;
>a foolish child brings grief to a mother.

Tainted wealth has no lasting value,
>but right living can save your life.

The LORD will not let the godly go hungry,
>but he refuses to satisfy the craving of the wicked.

Lazy people are soon poor;
>hard workers get rich.

A wise youth harvests in the summer,
>but one who sleeps during harvest is a disgrace.

The godly are showered with blessings;
>the words of the wicked conceal violent intentions.

We have happy memories of the godly,
>but the name of a wicked person rots away.

The wise are glad to be instructed,
  but babbling fools fall flat on their faces.

People with integrity walk safely,
  but those who follow crooked paths will be exposed.

People who wink at wrong cause trouble,
  but a bold reproof promotes peace.

The words of the godly are a life-giving fountain;
  the words of the wicked conceal violent intentions.

Hatred stirs up quarrels,
  but love makes up for all offenses.

Wise words come from the lips of people with understanding,
  but those lacking sense will be beaten with a rod.

Wise people treasure knowledge,
  but the babbling of a fool invites disaster.

The wealth of the rich is their fortress;
  the poverty of the poor is their destruction.

The earnings of the godly enhance their lives,
  but evil people squander their money on sin.

People who accept discipline are on the pathway to life,
  but those who ignore correction will go astray.

Hiding hatred makes you a liar;
  slandering others makes you a fool.

Too much talk leads to sin.
  Be sensible and keep your mouth shut.

The words of the godly are like sterling silver;
  the heart of a fool is worthless.

The words of the godly encourage many,
  but fools are destroyed by their lack of common sense.

The blessing of the LORD makes a person rich,
  and he adds no sorrow with it.

Doing wrong is fun for a fool,
  but living wisely brings pleasure to the sensible.

The fears of the wicked will be fulfilled;
  the hopes of the godly will be granted.

When the storms of life come, the wicked are whirled away,
    but the godly have a lasting foundation.

Lazy people irritate their employers,
    like vinegar to the teeth or smoke in the eyes.

Fear of the Lord lengthens one's life,
    but the years of the wicked are cut short.

The hopes of the godly result in happiness,
    but the expectations of the wicked come to nothing.

The way of the Lord is a stronghold to those with integrity,
    but it destroys the wicked.

The godly will never be disturbed,
    but the wicked will be removed from the land.

The mouth of the godly person gives wise advice,
    but the tongue that deceives will be cut off.

The lips of the godly speak helpful words,
    but the mouth of the wicked speaks perverse words.

The Lord detests the use of dishonest scales,
    but he delights in accurate weights.

Pride leads to disgrace,
    but with humility comes wisdom.

Honesty guides good people;
    dishonesty destroys treacherous people.

Riches won't help on the day of judgment,
    but right living can save you from death.

The godly are directed by honesty;
    the wicked fall beneath their load of sin.

The godliness of good people rescues them;
    the ambition of treacherous people traps them.

When the wicked die, their hopes die with them,
    for they rely on their own feeble strength.

The godly are rescued from trouble,
    and it falls on the wicked instead.

With their words, the godless destroy their friends,
    but knowledge will rescue the righteous.

The whole city celebrates when the godly succeed;
    they shout for joy when the wicked die.

Upright citizens are good for a city and make it prosper,
    but the talk of the wicked tears it apart.

It is foolish to belittle one's neighbor;
    a sensible person keeps quiet.

A gossip goes around telling secrets,
    but those who are trustworthy can keep a confidence.

Without wise leadership, a nation falls;
    there is safety in having many advisers.

There's danger in putting up security for a stranger's debt;
    it's safer not to guarantee another person's debt.

A gracious woman gains respect,
    but ruthless men gain only wealth.

Your kindness will reward you,
    but your cruelty will destroy you.

Evil people get rich for the moment,
    but the reward of the godly will last.

Godly people find life;
    evil people find death.

The LORD detests people with crooked hearts,
    but he delights in those with integrity.

Evil people will surely be punished,
    but the children of the godly will go free.

A beautiful woman who lacks discretion
    is like a gold ring in a pig's snout.

The godly can look forward to a reward,
    while the wicked can expect only judgment.

Give freely and become more wealthy;
    be stingy and lose everything.

The generous will prosper;
    those who refresh others will themselves be refreshed.

People curse those who hoard their grain,
    but they bless the one who sells in time of need.

If you search for good, you will find favor;
  but if you search for evil, it will find you!

Trust in your money and down you go!
  But the godly flourish like leaves in spring.

Those who bring trouble on their families inherit the wind.
  The fool will be a servant to the wise.

The seeds of good deeds become a tree of life;
  a wise person wins friends.

If the righteous are rewarded here on earth,
  what will happen to wicked sinners?

To learn, you must love discipline;
  it is stupid to hate correction.

The Lord approves of those who are good,
  but he condemns those who plan wickedness.

Wickedness never brings stability,
  but the godly have deep roots.

A worthy wife is a crown for her husband,
  but a disgraceful woman is like cancer in his bones.

The plans of the godly are just;
  the advice of the wicked is treacherous.

The words of the wicked are like a murderous ambush,
  but the words of the godly save lives.

The wicked die and disappear,
  but the family of the godly stands firm.

A sensible person wins admiration,
  but a warped mind is despised.

Better to be an ordinary person with a servant
  than to be self-important but have no food.

The godly care for their animals,
  but the wicked are always cruel.

A hard worker has plenty of food,
  but a person who chases fantasies has no sense.

Thieves are jealous of each other's loot,
  but the godly are well rooted and bear their own fruit.

The wicked are trapped by their own words,
    but the godly escape such trouble.

Wise words bring many benefits,
    and hard work brings rewards.

Fools think their own way is right,
    but the wise listen to others.

A fool is quick-tempered,
    but a wise person stays calm when insulted.

An honest witness tells the truth;
    a false witness tells lies.

Some people make cutting remarks,
    but the words of the wise bring healing.

Truthful words stand the test of time,
    but lies are soon exposed.

Deceit fills hearts that are plotting evil;
    joy fills hearts that are planning peace!

No harm comes to the godly,
    but the wicked have their fill of trouble.

The LORD detests lying lips,
    but he delights in those who tell the truth.

The wise don't make a show of their knowledge,
    but fools broadcast their foolishness.

Work hard and become a leader;
    be lazy and become a slave.

Worry weighs a person down;
    an encouraging word cheers a person up.

The godly give good advice to their friends;
    the wicked lead them astray.

Lazy people don't even cook the game they catch,
    but the diligent make use of everything they find.

The way of the godly leads to life;
    that path does not lead to death.

A wise child accepts a parent's discipline;
    a mocker refuses to listen to correction.

Wise words will win you a good meal,
but treacherous people have an appetite for violence.

Those who control their tongue will have a long life;
opening your mouth can ruin everything.

Lazy people want much but get little,
but those who work hard will prosper.

The godly hate lies;
the wicked cause shame and disgrace.

Godliness guards the path of the blameless,
but the evil are misled by sin.

Some who are poor pretend to be rich;
others who are rich pretend to be poor.

The rich can pay a ransom for their lives,
but the poor won't even get threatened.

The life of the godly is full of light and joy,
but the light of the wicked will be snuffed out.

Pride leads to conflict;
those who take advice are wise.

Wealth from get-rich-quick schemes quickly disappears;
wealth from hard work grows over time.

Hope deferred makes the heart sick,
but a dream fulfilled is a tree of life.

People who despise advice are asking for trouble;
those who respect a command will succeed.

The instruction of the wise is like a life-giving fountain;
those who accept it avoid the snares of death.

A person with good sense is respected;
a treacherous person is headed for destruction.

Wise people think before they act;
fools don't—and even brag about their foolishness.

An unreliable messenger stumbles into trouble,
but a reliable messenger brings healing.

If you ignore criticism, you will end in poverty and disgrace;
if you accept correction, you will be honored.

It is pleasant to see dreams come true,
  but fools refuse to turn from evil to attain them.

Walk with the wise and become wise;
  associate with fools and get in trouble.

Trouble chases sinners,
  while blessings reward the righteous.

Good people leave an inheritance to their grandchildren,
  but the sinner's wealth passes to the godly.

A poor person's farm may produce much food,
  but injustice sweeps it all away.

Those who spare the rod of discipline hate their children.
  Those who love their children care enough to discipline them.

The godly eat to their hearts' content,
  but the belly of the wicked goes hungry.

A wise woman builds her home,
  but a foolish woman tears it down with her own hands.

Those who follow the right path fear the LORD;
  those who take the wrong path despise him.

A fool's proud talk becomes a rod that beats him,
  but the words of the wise keep them safe.

Without oxen a stable stays clean,
  but you need a strong ox for a large harvest.

An honest witness does not lie;
  a false witness breathes lies.

A mocker seeks wisdom and never finds it,
  but knowledge comes easily to those with understanding.

Stay away from fools,
  for you won't find knowledge on their lips.

The prudent understand where they are going,
  but fools deceive themselves.

Fools make fun of guilt,
  but the godly acknowledge it and seek reconciliation.

Each heart knows its own bitterness,
  and no one else can fully share its joy.

The house of the wicked will be destroyed,
  but the tent of the godly will flourish.

There is a path before each person that seems right,
  but it ends in death.

Laughter can conceal a heavy heart,
  but when the laughter ends, the grief remains.

Backsliders get what they deserve;
  good people receive their reward.

Only simpletons believe everything they're told!
  The prudent carefully consider their steps.

The wise are cautious and avoid danger;
  fools plunge ahead with reckless confidence.

Short-tempered people do foolish things,
  and schemers are hated.

Simpletons are clothed with foolishness,
  but the prudent are crowned with knowledge.

Evil people will bow before good people;
  the wicked will bow at the gates of the godly.

The poor are despised even by their neighbors,
  while the rich have many "friends."

It is a sin to belittle one's neighbor;
  blessed are those who help the poor.

If you plan to do evil, you will be lost;
  if you plan to do good, you will receive unfailing love and
    faithfulness.

Work brings profit,
  but mere talk leads to poverty!

Wealth is a crown for the wise;
  the effort of fools yields only foolishness.

A truthful witness saves lives,
  but a false witness is a traitor.

Those who fear the LORD are secure;
  he will be a refuge for their children.

Fear of the LORD is a life-giving fountain;
  it offers escape from the snares of death.

A growing population is a king's glory;
  a prince without subjects has nothing.

People with understanding control their anger;
  a hot temper shows great foolishness.

A peaceful heart leads to a healthy body;
  jealousy is like cancer in the bones.

Those who oppress the poor insult their Maker,
  but helping the poor honors him.

The wicked are crushed by disaster,
  but the godly have a refuge when they die.

Wisdom is enshrined in an understanding heart;
  wisdom is not found among fools.

Godliness makes a nation great,
  but sin is a disgrace to any people.

A king rejoices in wise servants
  but is angry with those who disgrace him.

A gentle answer deflects anger,
  but harsh words make tempers flare.

The tongue of the wise makes knowledge appealing,
  but the mouth of a fool belches out foolishness.

The LORD is watching everywhere,
  keeping his eye on both the evil and the good.

Gentle words are a tree of life;
  a deceitful tongue crushes the spirit.

Only a fool despises a parent's discipline;
  whoever learns from correction is wise.

There is treasure in the house of the godly,
  but the earnings of the wicked bring trouble.

The lips of the wise give good advice;
  the heart of a fool has none to give.

The LORD detests the sacrifice of the wicked,
  but he delights in the prayers of the upright.

The LORD detests the way of the wicked,
  but he loves those who pursue godliness.

Whoever abandons the right path will be severely disciplined;
  whoever hates correction will die.

Even Death and Destruction hold no secrets from the LORD.
  How much more does he know the human heart!

Mockers hate to be corrected,
  so they stay away from the wise.

A glad heart makes a happy face;
  a broken heart crushes the spirit.

A wise person is hungry for knowledge,
  while the fool feeds on trash.

For the despondent, every day brings trouble;
  for the happy heart, life is a continual feast.

Better to have little, with fear for the LORD,
  than to have great treasure and inner turmoil.

A bowl of vegetables with someone you love
  is better than steak with someone you hate.

A hot-tempered person starts fights;
  a cool-tempered person stops them.

A lazy person's way is blocked with briers,
  but the path of the upright is an open highway.

Sensible children bring joy to their father;
  foolish children despise their mother.

Foolishness brings joy to those with no sense;
  a sensible person stays on the right path.

Plans go wrong for lack of advice;
  many advisers bring success.

Everyone enjoys a fitting reply;
  it is wonderful to say the right thing at the right time!

The path of life leads upward for the wise;
  they leave the grave behind.

The LORD tears down the house of the proud,
  but he protects the property of widows.

The LORD detests evil plans,
  but he delights in pure words.

Greed brings grief to the whole family,
  but those who hate bribes will live.

The heart of the godly thinks carefully before speaking;
  the mouth of the wicked overflows with evil words.

The Lord is far from the wicked,
  but he hears the prayers of the righteous.

+

A cheerful look brings joy to the heart;
  good news makes for good health.

If you listen to constructive criticism,
  you will be at home among the wise.

If you reject discipline, you only harm yourself;
  but if you listen to correction, you grow in understanding.

Fear of the Lord teaches wisdom;
  humility precedes honor.

We can make our own plans,
  but the Lord gives the right answer.

People may be pure in their own eyes,
  but the Lord examines their motives.

Commit your actions to the Lord,
  and your plans will succeed.

The Lord has made everything for his own purposes,
  even the wicked for a day of disaster.

The Lord detests the proud;
  they will surely be punished.

Unfailing love and faithfulness make atonement for sin.
  By fearing the Lord, people avoid evil.

When people's lives please the Lord,
  even their enemies are at peace with them.

Better to have little, with godliness,
  than to be rich and dishonest.

We can make our plans,
  but the Lord determines our steps.

The king speaks with divine wisdom;
   he must never judge unfairly.

The LORD demands accurate scales and balances;
   he sets the standards for fairness.

A king detests wrongdoing,
   for his rule is built on justice.

The king is pleased with words from righteous lips;
   he loves those who speak honestly.

The anger of the king is a deadly threat;
   the wise will try to appease it.

When the king smiles, there is life;
   his favor refreshes like a spring rain.

How much better to get wisdom than gold,
   and good judgment than silver!

The path of the virtuous leads away from evil;
   whoever follows that path is safe.

Pride goes before destruction,
   and haughtiness before a fall.

Better to live humbly with the poor
   than to share plunder with the proud.

Those who listen to instruction will prosper;
   those who trust the LORD will be joyful.

The wise are known for their understanding,
   and pleasant words are persuasive.

Discretion is a life-giving fountain to those who possess it,
   but discipline is wasted on fools.

From a wise mind comes wise speech;
   the words of the wise are persuasive.

Kind words are like honey—
   sweet to the soul and healthy for the body.

There is a path before each person that seems right,
   but it ends in death.

It is good for workers to have an appetite;
   an empty stomach drives them on.

Scoundrels create trouble;
    their words are a destructive blaze.

A troublemaker plants seeds of strife;
    gossip separates the best of friends.

Violent people mislead their companions,
    leading them down a harmful path.

With narrowed eyes, people plot evil;
    with a smirk, they plan their mischief.

Gray hair is a crown of glory;
    it is gained by living a godly life.

Better to be patient than powerful;
    better to have self-control than to conquer a city.

We may throw the dice,
    but the LORD determines how they fall.

Better a dry crust eaten in peace
    than a house filled with feasting—and conflict.

A wise servant will rule over the master's disgraceful son
    and will share the inheritance of the master's children.

Fire tests the purity of silver and gold,
    but the LORD tests the heart.

Wrongdoers eagerly listen to gossip;
    liars pay close attention to slander.

Those who mock the poor insult their Maker;
    those who rejoice at the misfortune of others will be punished.

Grandchildren are the crowning glory of the aged;
    parents are the pride of their children.

Eloquent words are not fitting for a fool;
    even less are lies fitting for a ruler.

A bribe is like a lucky charm;
    whoever gives one will prosper!

Love prospers when a fault is forgiven,
    but dwelling on it separates close friends.

A single rebuke does more for a person of understanding
    than a hundred lashes on the back of a fool.

Evil people are eager for rebellion,
  but they will be severely punished.

It is safer to meet a bear robbed of her cubs
  than to confront a fool caught in foolishness.

If you repay good with evil,
  evil will never leave your house.

Starting a quarrel is like opening a floodgate,
  so stop before a dispute breaks out.

Acquitting the guilty and condemning the innocent—
  both are detestable to the LORD.

It is senseless to pay to educate a fool,
  since he has no heart for learning.

A friend is always loyal,
  and a brother is born to help in time of need.

It's poor judgment to guarantee another person's debt
  or put up security for a friend.

Anyone who loves to quarrel loves sin;
  anyone who trusts in high walls invites disaster.

The crooked heart will not prosper;
  the lying tongue tumbles into trouble.

It is painful to be the parent of a fool;
  there is no joy for the father of a rebel.

A cheerful heart is good medicine,
  but a broken spirit saps a person's strength.

The wicked take secret bribes
  to pervert the course of justice.

Sensible people keep their eyes glued on wisdom,
  but a fool's eyes wander to the ends of the earth.

Foolish children bring grief to their father
  and bitterness to the one who gave them birth.

It is wrong to punish the godly for being good
  or to flog leaders for being honest.

A truly wise person uses few words;
  a person with understanding is even-tempered.

Even fools are thought wise when they keep silent;
   with their mouths shut, they seem intelligent.

Unfriendly people care only about themselves;
   they lash out at common sense.

Fools have no interest in understanding;
   they only want to air their own opinions.

Doing wrong leads to disgrace,
   and scandalous behavior brings contempt.

Wise words are like deep waters;
   wisdom flows from the wise like a bubbling brook.

It is not right to acquit the guilty
   or deny justice to the innocent.

Fools' words get them into constant quarrels;
   they are asking for a beating.

The mouths of fools are their ruin;
   they trap themselves with their lips.

Rumors are dainty morsels
   that sink deep into one's heart.

A lazy person is as bad as
   someone who destroys things.

The name of the LORD is a strong fortress;
   the godly run to him and are safe.

The rich think of their wealth as a strong defense;
   they imagine it to be a high wall of safety.

Haughtiness goes before destruction;
   humility precedes honor.

Spouting off before listening to the facts
   is both shameful and foolish.

The human spirit can endure a sick body,
   but who can bear a crushed spirit?

Intelligent people are always ready to learn.
   Their ears are open for knowledge.

Giving a gift can open doors;
   it gives access to important people!

The first to speak in court sounds right—
    until the cross-examination begins.

Flipping a coin can end arguments;
    it settles disputes between powerful opponents.

An offended friend is harder to win back than a fortified city.
    Arguments separate friends like a gate locked with bars.

Wise words satisfy like a good meal;
    the right words bring satisfaction.

The tongue can bring death or life;
    those who love to talk will reap the consequences.

The man who finds a wife finds a treasure,
    and he receives favor from the LORD.

The poor plead for mercy;
    the rich answer with insults.

There are "friends" who destroy each other,
    but a real friend sticks closer than a brother.

Better to be poor and honest
    than to be dishonest and a fool.

Enthusiasm without knowledge is no good;
    haste makes mistakes.

People ruin their lives by their own foolishness
    and then are angry at the LORD.

Wealth makes many "friends";
    poverty drives them all away.

A false witness will not go unpunished,
    nor will a liar escape.

Many seek favors from a ruler;
    everyone is the friend of a person who gives gifts!

The relatives of the poor despise them;
    how much more will their friends avoid them!
Though the poor plead with them,
    their friends are gone.

To acquire wisdom is to love yourself;
    people who cherish understanding will prosper.

A false witness will not go unpunished,
  and a liar will be destroyed.

It isn't right for a fool to live in luxury
  or for a slave to rule over princes!

Sensible people control their temper;
  they earn respect by overlooking wrongs.

The king's anger is like a lion's roar,
  but his favor is like dew on the grass.

A foolish child is a calamity to a father;
  a quarrelsome wife is as annoying as constant dripping.

Fathers can give their sons an inheritance of houses and wealth,
  but only the LORD can give an understanding wife.

Lazy people sleep soundly,
  but idleness leaves them hungry.

Keep the commandments and keep your life;
  despising them leads to death.

If you help the poor, you are lending to the LORD—
  and he will repay you!

Discipline your children while there is hope.
  Otherwise you will ruin their lives.

Hot-tempered people must pay the penalty.
  If you rescue them once, you will have to do it again.

Get all the advice and instruction you can,
  so you will be wise the rest of your life.

You can make many plans,
  but the LORD's purpose will prevail.

Loyalty makes a person attractive.
  It is better to be poor than dishonest.

Fear of the LORD leads to life,
  bringing security and protection from harm.

Lazy people take food in their hand
  but don't even lift it to their mouth.

If you punish a mocker, the simpleminded will learn a lesson;
  if you correct the wise, they will be all the wiser.

Children who mistreat their father or chase away their mother
    are an embarrassment and a public disgrace.

If you stop listening to instruction, my child,
    you will turn your back on knowledge.

A corrupt witness makes a mockery of justice;
    the mouth of the wicked gulps down evil.

Punishment is made for mockers,
    and the backs of fools are made to be beaten.

Wine produces mockers; alcohol leads to brawls.
    Those led astray by drink cannot be wise.

The king's fury is like a lion's roar;
    to rouse his anger is to risk your life.

Avoiding a fight is a mark of honor;
    only fools insist on quarreling.

Those too lazy to plow in the right season
    will have no food at the harvest.

Though good advice lies deep within the heart,
    a person with understanding will draw it out.

Many will say they are loyal friends,
    but who can find one who is truly reliable?

The godly walk with integrity;
    blessed are their children who follow them.

When a king sits in judgment, he weighs all the evidence,
    distinguishing the bad from the good.

Who can say, "I have cleansed my heart;
    I am pure and free from sin"?

False weights and unequal measures—
    the LORD detests double standards of every kind.

Even children are known by the way they act,
    whether their conduct is pure, and whether it is right.

Ears to hear and eyes to see—
    both are gifts from the LORD.

If you love sleep, you will end in poverty.
    Keep your eyes open, and there will be plenty to eat!

The buyer haggles over the price, saying, "It's worthless,"
  then brags about getting a bargain!

Wise words are more valuable
  than much gold and many rubies.

Get security from someone who guarantees a stranger's debt.
  Get a deposit if he does it for foreigners.

Stolen bread tastes sweet,
  but it turns to gravel in the mouth.

Plans succeed through good counsel;
  don't go to war without wise advice.

A gossip goes around telling secrets,
  so don't hang around with chatterers.

If you insult your father or mother,
  your light will be snuffed out in total darkness.

An inheritance obtained too early in life
  is not a blessing in the end.

Don't say, "I will get even for this wrong."
  Wait for the LORD to handle the matter.

The LORD detests double standards;
  he is not pleased by dishonest scales.

The LORD directs our steps,
  so why try to understand everything along the way?

Don't trap yourself by making a rash promise to God
  and only later counting the cost.

A wise king scatters the wicked like wheat,
  then runs his threshing wheel over them.

The LORD's light penetrates the human spirit,
  exposing every hidden motive.

Unfailing love and faithfulness protect the king;
  his throne is made secure through love.

The glory of the young is their strength;
  the gray hair of experience is the splendor of the old.

Physical punishment cleanses away evil;
  such discipline purifies the heart.

The king's heart is like a stream of water directed by the LORD;
  he guides it wherever he pleases.

People may be right in their own eyes,
  but the LORD examines their heart.

The LORD is more pleased when we do what is right and just
  than when we offer him sacrifices.

Haughty eyes, a proud heart,
  and evil actions are all sin.

Good planning and hard work lead to prosperity,
  but hasty shortcuts lead to poverty.

Wealth created by a lying tongue
  is a vanishing mist and a deadly trap.

The violence of the wicked sweeps them away,
  because they refuse to do what is just.

The guilty walk a crooked path;
  the innocent travel a straight road.

It's better to live alone in the corner of an attic
  than with a quarrelsome wife in a lovely home.

Evil people desire evil;
  their neighbors get no mercy from them.

If you punish a mocker, the simpleminded become wise;
  if you instruct the wise, they will be all the wiser.

The Righteous One knows what is going on in the homes of the
      wicked;
  he will bring disaster on them.

Those who shut their ears to the cries of the poor
  will be ignored in their own time of need.

A secret gift calms anger;
  a bribe under the table pacifies fury.

Justice is a joy to the godly,
  but it terrifies evildoers.

The person who strays from common sense
  will end up in the company of the dead.

Those who love pleasure become poor;
  those who love wine and luxury will never be rich.

The wicked are punished in place of the godly,
    and traitors in place of the honest.

It's better to live alone in the desert
    than with a quarrelsome, complaining wife.

The wise have wealth and luxury,
    but fools spend whatever they get.

Whoever pursues righteousness and unfailing love
    will find life, righteousness, and honor.

The wise conquer the city of the strong
    and level the fortress in which they trust.

Watch your tongue and keep your mouth shut,
    and you will stay out of trouble.

Mockers are proud and haughty;
    they act with boundless arrogance.

Despite their desires, the lazy will come to ruin,
    for their hands refuse to work.

Some people are always greedy for more,
    but the godly love to give!

The sacrifice of an evil person is detestable,
    especially when it is offered with wrong motives.

A false witness will be cut off,
    but a credible witness will be allowed to speak.

The wicked bluff their way through,
    but the virtuous think before they act.

No human wisdom or understanding or plan
    can stand against the LORD.

The horse is prepared for the day of battle,
    but the victory belongs to the LORD.

Choose a good reputation over great riches;
    being held in high esteem is better than silver or gold.

The rich and poor have this in common:
    The LORD made them both.

A prudent person foresees danger and takes precautions.
    The simpleton goes blindly on and suffers the consequences.

True humility and fear of the LORD
    lead to riches, honor, and long life.

Corrupt people walk a thorny, treacherous road;
    whoever values life will avoid it.

Direct your children onto the right path,
    and when they are older, they will not leave it.

Just as the rich rule the poor,
    so the borrower is servant to the lender.

Those who plant injustice will harvest disaster,
    and their reign of terror will come to an end.

Blessed are those who are generous,
    because they feed the poor.

Throw out the mocker, and fighting goes, too.
    Quarrels and insults will disappear.

Whoever loves a pure heart and gracious speech
    will have the king as a friend.

The LORD preserves those with knowledge,
    but he ruins the plans of the treacherous.

The lazy person claims, "There's a lion out there!
    If I go outside, I might be killed!"

The mouth of an immoral woman is a dangerous trap;
    those who make the LORD angry will fall into it.

A youngster's heart is filled with foolishness,
    but physical discipline will drive it far away.

A person who gets ahead by oppressing the poor
    or by showering gifts on the rich will end in poverty.

✢ ✢ ✢

Listen to the words of the wise;
    apply your heart to my instruction.
For it is good to keep these sayings in your heart
    and always ready on your lips.
I am teaching you today—yes, you—
    so you will trust in the LORD.
I have written thirty sayings for you,

filled with advice and knowledge.
In this way, you may know the truth
    and take an accurate report to those who sent you.

Don't rob the poor just because you can,
    or exploit the needy in court.
For the LORD is their defender.
    He will ruin anyone who ruins them.

Don't befriend angry people
    or associate with hot-tempered people,
or you will learn to be like them
    and endanger your soul.

Don't agree to guarantee another person's debt
    or put up security for someone else.
If you can't pay it,
    even your bed will be snatched from under you.

Don't cheat your neighbor by moving the ancient boundary markers
    set up by previous generations.

Do you see any truly competent workers?
    They will serve kings
    rather than working for ordinary people.

While dining with a ruler,
    pay attention to what is put before you.
If you are a big eater,
    put a knife to your throat;
don't desire all the delicacies,
    for he might be trying to trick you.

Don't wear yourself out trying to get rich.
    Be wise enough to know when to quit.
In the blink of an eye wealth disappears,
    for it will sprout wings
    and fly away like an eagle.

Don't eat with people who are stingy;
    don't desire their delicacies.
They are always thinking about how much it costs.
    "Eat and drink," they say, but they don't mean it.
You will throw up what little you've eaten,
    and your compliments will be wasted.

Don't waste your breath on fools,
   for they will despise the wisest advice.

Don't cheat your neighbor by moving the ancient boundary markers;
   don't take the land of defenseless orphans.
For their Redeemer is strong;
   he himself will bring their charges against you.

Commit yourself to instruction;
   listen carefully to words of knowledge.

Don't fail to discipline your children.
   The rod of punishment won't kill them.
Physical discipline
   may well save them from death.

My child, if your heart is wise,
   my own heart will rejoice!
Everything in me will celebrate
   when you speak what is right.

Don't envy sinners,
   but always continue to fear the LORD.
You will be rewarded for this;
   your hope will not be disappointed.

My child, listen and be wise:
   Keep your heart on the right course.
Do not carouse with drunkards
   or feast with gluttons,
for they are on their way to poverty,
   and too much sleep clothes them in rags.

Listen to your father, who gave you life,
   and don't despise your mother when she is old.
Get the truth and never sell it;
   also get wisdom, discipline, and good judgment.
The father of godly children has cause for joy.
   What a pleasure to have children who are wise.
So give your father and mother joy!
   May she who gave you birth be happy.

O my son, give me your heart.
   May your eyes take delight in following my ways.
A prostitute is a dangerous trap;
   a promiscuous woman is as dangerous as falling into a narrow well.

She hides and waits like a robber,
    eager to make more men unfaithful.

Who has anguish? Who has sorrow?
    Who is always fighting? Who is always complaining?
    Who has unnecessary bruises? Who has bloodshot eyes?
It is the one who spends long hours in the taverns,
    trying out new drinks.
Don't gaze at the wine, seeing how red it is,
    how it sparkles in the cup, how smoothly it goes down.
For in the end it bites like a poisonous snake;
    it stings like a viper.
You will see hallucinations,
    and you will say crazy things.
You will stagger like a sailor tossed at sea,
    clinging to a swaying mast.
And you will say, "They hit me, but I didn't feel it.
    I didn't even know it when they beat me up.
When will I wake up
    so I can look for another drink?"

Don't envy evil people
    or desire their company.
For their hearts plot violence,
    and their words always stir up trouble.

A house is built by wisdom
    and becomes strong through good sense.
Through knowledge its rooms are filled
    with all sorts of precious riches and valuables.

The wise are mightier than the strong,
    and those with knowledge grow stronger and stronger.
So don't go to war without wise guidance;
    victory depends on having many advisers.

Wisdom is too lofty for fools.
    Among leaders at the city gate, they have nothing to say.

A person who plans evil
    will get a reputation as a troublemaker.
The schemes of a fool are sinful;
    everyone detests a mocker.

If you fail under pressure,
    your strength is too small.

Rescue those who are unjustly sentenced to die;
  save them as they stagger to their death.
Don't excuse yourself by saying, "Look, we didn't know."
  For God understands all hearts, and he sees you.
He who guards your soul knows you knew.
  He will repay all people as their actions deserve.

My child, eat honey, for it is good, ·
  and the honeycomb is sweet to the taste.
In the same way, wisdom is sweet to your soul.
  If you find it, you will have a bright future,
  and your hopes will not be cut short.

Don't wait in ambush at the home of the godly,
  and don't raid the house where the godly live.
The godly may trip seven times, but they will get up again.
  But one disaster is enough to overthrow the wicked.

Don't rejoice when your enemies fall;
  don't be happy when they stumble.
For the LORD will be displeased with you
  and will turn his anger away from them.

Don't fret because of evildoers;
  don't envy the wicked.
For evil people have no future;
  the light of the wicked will be snuffed out.

My child, fear the LORD and the king.
Don't associate with rebels,
  for disaster will hit them suddenly.
Who knows what punishment will come
  from the LORD and the king?

✛ ✛ ✛

Here are some further sayings of the wise:

  It is wrong to show favoritism when passing judgment.
  A judge who says to the wicked, "You are innocent,"
    will be cursed by many people and denounced by the nations.
  But it will go well for those who convict the guilty;
    rich blessings will be showered on them.

  An honest answer
    is like a kiss of friendship.

Do your planning and prepare your fields
　　before building your house.

Don't testify against your neighbors without cause;
　　don't lie about them.
And don't say, "Now I can pay them back for what they've done to me!
　　I'll get even with them!"

I walked by the field of a lazy person,
　　the vineyard of one with no common sense.
I saw that it was overgrown with nettles.
　　It was covered with weeds,
　　and its walls were broken down.
Then, as I looked and thought about it,
　　I learned this lesson:
A little extra sleep, a little more slumber,
　　a little folding of the hands to rest—
then poverty will pounce on you like a bandit;
　　scarcity will attack you like an armed robber.

+ + +

These are more proverbs of Solomon, collected by the advisers of King
Hezekiah of Judah.

It is God's privilege to conceal things
　　and the king's privilege to discover them.

No one can comprehend the height of heaven, the depth of the earth,
　　or all that goes on in the king's mind!

Remove the impurities from silver,
　　and the sterling will be ready for the silversmith.
Remove the wicked from the king's court,
　　and his reign will be made secure by justice.

Don't demand an audience with the king
　　or push for a place among the great.
It's better to wait for an invitation to the head table
　　than to be sent away in public disgrace.

Just because you've seen something,
　　don't be in a hurry to go to court.
For what will you do in the end
　　if your neighbor deals you a shameful defeat?

When arguing with your neighbor,
    don't betray another person's secret.
Others may accuse you of gossip,
    and you will never regain your good reputation.

Timely advice is lovely,
    like golden apples in a silver basket.

To one who listens, valid criticism
    is like a gold earring or other gold jewelry.

Trustworthy messengers refresh like snow in summer.
    They revive the spirit of their employer.

A person who promises a gift but doesn't give it
    is like clouds and wind that bring no rain.

Patience can persuade a prince,
    and soft speech can break bones.

Do you like honey?
    Don't eat too much, or it will make you sick!

Don't visit your neighbors too often,
    or you will wear out your welcome.

Telling lies about others
    is as harmful as hitting them with an ax,
wounding them with a sword,
    or shooting them with a sharp arrow.

Putting confidence in an unreliable person in times of trouble
    is like chewing with a broken tooth or walking on a lame foot.

Singing cheerful songs to a person with a heavy heart
    is like taking someone's coat in cold weather
    or pouring vinegar in a wound.

If your enemies are hungry, give them food to eat.
    If they are thirsty, give them water to drink.
You will heap burning coals of shame on their heads,
    and the LORD will reward you.

As surely as a north wind brings rain,
    so a gossiping tongue causes anger!

It's better to live alone in the corner of an attic
    than with a quarrelsome wife in a lovely home.

Good news from far away
   is like cold water to the thirsty.

If the godly give in to the wicked,
   it's like polluting a fountain or muddying a spring.

It's not good to eat too much honey,
   and it's not good to seek honors for yourself.

A person without self-control
   is like a city with broken-down walls.

Honor is no more associated with fools
   than snow with summer or rain with harvest.

Like a fluttering sparrow or a darting swallow,
   an undeserved curse will not land on its intended victim.

Guide a horse with a whip, a donkey with a bridle,
   and a fool with a rod to his back!

Don't answer the foolish arguments of fools,
   or you will become as foolish as they are.

Be sure to answer the foolish arguments of fools,
   or they will become wise in their own estimation.

Trusting a fool to convey a message
   is like cutting off one's feet or drinking poison!

A proverb in the mouth of a fool
   is as useless as a paralyzed leg.

Honoring a fool
   is as foolish as tying a stone to a slingshot.

A proverb in the mouth of a fool
   is like a thorny branch brandished by a drunk.

An employer who hires a fool or a bystander
   is like an archer who shoots at random.

As a dog returns to its vomit,
   so a fool repeats his foolishness.

There is more hope for fools
   than for people who think they are wise.

The lazy person claims, "There's a lion on the road!
   Yes, I'm sure there's a lion out there!"

As a door swings back and forth on its hinges,
    so the lazy person turns over in bed.

Lazy people take food in their hand
    but don't even lift it to their mouth.

Lazy people consider themselves smarter
    than seven wise counselors.

Interfering in someone else's argument
    is as foolish as yanking a dog's ears.

Just as damaging
    as a madman shooting a deadly weapon
is someone who lies to a friend
    and then says, "I was only joking."

Fire goes out without wood,
    and quarrels disappear when gossip stops.

A quarrelsome person starts fights
    as easily as hot embers light charcoal or fire lights wood.

Rumors are dainty morsels
    that sink deep into one's heart.

Smooth words may hide a wicked heart,
    just as a pretty glaze covers a clay pot.

People may cover their hatred with pleasant words,
    but they're deceiving you.
They pretend to be kind, but don't believe them.
    Their hearts are full of many evils.
While their hatred may be concealed by trickery,
    their wrongdoing will be exposed in public.

If you set a trap for others,
    you will get caught in it yourself.
If you roll a boulder down on others,
    it will crush you instead.

A lying tongue hates its victims,
    and flattering words cause ruin.

Don't brag about tomorrow,
    since you don't know what the day will bring.

Let someone else praise you, not your own mouth—
    a stranger, not your own lips.

A stone is heavy and sand is weighty,
    but the resentment caused by a fool is even heavier.

Anger is cruel, and wrath is like a flood,
    but jealousy is even more dangerous.

An open rebuke
    is better than hidden love!

Wounds from a sincere friend
    are better than many kisses from an enemy.

A person who is full refuses honey,
    but even bitter food tastes sweet to the hungry.

A person who strays from home
    is like a bird that strays from its nest.

The heartfelt counsel of a friend
    is as sweet as perfume and incense.

Never abandon a friend—
    either yours or your father's.
When disaster strikes, you won't have to ask your brother for
      assistance.
    It's better to go to a neighbor than to a brother who lives far away.

Be wise, my child, and make my heart glad.
    Then I will be able to answer my critics.

A prudent person foresees danger and takes precautions.
    The simpleton goes blindly on and suffers the consequences.

Get security from someone who guarantees a stranger's debt.
    Get a deposit if he does it for foreigners.

A loud and cheerful greeting early in the morning
    will be taken as a curse!

A quarrelsome wife is as annoying
    as constant dripping on a rainy day.
Stopping her complaints is like trying to stop the wind
    or trying to hold something with greased hands.

As iron sharpens iron,
    so a friend sharpens a friend.

As workers who tend a fig tree are allowed to eat the fruit,
    so workers who protect their employer's interests will be rewarded.

As a face is reflected in water,
  so the heart reflects the real person.

Just as Death and Destruction are never satisfied,
  so human desire is never satisfied.

Fire tests the purity of silver and gold,
  but a person is tested by being praised.

You cannot separate fools from their foolishness,
  even though you grind them like grain with mortar and pestle.

Know the state of your flocks,
  and put your heart into caring for your herds,
for riches don't last forever,
  and the crown might not be passed to the next generation.
After the hay is harvested and the new crop appears
  and the mountain grasses are gathered in,
your sheep will provide wool for clothing,
  and your goats will provide the price of a field.
And you will have enough goats' milk for yourself,
  your family, and your servant girls.

+

The wicked run away when no one is chasing them,
  but the godly are as bold as lions.

When there is moral rot within a nation, its government topples easily.
  But wise and knowledgeable leaders bring stability.

A poor person who oppresses the poor
  is like a pounding rain that destroys the crops.

To reject the law is to praise the wicked;
  to obey the law is to fight them.

Evil people don't understand justice,
  but those who follow the LORD understand completely.

Better to be poor and honest
  than to be dishonest and rich.

Young people who obey the law are wise;
  those with wild friends bring shame to their parents.

Income from charging high interest rates
  will end up in the pocket of someone who is kind to the poor.

God detests the prayers
  of a person who ignores the law.

Those who lead good people along an evil path
  will fall into their own trap,
  but the honest will inherit good things.

Rich people may think they are wise,
  but a poor person with discernment can see right through them.

When the godly succeed, everyone is glad.
  When the wicked take charge, people go into hiding.

People who conceal their sins will not prosper,
  but if they confess and turn from them, they will receive mercy.

Blessed are those who fear to do wrong,
  but the stubborn are headed for serious trouble.

A wicked ruler is as dangerous to the poor
  as a roaring lion or an attacking bear.

A ruler with no understanding will oppress his people,
  but one who hates corruption will have a long life.

A murderer's tormented conscience will drive him into the grave.
  Don't protect him!

The blameless will be rescued from harm,
  but the crooked will be suddenly destroyed.

A hard worker has plenty of food,
  but a person who chases fantasies ends up in poverty.

The trustworthy person will get a rich reward,
  but a person who wants quick riches will get into trouble.

Showing partiality is never good,
  yet some will do wrong for a mere piece of bread.

Greedy people try to get rich quick
  but don't realize they're headed for poverty.

In the end, people appreciate honest criticism
  far more than flattery.

Anyone who steals from his father and mother
  and says, "What's wrong with that?"
  is no better than a murderer.

Greed causes fighting;
   trusting the Lord leads to prosperity.

Those who trust their own insight are foolish,
   but anyone who walks in wisdom is safe.

Whoever gives to the poor will lack nothing,
   but those who close their eyes to poverty will be cursed.

When the wicked take charge, people go into hiding.
   When the wicked meet disaster, the godly flourish.

Whoever stubbornly refuses to accept criticism
   will suddenly be destroyed beyond recovery.

When the godly are in authority, the people rejoice.
   But when the wicked are in power, they groan.

The man who loves wisdom brings joy to his father,
   but if he hangs around with prostitutes, his wealth is wasted.

A just king gives stability to his nation,
   but one who demands bribes destroys it.

To flatter friends
   is to lay a trap for their feet.

Evil people are trapped by sin,
   but the righteous escape, shouting for joy.

The godly care about the rights of the poor;
   the wicked don't care at all.

Mockers can get a whole town agitated,
   but the wise will calm anger.

If a wise person takes a fool to court,
   there will be ranting and ridicule but no satisfaction.

The bloodthirsty hate blameless people,
   but the upright seek to help them.

Fools vent their anger,
   but the wise quietly hold it back.

If a ruler pays attention to liars,
   all his advisers will be wicked.

The poor and the oppressor have this in common—
   the Lord gives sight to the eyes of both.

If a king judges the poor fairly,
  his throne will last forever.

To discipline a child produces wisdom,
  but a mother is disgraced by an undisciplined child.

When the wicked are in authority, sin flourishes,
  but the godly will live to see their downfall.

Discipline your children, and they will give you peace of mind
  and will make your heart glad.

When people do not accept divine guidance, they run wild.
  But whoever obeys the law is joyful.

Words alone will not discipline a servant;
  the words may be understood, but they are not heeded.

There is more hope for a fool
  than for someone who speaks without thinking.

A servant pampered from childhood
  will become a rebel.

An angry person starts fights;
  a hot-tempered person commits all kinds of sin.

Pride ends in humiliation,
  while humility brings honor.

If you assist a thief, you only hurt yourself.
  You are sworn to tell the truth, but you dare not testify.

Fearing people is a dangerous trap,
  but trusting the LORD means safety.

Many seek the ruler's favor,
  but justice comes from the LORD.

The righteous despise the unjust;
  the wicked despise the godly.

+ + +

The sayings of Agur son of Jakeh contain this message.

I am weary, O God;
  I am weary and worn out, O God.
I am too stupid to be human,

and I lack common sense.
I have not mastered human wisdom,
   nor do I know the Holy One.

Who but God goes up to heaven and comes back down?
   Who holds the wind in his fists?
Who wraps up the oceans in his cloak?
   Who has created the whole wide world?
What is his name—and his son's name?
   Tell me if you know!

Every word of God proves true.
   He is a shield to all who come to him for protection.
Do not add to his words,
   or he may rebuke you and expose you as a liar.

O God, I beg two favors from you;
   let me have them before I die.
First, help me never to tell a lie.
   Second, give me neither poverty nor riches!
   Give me just enough to satisfy my needs.
For if I grow rich, I may deny you and say, "Who is the LORD?"
   And if I am too poor, I may steal and thus insult God's holy name.

Never slander a worker to the employer,
   or the person will curse you, and you will pay for it.

Some people curse their father
   and do not thank their mother.
They are pure in their own eyes,
   but they are filthy and unwashed.
They look proudly around,
   casting disdainful glances.
They have teeth like swords
   and fangs like knives.
They devour the poor from the earth
   and the needy from among humanity.

The leech has two suckers
   that cry out, "More, more!"

There are three things that are never satisfied—
   no, four that never say, "Enough!":
the grave,
   the barren womb,

the thirsty desert,
the blazing fire.

The eye that mocks a father
and despises a mother's instructions
will be plucked out by ravens of the valley
and eaten by vultures.

There are three things that amaze me—
no, four things that I don't understand:
how an eagle glides through the sky,
how a snake slithers on a rock,
how a ship navigates the ocean,
how a man loves a woman.

An adulterous woman consumes a man,
then wipes her mouth and says, "What's wrong with that?"

There are three things that make the earth tremble—
no, four it cannot endure:
a slave who becomes a king,
an overbearing fool who prospers,
a bitter woman who finally gets a husband,
a servant girl who supplants her mistress.

There are four things on earth that are small but unusually wise:
Ants—they aren't strong,
but they store up food all summer.
Hyraxes—they aren't powerful,
but they make their homes among the rocks.
Locusts—they have no king,
but they march in formation.
Lizards—they are easy to catch,
but they are found even in kings' palaces.

There are three things that walk with stately stride—
no, four that strut about:
the lion, king of animals, who won't turn aside
for anything,
the strutting rooster,
the male goat,
a king as he leads his army.

If you have been a fool by being proud or plotting evil,
cover your mouth in shame.

As the beating of cream yields butter
    and striking the nose causes bleeding,
    so stirring up anger causes quarrels.

+ + +

The sayings of King Lemuel contain this message, which his mother taught
him.

O my son, O son of my womb,
    O son of my vows,
do not waste your strength on women,
    on those who ruin kings.

It is not for kings, O Lemuel, to guzzle wine.
    Rulers should not crave alcohol.
For if they drink, they may forget the law
    and not give justice to the oppressed.
Alcohol is for the dying,
    and wine for those in bitter distress.
Let them drink to forget their poverty
    and remember their troubles no more.

Speak up for those who cannot speak for themselves;
    ensure justice for those being crushed.
Yes, speak up for the poor and helpless,
    and see that they get justice.

+ + +

Who can find a virtuous and capable wife?
    She is more precious than rubies.
Her husband can trust her,
    and she will greatly enrich his life.
She brings him good, not harm,
    all the days of her life.

She finds wool and flax
    and busily spins it.
She is like a merchant's ship,
    bringing her food from afar.
She gets up before dawn to prepare breakfast for her household
    and plan the day's work for her servant girls.

She goes to inspect a field and buys it;
  with her earnings she plants a vineyard.
She is energetic and strong,
  a hard worker.
She makes sure her dealings are profitable;
  her lamp burns late into the night.

Her hands are busy spinning thread,
  her fingers twisting fiber.
She extends a helping hand to the poor
  and opens her arms to the needy.
She has no fear of winter for her household,
  for everyone has warm clothes.

She makes her own bedspreads.
  She dresses in fine linen and purple gowns.
Her husband is well known at the city gates,
  where he sits with the other civic leaders.
She makes belted linen garments
  and sashes to sell to the merchants.

She is clothed with strength and dignity,
  and she laughs without fear of the future.
When she speaks, her words are wise,
  and she gives instructions with kindness.
She carefully watches everything in her household
  and suffers nothing from laziness.

Her children stand and bless her.
  Her husband praises her:
"There are many virtuous and capable women in the world,
  but you surpass them all!"

Charm is deceptive, and beauty does not last;
  but a woman who fears the LORD will be greatly praised.
Reward her for all she has done.
  Let her deeds publicly declare her praise.

IMMERSED IN ECCLESIASTES

THE BOOKS OF THE BIBLE come together to tell the overarching story of God, the world, and the way back to life and blessing after humanity's rebellion against the Creator. We don't live in a world where everyone follows the wisdom of God's good ways. Many things have gone terribly wrong. Therefore our experience is a deep mystery: We know not only creation and life but also brokenness and death.

There is one place in the Bible where this mystery is addressed head-on: the book of Ecclesiastes. Here the author recognizes that things are more complex than the simple pattern generally found in Proverbs (if you do good, good things will happen to you). The more probing wisdom of Ecclesiastes acknowledges hard truths:

What is wrong cannot be made right.
What is missing cannot be recovered.

This somber statement proclaims that life is inscrutable and unpredictable in many ways. Ecclesiastes looks at the experience of life as it is really lived rather than trying to rationally explain everything. It relentlessly explores what actually happens "under the sun," that is, in the world as we know it.

Ecclesiastes contains the reflections of a man known as the Teacher, traditionally associated with Solomon, who should be respected because he "was considered wise, and he taught the people everything he knew. He listened carefully to many proverbs, studying and classifying them." The Teacher knows all about the helpful and compact wisdom sayings of the sages. Yet he is clearly frustrated by his experiences of life's injustices, absurdities, and impermanence. The thing that is so hard to find in our world is good and fulfilling meaning that lasts beyond a lifetime, or even a moment.

Often we find that significant portions of life are unfulfilling and superficial. The achievements and benefits of prolonged hard work can be quickly lost by unforeseen disasters and the poor stewardship of others. Even gaining wisdom itself doesn't necessarily help us have success in life. So what, then, is the point of it all?

The Teacher shares his insights over the course of seven reflections. In these reflections, he carefully observes various aspects of life on this earth and meditates on what he sees, alternating between poetry and prose in his explorations. On the surface, these reflections seem casual and rambling, mirroring life in a world where one never knows what to expect. But the book of Ecclesiastes presents them all inside an elegant framework:

> Prologue: The words of the Teacher (p. 253)
> > Theme statement: Everything is meaningless (p. 253)
> > > Poetic reflection (p. 253)
>
> > > > Seven major reflections (pp. 253-264)
>
> > > Poetic reflection (pp. 264-265)
> > Theme statement: Everything is meaningless (p. 265)
> Epilogue: The words of the Teacher (p. 265)

Ecclesiastes seems to offer two conclusions to its musings, one immediate and one more ultimate. In the short term, given the crookedness and futility that mark so much of life, the Teacher declares that it makes sense to find enjoyment in the present moment through the small pleasures of the day. As he says, "There is nothing better than to enjoy food and drink and to find satisfaction in work. . . . These pleasures are from the hand of God."

But at the book's end we find a bigger, more important lesson. Even though we cannot always see the deeper meaning of life in how things work out, it is crucial to know that God is watching and working in ways that we can't discern. Indeed, one day he will make everything clear, bringing all our actions to light. As we learn later in the Bible's story, on that day, the creation's futility will come to an end and all things in heaven and on earth will find their full restoration.

ECCLESIASTES

———— ✝ ————

These are the words of the Teacher, King David's son, who ruled in Jerusalem.

"Everything is meaningless," says the Teacher, "completely meaningless!"

What do people get for all their hard work under the sun? Generations come and generations go, but the earth never changes. The sun rises and the sun sets, then hurries around to rise again. The wind blows south, and then turns north. Around and around it goes, blowing in circles. Rivers run into the sea, but the sea is never full. Then the water returns again to the rivers and flows out again to the sea. Everything is wearisome beyond description. No matter how much we see, we are never satisfied. No matter how much we hear, we are not content.

History merely repeats itself. It has all been done before. Nothing under the sun is truly new. Sometimes people say, "Here is something new!" But actually it is old; nothing is ever truly new. We don't remember what happened in the past, and in future generations, no one will remember what we are doing now.

✝

I, the Teacher, was king of Israel, and I lived in Jerusalem. I devoted myself to search for understanding and to explore by wisdom everything being done under heaven. I soon discovered that God has dealt a tragic existence to the human race. I observed everything going on under the sun, and really, it is all meaningless—like chasing the wind.

What is wrong cannot be made right.
What is missing cannot be recovered.

I said to myself, "Look, I am wiser than any of the kings who ruled in Jerusalem before me. I have greater wisdom and knowledge than any of them." So I set out to learn everything from wisdom to madness and folly. But I learned firsthand that pursuing all this is like chasing the wind.

The greater my wisdom, the greater my grief.
To increase knowledge only increases sorrow.

I said to myself, "Come on, let's try pleasure. Let's look for the 'good things' in life." But I found that this, too, was meaningless. So I said, "Laughter is silly. What good does it do to seek pleasure?" After much thought, I decided to cheer myself with wine. And while still seeking wisdom, I clutched at foolishness. In this way, I tried to experience the only happiness most people find during their brief life in this world.

I also tried to find meaning by building huge homes for myself and by planting beautiful vineyards. I made gardens and parks, filling them with all kinds of fruit trees. I built reservoirs to collect the water to irrigate my many flourishing groves. I bought slaves, both men and women, and others were born into my household. I also owned large herds and flocks, more than any of the kings who had lived in Jerusalem before me. I collected great sums of silver and gold, the treasure of many kings and provinces. I hired wonderful singers, both men and women, and had many beautiful concubines. I had everything a man could desire!

So I became greater than all who had lived in Jerusalem before me, and my wisdom never failed me. Anything I wanted, I would take. I denied myself no pleasure. I even found great pleasure in hard work, a reward for all my labors. But as I looked at everything I had worked so hard to accomplish, it was all so meaningless—like chasing the wind. There was nothing really worthwhile anywhere.

So I decided to compare wisdom with foolishness and madness (for who can do this better than I, the king?). I thought, "Wisdom is better than foolishness, just as light is better than darkness. For the wise can see where they are going, but fools walk in the dark." Yet I saw that the wise and the foolish share the same fate. Both will die. So I said to myself, "Since I will end up the same as the fool, what's the value of all my wisdom? This is all so meaningless!" For the wise and the foolish both die. The wise will not be remembered any longer than the fool. In the days to come, both will be forgotten.

So I came to hate life because everything done here under the sun is so troubling. Everything is meaningless—like chasing the wind.

I came to hate all my hard work here on earth, for I must leave to others everything I have earned. And who can tell whether my successors will be wise or foolish? Yet they will control everything I have gained by my skill and hard work under the sun. How meaningless! So I gave up in despair, questioning the value of all my hard work in this world.

Some people work wisely with knowledge and skill, then must leave the fruit of their efforts to someone who hasn't worked for it. This, too, is meaningless, a great tragedy. So what do people get in this life for all their hard work and anxiety? Their days of labor are filled with pain and grief; even at night their minds cannot rest. It is all meaningless.

So I decided there is nothing better than to enjoy food and drink and to find satisfaction in work. Then I realized that these pleasures are from the hand of God. For who can eat or enjoy anything apart from him? God gives wisdom, knowledge, and joy to those who please him. But if a sinner becomes wealthy, God takes the wealth away and gives it to those who please him. This, too, is meaningless—like chasing the wind.

✛

For everything there is a season,
a time for every activity under heaven.
A time to be born and a time to die.
A time to plant and a time to harvest.
A time to kill and a time to heal.
A time to tear down and a time to build up.
A time to cry and a time to laugh.
A time to grieve and a time to dance.
A time to scatter stones and a time to gather stones.
A time to embrace and a time to turn away.
A time to search and a time to quit searching.
A time to keep and a time to throw away.
A time to tear and a time to mend.
A time to be quiet and a time to speak.
A time to love and a time to hate.
A time for war and a time for peace.

✛

What do people really get for all their hard work? I have seen the burden God has placed on us all. Yet God has made everything beautiful for its own time. He has planted eternity in the human heart, but even so, people cannot see the whole scope of God's work from beginning to end. So I concluded there is nothing better than to be happy and enjoy ourselves as long as we can. And people should eat and drink and enjoy the fruits of their labor, for these are gifts from God.

And I know that whatever God does is final. Nothing can be added to it or taken from it. God's purpose is that people should fear him. What is happening now has happened before, and what will happen in the future has happened before, because God makes the same things happen over and over again.

+

I also noticed that under the sun there is evil in the courtroom. Yes, even the courts of law are corrupt! I said to myself, "In due season God will judge everyone, both good and bad, for all their deeds."

I also thought about the human condition—how God proves to people that they are like animals. For people and animals share the same fate— both breathe and both must die. So people have no real advantage over the animals. How meaningless! Both go to the same place—they came from dust and they return to dust. For who can prove that the human spirit goes up and the spirit of animals goes down into the earth? So I saw that there is nothing better for people than to be happy in their work. That is our lot in life. And no one can bring us back to see what happens after we die.

+

Again, I observed all the oppression that takes place under the sun. I saw the tears of the oppressed, with no one to comfort them. The oppressors have great power, and their victims are helpless. So I concluded that the dead are better off than the living. But most fortunate of all are those who are not yet born. For they have not seen all the evil that is done under the sun.

Then I observed that most people are motivated to success because they envy their neighbors. But this, too, is meaningless—like chasing the wind.

> "Fools fold their idle hands,
>   leading them to ruin."

And yet,

> "Better to have one handful with quietness
>   than two handfuls with hard work
>   and chasing the wind."

I observed yet another example of something meaningless under the sun. This is the case of a man who is all alone, without a child or a brother, yet who works hard to gain as much wealth as he can. But then he asks himself, "Who am I working for? Why am I giving up so much pleasure now?" It is all so meaningless and depressing.

Two people are better off than one, for they can help each other succeed.

If one person falls, the other can reach out and help. But someone who falls alone is in real trouble. Likewise, two people lying close together can keep each other warm. But how can one be warm alone? A person standing alone can be attacked and defeated, but two can stand back-to-back and conquer. Three are even better, for a triple-braided cord is not easily broken.

It is better to be a poor but wise youth than an old and foolish king who refuses all advice. Such a youth could rise from poverty and succeed. He might even become king, though he has been in prison. But then everyone rushes to the side of yet another youth who replaces him. Endless crowds stand around him, but then another generation grows up and rejects him, too. So it is all meaningless—like chasing the wind.

As you enter the house of God, keep your ears open and your mouth shut. It is evil to make mindless offerings to God. Don't make rash promises, and don't be hasty in bringing matters before God. After all, God is in heaven, and you are here on earth. So let your words be few.

Too much activity gives you restless dreams; too many words make you a fool.

When you make a promise to God, don't delay in following through, for God takes no pleasure in fools. Keep all the promises you make to him. It is better to say nothing than to make a promise and not keep it. Don't let your mouth make you sin. And don't defend yourself by telling the Temple messenger that the promise you made was a mistake. That would make God angry, and he might wipe out everything you have achieved.

Talk is cheap, like daydreams and other useless activities. Fear God instead.

Don't be surprised if you see a poor person being oppressed by the powerful and if justice is being miscarried throughout the land. For every official is under orders from higher up, and matters of justice get lost in red tape and bureaucracy. Even the king milks the land for his own profit!

Those who love money will never have enough. How meaningless to think that wealth brings true happiness! The more you have, the more people come to help you spend it. So what good is wealth—except perhaps to watch it slip through your fingers!

People who work hard sleep well, whether they eat little or much. But the rich seldom get a good night's sleep.

There is another serious problem I have seen under the sun. Hoarding riches harms the saver. Money is put into risky investments that turn sour, and everything is lost. In the end, there is nothing left to pass on to one's children. We all come to the end of our lives as naked and empty-handed as on the day we were born. We can't take our riches with us.

And this, too, is a very serious problem. People leave this world no better off than when they came. All their hard work is for nothing—like working for the wind. Throughout their lives, they live under a cloud—frustrated, discouraged, and angry.

Even so, I have noticed one thing, at least, that is good. It is good for people to eat, drink, and enjoy their work under the sun during the short life God has given them, and to accept their lot in life. And it is a good thing to receive wealth from God and the good health to enjoy it. To enjoy your work and accept your lot in life—this is indeed a gift from God. God keeps such people so busy enjoying life that they take no time to brood over the past.

+

There is another serious tragedy I have seen under the sun, and it weighs heavily on humanity. God gives some people great wealth and honor and everything they could ever want, but then he doesn't give them the chance to enjoy these things. They die, and someone else, even a stranger, ends up enjoying their wealth! This is meaningless—a sickening tragedy.

A man might have a hundred children and live to be very old. But if he finds no satisfaction in life and doesn't even get a decent burial, it would have been better for him to be born dead. His birth would have been meaningless, and he would have ended in darkness. He wouldn't even have had a name, and he would never have seen the sun or known of its existence. Yet he would have had more peace than in growing up to be an unhappy man. He might live a thousand years twice over but still not find contentment. And since he must die like everyone else—well, what's the use?

All people spend their lives scratching for food, but they never seem to have enough. So are wise people really better off than fools? Do poor people gain anything by being wise and knowing how to act in front of others?

Enjoy what you have rather than desiring what you don't have. Just dreaming about nice things is meaningless—like chasing the wind.

Everything has already been decided. It was known long ago what each person would be. So there's no use arguing with God about your destiny.

The more words you speak, the less they mean. So what good are they?

In the few days of our meaningless lives, who knows how our days can best be spent? Our lives are like a shadow. Who can tell what will happen on this earth after we are gone?

A good reputation is more valuable than costly perfume.
    And the day you die is better than the day you are born.
Better to spend your time at funerals than at parties.
    After all, everyone dies—
    so the living should take this to heart.
Sorrow is better than laughter,
    for sadness has a refining influence on us.
A wise person thinks a lot about death,
    while a fool thinks only about having a good time.

Better to be criticized by a wise person
    than to be praised by a fool.
A fool's laughter is quickly gone,
    like thorns crackling in a fire.
    This also is meaningless.

Extortion turns wise people into fools,
    and bribes corrupt the heart.

Finishing is better than starting.
    Patience is better than pride.

Control your temper,
    for anger labels you a fool.

Don't long for "the good old days."
    This is not wise.

Wisdom is even better when you have money.
    Both are a benefit as you go through life.
Wisdom and money can get you almost anything,
    but only wisdom can save your life.

Accept the way God does things,
    for who can straighten what he has made crooked?
Enjoy prosperity while you can,
    but when hard times strike, realize that both come from God.
    Remember that nothing is certain in this life.

I have seen everything in this meaningless life, including the death of good young people and the long life of wicked people. So don't be too good or too wise! Why destroy yourself? On the other hand, don't be too wicked either. Don't be a fool! Why die before your time? Pay attention to these instructions, for anyone who fears God will avoid both extremes.

One wise person is stronger than ten leading citizens of a town!

Not a single person on earth is always good and never sins.

Don't eavesdrop on others—you may hear your servant curse you. For you know how often you yourself have cursed others.

I have always tried my best to let wisdom guide my thoughts and actions. I said to myself, "I am determined to be wise." But it didn't work. Wisdom is always distant and difficult to find.

I searched everywhere, determined to find wisdom and to understand the reason for things. I was determined to prove to myself that wickedness is stupid and that foolishness is madness.

I discovered that a seductive woman is a trap more bitter than death. Her passion is a snare, and her soft hands are chains. Those who are pleasing to God will escape her, but sinners will be caught in her snare.

"This is my conclusion," says the Teacher. "I discovered this after looking at the matter from every possible angle. Though I have searched repeatedly, I have not found what I was looking for. Only one out of a thousand men is virtuous, but not one woman! But I did find this: God created people to be virtuous, but they have each turned to follow their own downward path."

How wonderful to be wise,
    to analyze and interpret things.
Wisdom lights up a person's face,
    softening its harshness.

Obey the king since you vowed to God that you would. Don't try to avoid doing your duty, and don't stand with those who plot evil, for the king can do whatever he wants. His command is backed by great power. No one can resist or question it. Those who obey him will not be punished. Those who are wise will find a time and a way to do what is right, for there is a time and a way for everything, even when a person is in trouble.

Indeed, how can people avoid what they don't know is going to happen? None of us can hold back our spirit from departing. None of us has the power to prevent the day of our death. There is no escaping that obligation, that dark battle. And in the face of death, wickedness will certainly not rescue the wicked.

I have thought deeply about all that goes on here under the sun, where people have the power to hurt each other. I have seen wicked people buried with honor. Yet they were the very ones who frequented the Temple and are now praised in the same city where they committed their crimes! This, too, is meaningless. When a crime is not punished quickly, people feel it is safe to do wrong. But even though a person sins a hundred times and still lives a long time, I know that those who fear God will be better off. The wicked will not prosper, for they do not fear God. Their days will never grow long like the evening shadows.

And this is not all that is meaningless in our world. In this life, good people are often treated as though they were wicked, and wicked people are often treated as though they were good. This is so meaningless!

So I recommend having fun, because there is nothing better for people in this world than to eat, drink, and enjoy life. That way they will experience some happiness along with all the hard work God gives them under the sun.

In my search for wisdom and in my observation of people's burdens here on earth, I discovered that there is ceaseless activity, day and night. I realized that no one can discover everything God is doing under the sun. Not even the wisest people discover everything, no matter what they claim.

+

This, too, I carefully explored: Even though the actions of godly and wise people are in God's hands, no one knows whether God will show them favor. The same destiny ultimately awaits everyone, whether righteous or wicked, good or bad, ceremonially clean or unclean, religious or irreligious. Good people receive the same treatment as sinners, and people who make promises to God are treated like people who don't.

It seems so wrong that everyone under the sun suffers the same fate. Already twisted by evil, people choose their own mad course, for they have no hope. There is nothing ahead but death anyway. There is hope only for the living. As they say, "It's better to be a live dog than a dead lion!"

The living at least know they will die, but the dead know nothing. They have no further reward, nor are they remembered. Whatever they did in their lifetime—loving, hating, envying—is all long gone. They no longer play a part in anything here on earth. So go ahead. Eat your food with joy, and drink your wine with a happy heart, for God approves of this! Wear fine clothes, with a splash of cologne!

Live happily with the woman you love through all the meaningless days of life that God has given you under the sun. The wife God gives you is your reward for all your earthly toil. Whatever you do, do well. For when you go to the grave, there will be no work or planning or knowledge or wisdom.

+

I have observed something else under the sun. The fastest runner doesn't always win the race, and the strongest warrior doesn't always win the battle. The wise sometimes go hungry, and the skillful are not necessarily wealthy. And those who are educated don't always lead successful lives. It is all decided by chance, by being in the right place at the right time.

People can never predict when hard times might come. Like fish in a net or birds in a trap, people are caught by sudden tragedy.

Here is another bit of wisdom that has impressed me as I have watched the way our world works. There was a small town with only a few people, and a great king came with his army and besieged it. A poor, wise man knew how to save the town, and so it was rescued. But afterward no one thought to thank him. So even though wisdom is better than strength, those who are wise will be despised if they are poor. What they say will not be appreciated for long.

> Better to hear the quiet words of a wise person
>   than the shouts of a foolish king.
> Better to have wisdom than weapons of war,
>   but one sinner can destroy much that is good.

> As dead flies cause even a bottle of perfume to stink,
>   so a little foolishness spoils great wisdom and honor.

> A wise person chooses the right road;
>   a fool takes the wrong one.

> You can identify fools
>   just by the way they walk down the street!

> If your boss is angry at you, don't quit!
>   A quiet spirit can overcome even great mistakes.

There is another evil I have seen under the sun. Kings and rulers make a grave mistake when they give great authority to foolish people and low positions to people of proven worth. I have even seen servants riding horseback like princes—and princes walking like servants!

> When you dig a well,
>   you might fall in.
> When you demolish an old wall,
>   you could be bitten by a snake.
> When you work in a quarry,
>   stones might fall and crush you.
> When you chop wood,
>   there is danger with each stroke of your ax.

Using a dull ax requires great strength,
  so sharpen the blade.
That's the value of wisdom;
  it helps you succeed.

If a snake bites before you charm it,
  what's the use of being a snake charmer?

Wise words bring approval,
  but fools are destroyed by their own words.

Fools base their thoughts on foolish assumptions,
  so their conclusions will be wicked madness;
  they chatter on and on.

No one really knows what is going to happen;
  no one can predict the future.

Fools are so exhausted by a little work
  that they can't even find their way home.

What sorrow for the land ruled by a servant,
  the land whose leaders feast in the morning.
Happy is the land whose king is a noble leader
  and whose leaders feast at the proper time
  to gain strength for their work, not to get drunk.

Laziness leads to a sagging roof;
  idleness leads to a leaky house.

A party gives laughter,
  wine gives happiness,
  and money gives everything!

Never make light of the king, even in your thoughts.
  And don't make fun of the powerful, even in your own
    bedroom.
For a little bird might deliver your message
  and tell them what you said.

Send your grain across the seas,
  and in time, profits will flow back to you.
But divide your investments among many places,
  for you do not know what risks might lie ahead.

When clouds are heavy, the rains come down.
  Whether a tree falls north or south, it stays where it falls.

Farmers who wait for perfect weather never plant.
  If they watch every cloud, they never harvest.

Just as you cannot understand the path of the wind or the mystery of
a tiny baby growing in its mother's womb, so you cannot understand the
activity of God, who does all things.

Plant your seed in the morning and keep busy all afternoon, for you
don't know if profit will come from one activity or another—or maybe
both.

Light is sweet; how pleasant to see a new day dawning.

When people live to be very old, let them rejoice in every day of life. But
let them also remember there will be many dark days. Everything still to
come is meaningless.

Young people, it's wonderful to be young! Enjoy every minute of it. Do
everything you want to do; take it all in. But remember that you must give
an account to God for everything you do. So refuse to worry, and keep
your body healthy. But remember that youth, with a whole life before you,
is meaningless.

+

Don't let the excitement of youth cause you to forget your Creator.
Honor him in your youth before you grow old and say, "Life is not
pleasant anymore." Remember him before the light of the sun, moon,
and stars is dim to your old eyes, and rain clouds continually darken
your sky. Remember him before your legs—the guards of your house—
start to tremble; and before your shoulders—the strong men—stoop.
Remember him before your teeth—your few remaining servants—
stop grinding; and before your eyes—the women looking through the
windows—see dimly.

Remember him before the door to life's opportunities is closed and the
sound of work fades. Now you rise at the first chirping of the birds, but
then all their sounds will grow faint.

Remember him before you become fearful of falling and worry about
danger in the streets; before your hair turns white like an almond tree in
bloom, and you drag along without energy like a dying grasshopper, and
the caperberry no longer inspires sexual desire. Remember him before
you near the grave, your everlasting home, when the mourners will weep
at your funeral.

Yes, remember your Creator now while you are young, before the silver
cord of life snaps and the golden bowl is broken. Don't wait until the water
jar is smashed at the spring and the pulley is broken at the well. For then

the dust will return to the earth, and the spirit will return to God who gave it.

"Everything is meaningless," says the Teacher, "completely meaningless."

+

Keep this in mind: The Teacher was considered wise, and he taught the people everything he knew. He listened carefully to many proverbs, studying and classifying them. The Teacher sought to find just the right words to express truths clearly.

The words of the wise are like cattle prods—painful but helpful. Their collected sayings are like a nail-studded stick with which a shepherd drives the sheep.

But, my child, let me give you some further advice: Be careful, for writing books is endless, and much study wears you out.

That's the whole story. Here now is my final conclusion: Fear God and obey his commands, for this is everyone's duty. God will judge us for everything we do, including every secret thing, whether good or bad.

IMMERSED IN JOB

THE STORY OF JOB BEGINS by telling us "he was blameless—a man of complete integrity. He feared God and stayed away from evil." Job is exactly the kind of person the book of Proverbs envisions when it urges its readers to embrace wisdom. According to Israel's wisdom tradition, such godly character should lead to success and prosperity in life. And when we first meet Job, he is indeed prosperous and wealthy, surrounded by a large family and respected for his wisdom. But a sudden series of catastrophes takes everything away, and he's left in poverty, disfigured by disease and disgraced in the eyes of the community.

The book then presents an extended dialogue between Job and three of his friends who come to "comfort and console him." But as it turns out, they have come mostly to confront him with his guilt, which they believe caused his troubles. In their unbending moral universe, goodness is always rewarded and wrongdoing is invariably punished. So if Job has gone from prosperity to suffering, there must certainly be some great sin or failure in his life.

For his part, Job relentlessly protests that he is innocent, that the Almighty has made some mistake in allowing these tragedies into Job's life. In the strength of his moral certainty, Job demands to meet with God and present his case directly.

The reader learns at the start of the book that there's more to this story than any of the players on earth know. But the drama of Job's arguments with his friends and his extended complaint to God has to play itself out, since the secret remains unknown to them.

The book of Job is a daring exploration of the deepest questions regarding our faith in God and his role in the world. According to the Bible, wisdom gives us the ability to understand the order God gave to the world. But what happens when that ability is stretched to its limits? What are we to do when our explanations fail? What if the order in the world itself seems to be fractured?

The book of Job is made up of a series of long poetic dialogues that are bookended by brief explanatory narratives. The poetic dialogues are marked by powerful imagery and elegant, serious tones. There are three rounds of these speeches between Job and his three friends, and all are contained within Job's overall protest, which is really directed toward God.

The discussion is not merely theoretical or abstract; rather, it is set in an ongoing drama with Job's unexplained catastrophes squarely at the center. As readers we will see this drama worked out as the conflict continues throughout the course of the book.

But Job wearies of listening to others speaking for God; he wants to confront God in person. And then it happens. There is no more talking about God; a theophany occurs—God appears! Now the questioning is reversed. In a series of magnificent poems, God declares his creative power and mastery over the entire creation. God questions Job on things he knows nothing about, and Job's protests now appear to be small and uninformed.

The question "Am I being treated justly?" takes on new meaning in relation to the larger context of God's intimate knowledge and over-sight of all things. The book of Job teaches us that any good under-standing of the mystery of our lives begins with the knowledge that God alone is the Creator and Sustainer of the world.

We learn much at the end of Job's drama. Those who claimed to speak for God, confidently attributing guilt to those who suffer, are shown to be gravely mistaken. God is always free, unbound by any human formulation about what he must do in a particular situation. He is above and beyond us, doing things we know nothing about. Job's suffering was not because of his sin, and his honest protests about his innocence are shown to have been legitimate. And even in his com-plaints to God, Job has been rooted in faith. He never lost his trust that only God could intervene to justify him and make things right.

This profound wisdom drama concludes with God's intervention as he changes Job's circumstances once again. But the lesson has been learned. We are to find no easy comfort or blame in our formulas about God. The Creator alone sees all things. Our lives are to be lived in faith, trusting the God who is good to set all things right in the end.

JOB

✛

There once was a man named Job who lived in the land of Uz. He was blameless—a man of complete integrity. He feared God and stayed away from evil. He had seven sons and three daughters. He owned 7,000 sheep, 3,000 camels, 500 teams of oxen, and 500 female donkeys. He also had many servants. He was, in fact, the richest person in that entire area.

Job's sons would take turns preparing feasts in their homes, and they would also invite their three sisters to celebrate with them. When these celebrations ended—sometimes after several days—Job would purify his children. He would get up early in the morning and offer a burnt offering for each of them. For Job said to himself, "Perhaps my children have sinned and have cursed God in their hearts." This was Job's regular practice.

One day the members of the heavenly court came to present themselves before the LORD, and the Accuser, Satan, came with them. "Where have you come from?" the LORD asked Satan.

Satan answered the LORD, "I have been patrolling the earth, watching everything that's going on."

Then the LORD asked Satan, "Have you noticed my servant Job? He is the finest man in all the earth. He is blameless—a man of complete integrity. He fears God and stays away from evil."

Satan replied to the LORD, "Yes, but Job has good reason to fear God. You have always put a wall of protection around him and his home and his property. You have made him prosper in everything he does. Look how rich he is! But reach out and take away everything he has, and he will surely curse you to your face!"

"All right, you may test him," the LORD said to Satan. "Do whatever you want with everything he possesses, but don't harm him physically." So Satan left the LORD's presence.

One day when Job's sons and daughters were feasting at the oldest brother's house, a messenger arrived at Job's home with this news: "Your oxen were plowing, with the donkeys feeding beside them, when the Sabeans raided us. They stole all the animals and killed all the farmhands. I am the only one who escaped to tell you."

While he was still speaking, another messenger arrived with this news: "The fire of God has fallen from heaven and burned up your sheep and all the shepherds. I am the only one who escaped to tell you."

While he was still speaking, a third messenger arrived with this news: "Three bands of Chaldean raiders have stolen your camels and killed your servants. I am the only one who escaped to tell you."

While he was still speaking, another messenger arrived with this news: "Your sons and daughters were feasting in their oldest brother's home. Suddenly, a powerful wind swept in from the wilderness and hit the house on all sides. The house collapsed, and all your children are dead. I am the only one who escaped to tell you."

Job stood up and tore his robe in grief. Then he shaved his head and fell to the ground to worship. He said,

"I came naked from my mother's womb,
    and I will be naked when I leave.
The LORD gave me what I had,
    and the LORD has taken it away.
Praise the name of the LORD!"

In all of this, Job did not sin by blaming God.

One day the members of the heavenly court came again to present themselves before the LORD, and the Accuser, Satan, came with them. "Where have you come from?" the LORD asked Satan.

Satan answered the LORD, "I have been patrolling the earth, watching everything that's going on."

Then the LORD asked Satan, "Have you noticed my servant Job? He is the finest man in all the earth. He is blameless—a man of complete integrity. He fears God and stays away from evil. And he has maintained his integrity, even though you urged me to harm him without cause."

Satan replied to the LORD, "Skin for skin! A man will give up everything he has to save his life. But reach out and take away his health, and he will surely curse you to your face!"

"All right, do with him as you please," the LORD said to Satan. "But spare his life." So Satan left the LORD's presence, and he struck Job with terrible boils from head to foot.

Job scraped his skin with a piece of broken pottery as he sat among the ashes. His wife said to him, "Are you still trying to maintain your integrity? Curse God and die."

But Job replied, "You talk like a foolish woman. Should we accept only good things from the hand of God and never anything bad?" So in all this, Job said nothing wrong.

When three of Job's friends heard of the tragedy he had suffered, they got together and traveled from their homes to comfort and console him. Their names were Eliphaz the Temanite, Bildad the Shuhite, and Zophar the Naamathite. When they saw Job from a distance, they scarcely recognized him. Wailing loudly, they tore their robes and threw dust into the air over their heads to show their grief. Then they sat on the ground with him for seven days and nights. No one said a word to Job, for they saw that his suffering was too great for words.

+ + +

At last Job spoke, and he cursed the day of his birth. He said:

"Let the day of my birth be erased,
    and the night I was conceived.
Let that day be turned to darkness.
    Let it be lost even to God on high,
    and let no light shine on it.
Let the darkness and utter gloom claim that day for its own.
    Let a black cloud overshadow it,
    and let the darkness terrify it.
Let that night be blotted off the calendar,
    never again to be counted among the days of the year,
    never again to appear among the months.
Let that night be childless.
    Let it have no joy.
Let those who are experts at cursing—
    whose cursing could rouse Leviathan—
    curse that day.
Let its morning stars remain dark.
    Let it hope for light, but in vain;
    may it never see the morning light.
Curse that day for failing to shut my mother's womb,
    for letting me be born to see all this trouble.

"Why wasn't I born dead?
    Why didn't I die as I came from the womb?
Why was I laid on my mother's lap?
    Why did she nurse me at her breasts?
Had I died at birth, I would now be at peace.

I would be asleep and at rest.
I would rest with the world's kings and prime ministers,
  whose great buildings now lie in ruins.
I would rest with princes, rich in gold,
  whose palaces were filled with silver.
Why wasn't I buried like a stillborn child,
  like a baby who never lives to see the light?
For in death the wicked cause no trouble,
  and the weary are at rest.
Even captives are at ease in death,
  with no guards to curse them.
Rich and poor are both there,
  and the slave is free from his master.

"Oh, why give light to those in misery,
  and life to those who are bitter?
They long for death, and it won't come.
  They search for death more eagerly than for hidden treasure.
They're filled with joy when they finally die,
  and rejoice when they find the grave.
Why is life given to those with no future,
  those God has surrounded with difficulties?
I cannot eat for sighing;
  my groans pour out like water.
What I always feared has happened to me.
  What I dreaded has come true.
I have no peace, no quietness.
  I have no rest; only trouble comes."

+

Then Eliphaz the Temanite replied to Job:

"Will you be patient and let me say a word?
  For who could keep from speaking out?

"In the past you have encouraged many people;
  you have strengthened those who were weak.
Your words have supported those who were falling;
  you encouraged those with shaky knees.
But now when trouble strikes, you lose heart.
  You are terrified when it touches you.
Doesn't your reverence for God give you confidence?
  Doesn't your life of integrity give you hope?

"Stop and think! Do the innocent die?
  When have the upright been destroyed?
My experience shows that those who plant trouble
  and cultivate evil will harvest the same.
A breath from God destroys them.
  They vanish in a blast of his anger.
The lion roars and the wildcat snarls,
  but the teeth of strong lions will be broken.
The fierce lion will starve for lack of prey,
  and the cubs of the lioness will be scattered.

"This truth was given to me in secret,
  as though whispered in my ear.
It came to me in a disturbing vision at night,
  when people are in a deep sleep.
Fear gripped me,
  and my bones trembled.
A spirit swept past my face,
  and my hair stood on end.
The spirit stopped, but I couldn't see its shape.
  There was a form before my eyes.
In the silence I heard a voice say,
'Can a mortal be innocent before God?
  Can anyone be pure before the Creator?'

"If God does not trust his own angels
  and has charged his messengers with foolishness,
how much less will he trust people made of clay!
  They are made of dust, crushed as easily as a moth.
They are alive in the morning but dead by evening,
  gone forever without a trace.
Their tent-cords are pulled and the tent collapses,
  and they die in ignorance.

"Cry for help, but will anyone answer you?
  Which of the angels will help you?
Surely resentment destroys the fool,
  and jealousy kills the simple.
I have seen that fools may be successful for the moment,
  but then comes sudden disaster.
Their children are abandoned far from help;
  they are crushed in court with no one to defend them.
The hungry devour their harvest,

even when it is guarded by brambles.
The thirsty pant after their wealth.
But evil does not spring from the soil,
and trouble does not sprout from the earth.
People are born for trouble
as readily as sparks fly up from a fire.

"If I were you, I would go to God
and present my case to him.
He does great things too marvelous to understand.
He performs countless miracles.
He gives rain for the earth
and water for the fields.
He gives prosperity to the poor
and protects those who suffer.
He frustrates the plans of schemers
so the work of their hands will not succeed.
He traps the wise in their own cleverness
so their cunning schemes are thwarted.
They find it is dark in the daytime,
and they grope at noon as if it were night.
He rescues the poor from the cutting words of the strong,
and rescues them from the clutches of the powerful.
And so at last the poor have hope,
and the snapping jaws of the wicked are shut.

"But consider the joy of those corrected by God!
Do not despise the discipline of the Almighty when you sin.
For though he wounds, he also bandages.
He strikes, but his hands also heal.
From six disasters he will rescue you;
even in the seventh, he will keep you from evil.
He will save you from death in time of famine,
from the power of the sword in time of war.
You will be safe from slander
and have no fear when destruction comes.
You will laugh at destruction and famine;
wild animals will not terrify you.
You will be at peace with the stones of the field,
and its wild animals will be at peace with you.
You will know that your home is safe.
When you survey your possessions, nothing will be missing.
You will have many children;

your descendants will be as plentiful as grass!
You will go to the grave at a ripe old age,
    like a sheaf of grain harvested at the proper time!

"We have studied life and found all this to be true.
    Listen to my counsel, and apply it to yourself."

+

Then Job spoke again:

"If my misery could be weighed
    and my troubles be put on the scales,
they would outweigh all the sands of the sea.
    That is why I spoke impulsively.
For the Almighty has struck me down with his arrows.
    Their poison infects my spirit.
    God's terrors are lined up against me.
Don't I have a right to complain?
    Don't wild donkeys bray when they find no grass,
    and oxen bellow when they have no food?
Don't people complain about unsalted food?
    Does anyone want the tasteless white of an egg?
My appetite disappears when I look at it;
    I gag at the thought of eating it!

"Oh, that I might have my request,
    that God would grant my desire.
I wish he would crush me.
    I wish he would reach out his hand and kill me.
At least I can take comfort in this:
    Despite the pain,
    I have not denied the words of the Holy One.
But I don't have the strength to endure.
    I have nothing to live for.
Do I have the strength of a stone?
    Is my body made of bronze?
No, I am utterly helpless,
    without any chance of success.

"One should be kind to a fainting friend,
    but you accuse me without any fear of the Almighty.
My brothers, you have proved as unreliable as a seasonal brook
    that overflows its banks in the spring

when it is swollen with ice and melting snow.
But when the hot weather arrives, the water disappears.
   The brook vanishes in the heat.
The caravans turn aside to be refreshed,
   but there is nothing to drink, so they die.
The caravans from Tema search for this water;
   the travelers from Sheba hope to find it.
They count on it but are disappointed.
   When they arrive, their hopes are dashed.
You, too, have given no help.
   You have seen my calamity, and you are afraid.
But why? Have I ever asked you for a gift?
   Have I begged for anything of yours for myself?
Have I asked you to rescue me from my enemies,
   or to save me from ruthless people?
Teach me, and I will keep quiet.
   Show me what I have done wrong.
Honest words can be painful,
   but what do your criticisms amount to?
Do you think your words are convincing
   when you disregard my cry of desperation?
You would even send an orphan into slavery
   or sell a friend.
Look at me!
   Would I lie to your face?
Stop assuming my guilt,
   for I have done no wrong.
Do you think I am lying?
   Don't I know the difference between right and wrong?

"Is not all human life a struggle?
   Our lives are like that of a hired hand,
like a worker who longs for the shade,
   like a servant waiting to be paid.
I, too, have been assigned months of futility,
   long and weary nights of misery.
Lying in bed, I think, 'When will it be morning?'
   But the night drags on, and I toss till dawn.
My body is covered with maggots and scabs.
   My skin breaks open, oozing with pus.

"My days fly faster than a weaver's shuttle.
   They end without hope.

O God, remember that my life is but a breath,
    and I will never again feel happiness.
You see me now, but not for long.
    You will look for me, but I will be gone.
Just as a cloud dissipates and vanishes,
    those who die will not come back.
They are gone forever from their home—
    never to be seen again.

"I cannot keep from speaking.
    I must express my anguish.
    My bitter soul must complain.
Am I a sea monster or a dragon
    that you must place me under guard?
I think, 'My bed will comfort me,
    and sleep will ease my misery,'
but then you shatter me with dreams
    and terrify me with visions.
I would rather be strangled—
    rather die than suffer like this.
I hate my life and don't want to go on living.
    Oh, leave me alone for my few remaining days.

"What are people, that you should make so much of us,
    that you should think of us so often?
For you examine us every morning
    and test us every moment.
Why won't you leave me alone,
    at least long enough for me to swallow!
If I have sinned, what have I done to you,
    O watcher of all humanity?
Why make me your target?
    Am I a burden to you?
Why not just forgive my sin
    and take away my guilt?
For soon I will lie down in the dust and die.
    When you look for me, I will be gone."

+

Then Bildad the Shuhite replied to Job:

"How long will you go on like this?
    You sound like a blustering wind.

Does God twist justice?
    Does the Almighty twist what is right?
Your children must have sinned against him,
    so their punishment was well deserved.
But if you pray to God
    and seek the favor of the Almighty,
and if you are pure and live with integrity,
    he will surely rise up and restore your happy home.
And though you started with little,
    you will end with much.

"Just ask the previous generation.
    Pay attention to the experience of our ancestors.
For we were born but yesterday and know nothing.
    Our days on earth are as fleeting as a shadow.
But those who came before us will teach you.
    They will teach you the wisdom of old.

"Can papyrus reeds grow tall without a marsh?
    Can marsh grass flourish without water?
While they are still flowering, not ready to be cut,
    they begin to wither more quickly than grass.
The same happens to all who forget God.
    The hopes of the godless evaporate.
Their confidence hangs by a thread.
    They are leaning on a spider's web.
They cling to their home for security, but it won't last.
    They try to hold it tight, but it will not endure.
The godless seem like a lush plant growing in the sunshine,
    its branches spreading across the garden.
Its roots grow down through a pile of stones;
    it takes hold on a bed of rocks.
But when it is uprooted,
    it's as though it never existed!
That's the end of its life,
    and others spring up from the earth to replace it.

"But look, God will not reject a person of integrity,
    nor will he lend a hand to the wicked.
He will once again fill your mouth with laughter
    and your lips with shouts of joy.
Those who hate you will be clothed with shame,
    and the home of the wicked will be destroyed."

+

Then Job spoke again:

"Yes, I know all this is true in principle.
But how can a person be declared innocent in God's sight?
If someone wanted to take God to court,
would it be possible to answer him even once in a thousand
times?
For God is so wise and so mighty.
Who has ever challenged him successfully?

"Without warning, he moves the mountains,
overturning them in his anger.
He shakes the earth from its place,
and its foundations tremble.
If he commands it, the sun won't rise
and the stars won't shine.
He alone has spread out the heavens
and marches on the waves of the sea.
He made all the stars—the Bear and Orion,
the Pleiades and the constellations of the southern sky.
He does great things too marvelous to understand.
He performs countless miracles.

"Yet when he comes near, I cannot see him.
When he moves by, I do not see him go.
If he snatches someone in death, who can stop him?
Who dares to ask, 'What are you doing?'
And God does not restrain his anger.
Even the monsters of the sea are crushed beneath his feet.

"So who am I, that I should try to answer God
or even reason with him?
Even if I were right, I would have no defense.
I could only plead for mercy.
And even if I summoned him and he responded,
I'm not sure he would listen to me.
For he attacks me with a storm
and repeatedly wounds me without cause.
He will not let me catch my breath,
but fills me instead with bitter sorrows.
If it's a question of strength, he's the strong one.
If it's a matter of justice, who dares to summon him to court?

Though I am innocent, my own mouth would pronounce me guilty.
  Though I am blameless, it would prove me wicked.

"I am innocent,
  but it makes no difference to me—
  I despise my life.
Innocent or wicked, it is all the same to God.
  That's why I say, 'He destroys both the blameless and the
    wicked.'
When a plague sweeps through,
  he laughs at the death of the innocent.
The whole earth is in the hands of the wicked,
  and God blinds the eyes of the judges.
  If he's not the one who does it, who is?

"My life passes more swiftly than a runner.
  It flees away without a glimpse of happiness.
It disappears like a swift papyrus boat,
  like an eagle swooping down on its prey.
If I decided to forget my complaints,
  to put away my sad face and be cheerful,
I would still dread all the pain,
  for I know you will not find me innocent, O God.
Whatever happens, I will be found guilty.
  So what's the use of trying?
Even if I were to wash myself with soap
  and clean my hands with lye,
you would plunge me into a muddy ditch,
  and my own filthy clothing would hate me.

"God is not a mortal like me,
  so I cannot argue with him or take him to trial.
If only there were a mediator between us,
  someone who could bring us together.
The mediator could make God stop beating me,
  and I would no longer live in terror of his punishment.
Then I could speak to him without fear,
  but I cannot do that in my own strength.

"I am disgusted with my life.
  Let me complain freely.
  My bitter soul must complain.
I will say to God, 'Don't simply condemn me—
  tell me the charge you are bringing against me.

What do you gain by oppressing me?
  Why do you reject me, the work of your own hands,
    while smiling on the schemes of the wicked?
Are your eyes like those of a human?
  Do you see things only as people see them?
Is your lifetime only as long as ours?
  Is your life so short
that you must quickly probe for my guilt
  and search for my sin?
Although you know I am not guilty,
  no one can rescue me from your hands.

"'You formed me with your hands; you made me,
  yet now you completely destroy me.
Remember that you made me from dust—
  will you turn me back to dust so soon?
You guided my conception
  and formed me in the womb.
You clothed me with skin and flesh,
  and you knit my bones and sinews together.
You gave me life and showed me your unfailing love.
  My life was preserved by your care.

"'Yet your real motive—
  your true intent—
was to watch me, and if I sinned,
  you would not forgive my guilt.
If I am guilty, too bad for me;
  and even if I'm innocent, I can't hold my head high,
    because I am filled with shame and misery.
And if I hold my head high, you hunt me like a lion
  and display your awesome power against me.
Again and again you witness against me.
  You pour out your growing anger on me
  and bring fresh armies against me.

"'Why, then, did you deliver me from my mother's womb?
  Why didn't you let me die at birth?
It would be as though I had never existed,
  going directly from the womb to the grave.
I have only a few days left, so leave me alone,
  that I may have a moment of comfort
before I leave—never to return—
  for the land of darkness and utter gloom.

It is a land as dark as midnight,
  a land of gloom and confusion,
  where even the light is dark as midnight.'"

+

Then Zophar the Naamathite replied to Job:

"Shouldn't someone answer this torrent of words?
  Is a person proved innocent just by a lot of talking?
Should I remain silent while you babble on?
  When you mock God, shouldn't someone make you ashamed?
You claim, 'My beliefs are pure,'
  and 'I am clean in the sight of God.'
If only God would speak;
  if only he would tell you what he thinks!
If only he would tell you the secrets of wisdom,
  for true wisdom is not a simple matter.
Listen! God is doubtless punishing you
  far less than you deserve!

"Can you solve the mysteries of God?
  Can you discover everything about the Almighty?
Such knowledge is higher than the heavens—
  and who are you?
It is deeper than the underworld—
  what do you know?
It is broader than the earth
  and wider than the sea.
If God comes and puts a person in prison
  or calls the court to order, who can stop him?
For he knows those who are false,
  and he takes note of all their sins.
An empty-headed person won't become wise
  any more than a wild donkey can bear a human child.

"If only you would prepare your heart
  and lift up your hands to him in prayer!
Get rid of your sins,
  and leave all iniquity behind you.
Then your face will brighten with innocence.
  You will be strong and free of fear.
You will forget your misery;
  it will be like water flowing away.

Your life will be brighter than the noonday.
    Even darkness will be as bright as morning.
Having hope will give you courage.
    You will be protected and will rest in safety.
You will lie down unafraid,
    and many will look to you for help.
But the wicked will be blinded.
    They will have no escape.
    Their only hope is death."

+

Then Job spoke again:

"You people really know everything, don't you?
    And when you die, wisdom will die with you!
Well, I know a few things myself—
    and you're no better than I am.
    Who doesn't know these things you've been saying?
Yet my friends laugh at me,
    for I call on God and expect an answer.
I am a just and blameless man,
    yet they laugh at me.
People who are at ease mock those in trouble.
    They give a push to people who are stumbling.
But robbers are left in peace,
    and those who provoke God live in safety—
    though God keeps them in his power.

"Just ask the animals, and they will teach you.
    Ask the birds of the sky, and they will tell you.
Speak to the earth, and it will instruct you.
    Let the fish in the sea speak to you.
For they all know
    that my disaster has come from the hand of the LORD.
For the life of every living thing is in his hand,
    and the breath of every human being.
The ear tests the words it hears
    just as the mouth distinguishes between foods.
Wisdom belongs to the aged,
    and understanding to the old.

"But true wisdom and power are found in God;
    counsel and understanding are his.

What he destroys cannot be rebuilt.
When he puts someone in prison, there is no escape.
If he holds back the rain, the earth becomes a desert.
If he releases the waters, they flood the earth.
Yes, strength and wisdom are his;
deceivers and deceived are both in his power.
He leads counselors away, stripped of good judgment;
wise judges become fools.
He removes the royal robe of kings.
They are led away with ropes around their waist.
He leads priests away, stripped of status;
he overthrows those with long years in power.
He silences the trusted adviser
and removes the insight of the elders.
He pours disgrace upon princes
and disarms the strong.

"He uncovers mysteries hidden in darkness;
he brings light to the deepest gloom.
He builds up nations, and he destroys them.
He expands nations, and he abandons them.
He strips kings of understanding
and leaves them wandering in a pathless wasteland.
They grope in the darkness without a light.
He makes them stagger like drunkards.

"Look, I have seen all this with my own eyes
and heard it with my own ears, and now I understand.
I know as much as you do.
You are no better than I am.
As for me, I would speak directly to the Almighty.
I want to argue my case with God himself.
As for you, you smear me with lies.
As physicians, you are worthless quacks.
If only you could be silent!
That's the wisest thing you could do.
Listen to my charge;
pay attention to my arguments.

"Are you defending God with lies?
Do you make your dishonest arguments for his sake?
Will you slant your testimony in his favor?
Will you argue God's case for him?

What will happen when he finds out what you are doing?
  Can you fool him as easily as you fool people?
No, you will be in trouble with him
  if you secretly slant your testimony in his favor.
Doesn't his majesty terrify you?
  Doesn't your fear of him overwhelm you?
Your platitudes are as valuable as ashes.
  Your defense is as fragile as a clay pot.

"Be silent now and leave me alone.
  Let me speak, and I will face the consequences.
Why should I put myself in mortal danger
  and take my life in my own hands?
God might kill me, but I have no other hope.
  I am going to argue my case with him.
But this is what will save me—I am not godless.
  If I were, I could not stand before him.

"Listen closely to what I am about to say.
  Hear me out.
I have prepared my case;
  I will be proved innocent.
Who can argue with me over this?
  And if you prove me wrong, I will remain silent
    and die.

"O God, grant me these two things,
  and then I will be able to face you.
Remove your heavy hand from me,
  and don't terrify me with your awesome presence.
Now summon me, and I will answer!
  Or let me speak to you, and you reply.
Tell me, what have I done wrong?
  Show me my rebellion and my sin.
Why do you turn away from me?
  Why do you treat me as your enemy?
Would you terrify a leaf blown by the wind?
  Would you chase dry straw?

"You write bitter accusations against me
  and bring up all the sins of my youth.
You put my feet in stocks.
  You examine all my paths.
  You trace all my footprints.

I waste away like rotting wood,
   like a moth-eaten coat.

"How frail is humanity!
   How short is life, how full of trouble!
We blossom like a flower and then wither.
   Like a passing shadow, we quickly disappear.
Must you keep an eye on such a frail creature
   and demand an accounting from me?
Who can bring purity out of an impure person?
   No one!
You have decided the length of our lives.
   You know how many months we will live,
   and we are not given a minute longer.
So leave us alone and let us rest!
   We are like hired hands, so let us finish our work in peace.

"Even a tree has more hope!
   If it is cut down, it will sprout again
   and grow new branches.
Though its roots have grown old in the earth
   and its stump decays,
at the scent of water it will bud
   and sprout again like a new seedling.

"But when people die, their strength is gone.
   They breathe their last, and then where are they?
As water evaporates from a lake
   and a river disappears in drought,
people are laid to rest and do not rise again.
   Until the heavens are no more, they will not wake up
   nor be roused from their sleep.

"I wish you would hide me in the grave
   and forget me there until your anger has passed.
   But mark your calendar to think of me again!
Can the dead live again?
   If so, this would give me hope through all my years
      of struggle,
   and I would eagerly await the release of death.
You would call and I would answer,
   and you would yearn for me, your handiwork.
For then you would guard my steps,
   instead of watching for my sins.

My sins would be sealed in a pouch,
    and you would cover my guilt.

"But instead, as mountains fall and crumble
    and as rocks fall from a cliff,
as water wears away the stones
    and floods wash away the soil,
    so you destroy people's hope.
You always overpower them, and they pass from the scene.
    You disfigure them in death and send them away.
They never know if their children grow up in honor
    or sink to insignificance.
They suffer painfully;
    their life is full of trouble."

+

Then Eliphaz the Temanite replied:

"A wise man wouldn't answer with such empty talk!
    You are nothing but a windbag.
The wise don't engage in empty chatter.
    What good are such words?
Have you no fear of God,
    no reverence for him?
Your sins are telling your mouth what to say.
    Your words are based on clever deception.
Your own mouth condemns you, not I.
    Your own lips testify against you.

"Were you the first person ever born?
    Were you born before the hills were made?
Were you listening at God's secret council?
    Do you have a monopoly on wisdom?
What do you know that we don't?
    What do you understand that we do not?
On our side are aged, gray-haired men
    much older than your father!

"Is God's comfort too little for you?
    Is his gentle word not enough?
What has taken away your reason?
    What has weakened your vision,
that you turn against God

and say all these evil things?
Can any mortal be pure?
    Can anyone born of a woman be just?
Look, God does not even trust the angels.
    Even the heavens are not absolutely pure in his sight.
How much less pure is a corrupt and sinful person
    with a thirst for wickedness!

"If you will listen, I will show you.
    I will answer you from my own experience.
And it is confirmed by the reports of wise men
    who have heard the same thing from their fathers—
from those to whom the land was given
    long before any foreigners arrived.

"The wicked writhe in pain throughout their lives.
    Years of trouble are stored up for the ruthless.
The sound of terror rings in their ears,
    and even on good days they fear the attack of the destroyer.
They dare not go out into the darkness
    for fear they will be murdered.
They wander around, saying, 'Where can I find bread?'
    They know their day of destruction is near.
That dark day terrifies them.
    They live in distress and anguish,
    like a king preparing for battle.
For they shake their fists at God,
    defying the Almighty.
Holding their strong shields,
    they defiantly charge against him.

"These wicked people are heavy and prosperous;
    their waists bulge with fat.
But their cities will be ruined.
    They will live in abandoned houses
    that are ready to tumble down.
Their riches will not last,
    and their wealth will not endure.
    Their possessions will no longer spread across
        the horizon.

"They will not escape the darkness.
    The burning sun will wither their shoots,
    and the breath of God will destroy them.

Let them no longer fool themselves by trusting in empty riches,
    for emptiness will be their only reward.
They will be cut down in the prime of life;
    their branches will never again be green.
They will be like a vine whose grapes are harvested too early,
    like an olive tree that loses its blossoms before the fruit can
       form.
For the godless are barren.
    Their homes, enriched through bribery, will burn.
They conceive trouble and give birth to evil.
    Their womb produces deceit."

+

Then Job spoke again:

"I have heard all this before.
    What miserable comforters you are!
Won't you ever stop blowing hot air?
    What makes you keep on talking?
I could say the same things if you were in my place.
    I could spout off criticism and shake my head at you.
But if it were me, I would encourage you.
    I would try to take away your grief.
Instead, I suffer if I defend myself,
    and I suffer no less if I refuse to speak.

"O God, you have ground me down
    and devastated my family.
As if to prove I have sinned, you've reduced me to skin and bones.
    My gaunt flesh testifies against me.
God hates me and angrily tears me apart.
    He snaps his teeth at me
    and pierces me with his eyes.
People jeer and laugh at me.
    They slap my cheek in contempt.
    A mob gathers against me.
God has handed me over to sinners.
    He has tossed me into the hands of the wicked.

"I was living quietly until he shattered me.
    He took me by the neck and broke me in pieces.
Then he set me up as his target,

and now his archers surround me.
His arrows pierce me without mercy.
   The ground is wet with my blood.
Again and again he smashes against me,
   charging at me like a warrior.
I wear burlap to show my grief.
   My pride lies in the dust.
My eyes are red with weeping;
   dark shadows circle my eyes.
Yet I have done no wrong,
   and my prayer is pure.

"O earth, do not conceal my blood.
   Let it cry out on my behalf.
Even now my witness is in heaven.
   My advocate is there on high.
My friends scorn me,
   but I pour out my tears to God.
I need someone to mediate between God and me,
   as a person mediates between friends.
For soon I must go down that road
   from which I will never return.

"My spirit is crushed,
   and my life is nearly snuffed out.
   The grave is ready to receive me.
I am surrounded by mockers.
   I watch how bitterly they taunt me.

"You must defend my innocence, O God,
   since no one else will stand up for me.
You have closed their minds to understanding,
   but do not let them triumph.
They betray their friends for their own advantage,
   so let their children faint with hunger.

"God has made a mockery of me among the people;
   they spit in my face.
My eyes are swollen with weeping,
   and I am but a shadow of my former self.
The virtuous are horrified when they see me.
   The innocent rise up against the ungodly.
The righteous keep moving forward,
   and those with clean hands become stronger and stronger.

"As for all of you, come back with a better argument,
  though I still won't find a wise man among you.
My days are over.
  My hopes have disappeared.
  My heart's desires are broken.
These men say that night is day;
  they claim that the darkness is light.
What if I go to the grave
  and make my bed in darkness?
What if I call the grave my father,
  and the maggot my mother or my sister?
Where then is my hope?
  Can anyone find it?
No, my hope will go down with me to the grave.
  We will rest together in the dust!"

✢

Then Bildad the Shuhite replied:

"How long before you stop talking?
  Speak sense if you want us to answer!
Do you think we are mere animals?
  Do you think we are stupid?
You may tear out your hair in anger,
  but will that destroy the earth?
  Will it make the rocks tremble?

"Surely the light of the wicked will be snuffed out.
  The sparks of their fire will not glow.
The light in their tent will grow dark.
  The lamp hanging above them will be quenched.
The confident stride of the wicked will be shortened.
  Their own schemes will be their downfall.
The wicked walk into a net.
  They fall into a pit.
A trap grabs them by the heel.
  A snare holds them tight.
A noose lies hidden on the ground.
  A rope is stretched across their path.

"Terrors surround the wicked
  and trouble them at every step.

Hunger depletes their strength,
    and calamity waits for them to stumble.
Disease eats their skin;
    death devours their limbs.
They are torn from the security of their homes
    and are brought down to the king of terrors.
The homes of the wicked will burn down;
    burning sulfur rains on their houses.
Their roots will dry up,
    and their branches will wither.
All memory of their existence will fade from the earth;
    no one will remember their names.
They will be thrust from light into darkness,
    driven from the world.
They will have neither children nor grandchildren,
    nor any survivor in the place where they lived.
People in the west are appalled at their fate;
    people in the east are horrified.
They will say, 'This was the home of a wicked person,
    the place of one who rejected God.'"

✛

Then Job spoke again:

"How long will you torture me?
    How long will you try to crush me with your words?
You have already insulted me ten times.
    You should be ashamed of treating me so badly.
Even if I have sinned,
    that is my concern, not yours.
You think you're better than I am,
    using my humiliation as evidence of my sin.
But it is God who has wronged me,
    capturing me in his net.

"I cry out, 'Help!' but no one answers me.
    I protest, but there is no justice.
God has blocked my way so I cannot move.
    He has plunged my path into darkness.
He has stripped me of my honor
    and removed the crown from my head.
He has demolished me on every side, and I am finished.

He has uprooted my hope like a fallen tree.
His fury burns against me;
  he counts me as an enemy.
His troops advance.
  They build up roads to attack me.
  They camp all around my tent.

"My relatives stay far away,
  and my friends have turned against me.
My family is gone,
  and my close friends have forgotten me.
My servants and maids consider me a stranger.
  I am like a foreigner to them.
When I call my servant, he doesn't come;
  I have to plead with him!
My breath is repulsive to my wife.
  I am rejected by my own family.
Even young children despise me.
  When I stand to speak, they turn their backs on me.
My close friends detest me.
  Those I loved have turned against me.
I have been reduced to skin and bones
  and have escaped death by the skin of my teeth.

"Have mercy on me, my friends, have mercy,
  for the hand of God has struck me.
Must you also persecute me, like God does?
  Haven't you chewed me up enough?

"Oh, that my words could be recorded.
  Oh, that they could be inscribed on a monument,
carved with an iron chisel and filled with lead,
  engraved forever in the rock.

"But as for me, I know that my Redeemer lives,
  and he will stand upon the earth at last.
And after my body has decayed,
  yet in my body I will see God!
I will see him for myself.
  Yes, I will see him with my own eyes.
  I am overwhelmed at the thought!

"How dare you go on persecuting me,
  saying, 'It's his own fault'?

You should fear punishment yourselves,
    for your attitude deserves punishment.
    Then you will know that there is indeed a judgment."

+

Then Zophar the Naamathite replied:

"I must reply
    because I am greatly disturbed.
I've had to endure your insults,
    but now my spirit prompts me to reply.

"Don't you realize that from the beginning of time,
    ever since people were first placed on the earth,
the triumph of the wicked has been short lived
    and the joy of the godless has been only temporary?
Though the pride of the godless reaches to the heavens
    and their heads touch the clouds,
yet they will vanish forever,
    thrown away like their own dung.
Those who knew them will ask,
    'Where are they?'
They will fade like a dream and not be found.
    They will vanish like a vision in the night.
Those who once saw them will see them no more.
    Their families will never see them again.
Their children will beg from the poor,
    for they must give back their stolen riches.
Though they are young,
    their bones will lie in the dust.

"They enjoyed the sweet taste of wickedness,
    letting it melt under their tongue.
They savored it,
    holding it long in their mouths.
But suddenly the food in their bellies turns sour,
    a poisonous venom in their stomach.
They will vomit the wealth they swallowed.
    God won't let them keep it down.
They will suck the poison of cobras.
    The viper will kill them.
They will never again enjoy streams of olive oil
    or rivers of milk and honey.

They will give back everything they worked for.
  Their wealth will bring them no joy.
For they oppressed the poor and left them destitute.
  They foreclosed on their homes.
They were always greedy and never satisfied.
  Nothing remains of all the things they dreamed about.
Nothing is left after they finish gorging themselves.
  Therefore, their prosperity will not endure.

"In the midst of plenty, they will run into trouble
  and be overcome by misery.
May God give them a bellyful of trouble.
  May God rain down his anger upon them.
When they try to escape an iron weapon,
  a bronze-tipped arrow will pierce them.
The arrow is pulled from their back,
  and the arrowhead glistens with blood.
The terrors of death are upon them.
  Their treasures will be thrown into deepest darkness.
A wildfire will devour their goods,
  consuming all they have left.
The heavens will reveal their guilt,
  and the earth will testify against them.
A flood will sweep away their house.
  God's anger will descend on them in torrents.
This is the reward that God gives the wicked.
  It is the inheritance decreed by God."

✛

Then Job spoke again:

"Listen closely to what I am saying.
  That's one consolation you can give me.
Bear with me, and let me speak.
  After I have spoken, you may resume mocking me.

"My complaint is with God, not with people.
  I have good reason to be so impatient.
Look at me and be stunned.
  Put your hand over your mouth in shock.
When I think about what I am saying, I shudder.
  My body trembles.

"Why do the wicked prosper,
    growing old and powerful?
They live to see their children grow up and settle down,
    and they enjoy their grandchildren.
Their homes are safe from every fear,
    and God does not punish them.
Their bulls never fail to breed.
    Their cows bear calves and never miscarry.
They let their children frisk about like lambs.
    Their little ones skip and dance.
They sing with tambourine and harp.
    They celebrate to the sound of the flute.
They spend their days in prosperity,
    then go down to the grave in peace.
And yet they say to God, 'Go away.
    We want no part of you and your ways.
Who is the Almighty, and why should we obey him?
    What good will it do us to pray?'
(They think their prosperity is of their own doing,
    but I will have nothing to do with that kind of thinking.)

"Yet the light of the wicked never seems to be extinguished.
    Do they ever have trouble?
    Does God distribute sorrows to them in anger?
Are they driven before the wind like straw?
    Are they carried away by the storm like chaff?
    Not at all!

"'Well,' you say, 'at least God will punish their children!'
    But I say he should punish the ones who sin,
    so that they understand his judgment.
Let them see their destruction with their own eyes.
    Let them drink deeply of the anger of the Almighty.
For they will not care what happens to their family
    after they are dead.

"But who can teach a lesson to God,
    since he judges even the most powerful?
One person dies in prosperity,
    completely comfortable and secure,
the picture of good health,
    vigorous and fit.
Another person dies in bitter poverty,
    never having tasted the good life.

But both are buried in the same dust,
  both eaten by the same maggots.

"Look, I know what you're thinking.
  I know the schemes you plot against me.
You will tell me of rich and wicked people
  whose houses have vanished because of their sins.
But ask those who have been around,
  and they will tell you the truth.
Evil people are spared in times of calamity
  and are allowed to escape disaster.
No one criticizes them openly
  or pays them back for what they have done.
When they are carried to the grave,
  an honor guard keeps watch at their tomb.
A great funeral procession goes to the cemetery.
  Many pay their respects as the body is laid to rest,
  and the earth gives sweet repose.

"How can your empty clichés comfort me?
  All your explanations are lies!"

✛

Then Eliphaz the Temanite replied:

"Can a person do anything to help God?
  Can even a wise person be helpful to him?
Is it any advantage to the Almighty if you are righteous?
  Would it be any gain to him if you were perfect?
Is it because you're so pious that he accuses you
  and brings judgment against you?
No, it's because of your wickedness!
  There's no limit to your sins.

"For example, you must have lent money to your friend
  and demanded clothing as security.
  Yes, you stripped him to the bone.
You must have refused water for the thirsty
  and food for the hungry.
You probably think the land belongs to the powerful
  and only the privileged have a right to it!
You must have sent widows away empty-handed
  and crushed the hopes of orphans.

That is why you are surrounded by traps
   and tremble from sudden fears.
That is why you cannot see in the darkness,
   and waves of water cover you.

"God is so great—higher than the heavens,
   higher than the farthest stars.
But you reply, 'That's why God can't see what I am doing!
   How can he judge through the thick darkness?
For thick clouds swirl about him, and he cannot see us.
   He is way up there, walking on the vault of heaven.'

"Will you continue on the old paths
   where evil people have walked?
They were snatched away in the prime of life,
   the foundations of their lives washed away.
For they said to God, 'Leave us alone!
   What can the Almighty do to us?'
Yet he was the one who filled their homes with good things,
   so I will have nothing to do with that kind of thinking.

"The righteous will be happy to see the wicked destroyed,
   and the innocent will laugh in contempt.
They will say, 'See how our enemies have been destroyed.
   The last of them have been consumed in the fire.'

"Submit to God, and you will have peace;
   then things will go well for you.
Listen to his instructions,
   and store them in your heart.
If you return to the Almighty, you will be restored—
   so clean up your life.
If you give up your lust for money
   and throw your precious gold into the river,
the Almighty himself will be your treasure.
   He will be your precious silver!

"Then you will take delight in the Almighty
   and look up to God.
You will pray to him, and he will hear you,
   and you will fulfill your vows to him.
You will succeed in whatever you choose to do,
   and light will shine on the road ahead of you.
If people are in trouble and you say, 'Help them,'
   God will save them.

Even sinners will be rescued;
>   they will be rescued because your hands are pure."

+

Then Job spoke again:

> "My complaint today is still a bitter one,
>   and I try hard not to groan aloud.
> If only I knew where to find God,
>   I would go to his court.
> I would lay out my case
>   and present my arguments.
> Then I would listen to his reply
>   and understand what he says to me.
> Would he use his great power to argue with me?
>   No, he would give me a fair hearing.
> Honest people can reason with him,
>   so I would be forever acquitted by my judge.
> I go east, but he is not there.
>   I go west, but I cannot find him.
> I do not see him in the north, for he is hidden.
>   I look to the south, but he is concealed.

> "But he knows where I am going.
>   And when he tests me, I will come out as pure as gold.
> For I have stayed on God's paths;
>   I have followed his ways and not turned aside.
> I have not departed from his commands,
>   but have treasured his words more than daily food.
> But once he has made his decision, who can change his mind?
>   Whatever he wants to do, he does.
> So he will do to me whatever he has planned.
>   He controls my destiny.
> No wonder I am so terrified in his presence.
>   When I think of it, terror grips me.
> God has made me sick at heart;
>   the Almighty has terrified me.
> Darkness is all around me;
>   thick, impenetrable darkness is everywhere.

> "Why doesn't the Almighty bring the wicked to judgment?
>   Why must the godly wait for him in vain?

Evil people steal land by moving the boundary markers.
  They steal livestock and put them in their own pastures.
They take the orphan's donkey
  and demand the widow's ox as security for a loan.
The poor are pushed off the path;
  the needy must hide together for safety.
Like wild donkeys in the wilderness,
  the poor must spend all their time looking for food,
  searching even in the desert for food for their children.
They harvest a field they do not own,
  and they glean in the vineyards of the wicked.
All night they lie naked in the cold,
  without clothing or covering.
They are soaked by mountain showers,
  and they huddle against the rocks for want of a home.

"The wicked snatch a widow's child from her breast,
  taking the baby as security for a loan.
The poor must go about naked, without any clothing.
  They harvest food for others while they themselves are starving.
They press out olive oil without being allowed to taste it,
  and they tread in the winepress as they suffer from thirst.
The groans of the dying rise from the city,
  and the wounded cry for help,
  yet God ignores their moaning.

"Wicked people rebel against the light.
  They refuse to acknowledge its ways
  or stay in its paths.
The murderer rises in the early dawn
  to kill the poor and needy;
  at night he is a thief.
The adulterer waits for the twilight,
  saying, 'No one will see me then.'
  He hides his face so no one will know him.
Thieves break into houses at night
  and sleep in the daytime.
  They are not acquainted with the light.
The black night is their morning.
  They ally themselves with the terrors of the darkness.

"But they disappear like foam down a river.
  Everything they own is cursed,
  and they are afraid to enter their own vineyards.

The grave consumes sinners
    just as drought and heat consume snow.
Their own mothers will forget them.
    Maggots will find them sweet to eat.
No one will remember them.
    Wicked people are broken like a tree in the storm.
They cheat the woman who has no son to help her.
    They refuse to help the needy widow.

"God, in his power, drags away the rich.
    They may rise high, but they have no assurance of life.
They may be allowed to live in security,
    but God is always watching them.
And though they are great now,
    in a moment they will be gone like all others,
    cut off like heads of grain.
Can anyone claim otherwise?
    Who can prove me wrong?"

+

Then Bildad the Shuhite replied:

"God is powerful and dreadful.
    He enforces peace in the heavens.
Who is able to count his heavenly army?
    Doesn't his light shine on all the earth?
How can a mortal be innocent before God?
    Can anyone born of a woman be pure?
God is more glorious than the moon;
    he shines brighter than the stars.
In comparison, people are maggots;
    we mortals are mere worms."

+

Then Job spoke again:

"How you have helped the powerless!
    How you have saved the weak!
How you have enlightened my stupidity!
    What wise advice you have offered!
Where have you gotten all these wise sayings?
    Whose spirit speaks through you?

"The dead tremble—
   those who live beneath the waters.
The underworld is naked in God's presence.
   The place of destruction is uncovered.
God stretches the northern sky over empty space
   and hangs the earth on nothing.
He wraps the rain in his thick clouds,
   and the clouds don't burst with the weight.
He covers the face of the moon,
   shrouding it with his clouds.
He created the horizon when he separated the waters;
   he set the boundary between day and night.
The foundations of heaven tremble;
   they shudder at his rebuke.
By his power the sea grew calm.
   By his skill he crushed the great sea monster.
His Spirit made the heavens beautiful,
   and his power pierced the gliding serpent.
These are just the beginning of all that he does,
   merely a whisper of his power.
   Who, then, can comprehend the thunder of his power?"

+

Job continued speaking:

"I vow by the living God, who has taken away my rights,
   by the Almighty who has embittered my soul—
As long as I live,
   while I have breath from God,
my lips will speak no evil,
   and my tongue will speak no lies.
I will never concede that you are right;
   I will defend my integrity until I die.
I will maintain my innocence without wavering.
   My conscience is clear for as long as I live.

"May my enemy be punished like the wicked,
   my adversary like those who do evil.
For what hope do the godless have when God cuts them off
   and takes away their life?
Will God listen to their cry
   when trouble comes upon them?

Can they take delight in the Almighty?
   Can they call to God at any time?
I will teach you about God's power.
   I will not conceal anything concerning the Almighty.
But you have seen all this,
   yet you say all these useless things to me.

"This is what the wicked will receive from God;
   this is their inheritance from the Almighty.
They may have many children,
   but the children will die in war or starve to death.
Those who survive will die of a plague,
   and not even their widows will mourn them.

"Evil people may have piles of money
   and may store away mounds of clothing.
But the righteous will wear that clothing,
   and the innocent will divide that money.
The wicked build houses as fragile as a spider's web,
   as flimsy as a shelter made of branches.
The wicked go to bed rich
   but wake to find that all their wealth is gone.
Terror overwhelms them like a flood,
   and they are blown away in the storms of the night.
The east wind carries them away, and they are gone.
   It sweeps them away.
It whirls down on them without mercy.
   They struggle to flee from its power.
But everyone jeers at them
   and mocks them.

+

"People know where to mine silver
   and how to refine gold.
They know where to dig iron from the earth
   and how to smelt copper from rock.
They know how to shine light in the darkness
   and explore the farthest regions of the earth
   as they search in the dark for ore.
They sink a mine shaft into the earth
   far from where anyone lives.
   They descend on ropes, swinging back and forth.

Food is grown on the earth above,
    but down below, the earth is melted as by fire.
Here the rocks contain precious lapis lazuli,
    and the dust contains gold.
These are treasures no bird of prey can see,
    no falcon's eye observe.
No wild animal has walked upon these treasures;
    no lion has ever set his paw there.
People know how to tear apart flinty rocks
    and overturn the roots of mountains.
They cut tunnels in the rocks
    and uncover precious stones.
They dam up the trickling streams
    and bring to light the hidden treasures.

"But do people know where to find wisdom?
    Where can they find understanding?
No one knows where to find it,
    for it is not found among the living.
'It is not here,' says the ocean.
    'Nor is it here,' says the sea.
It cannot be bought with gold.
    It cannot be purchased with silver.
It's worth more than all the gold of Ophir,
    greater than precious onyx or lapis lazuli.
Wisdom is more valuable than gold and crystal.
    It cannot be purchased with jewels mounted in fine gold.
Coral and jasper are worthless in trying to get it.
    The price of wisdom is far above rubies.
Precious peridot from Ethiopia cannot be exchanged for it.
    It's worth more than the purest gold.

"But do people know where to find wisdom?
    Where can they find understanding?
It is hidden from the eyes of all humanity.
    Even the sharp-eyed birds in the sky cannot discover it.
Destruction and Death say,
    'We've heard only rumors of where wisdom can be found.'

"God alone understands the way to wisdom;
    he knows where it can be found,
for he looks throughout the whole earth
    and sees everything under the heavens.

He decided how hard the winds should blow
    and how much rain should fall.
He made the laws for the rain
    and laid out a path for the lightning.
Then he saw wisdom and evaluated it.
    He set it in place and examined it thoroughly.
And this is what he says to all humanity:
'The fear of the Lord is true wisdom;
    to forsake evil is real understanding.'"

+

Job continued speaking:

"I long for the years gone by
    when God took care of me,
when he lit up the way before me
    and I walked safely through the darkness.
When I was in my prime,
    God's friendship was felt in my home.
The Almighty was still with me,
    and my children were around me.
My steps were awash in cream,
    and the rocks gushed olive oil for me.

"Those were the days when I went to the city gate
    and took my place among the honored leaders.
The young stepped aside when they saw me,
    and even the aged rose in respect at my coming.
The princes stood in silence
    and put their hands over their mouths.
The highest officials of the city stood quietly,
    holding their tongues in respect.

"All who heard me praised me.
    All who saw me spoke well of me.
For I assisted the poor in their need
    and the orphans who required help.
I helped those without hope, and they blessed me.
    And I caused the widows' hearts to sing for joy.
Everything I did was honest.
    Righteousness covered me like a robe,
    and I wore justice like a turban.

I served as eyes for the blind
   and feet for the lame.
I was a father to the poor
   and assisted strangers who needed help.
I broke the jaws of godless oppressors
   and plucked their victims from their teeth.

"I thought, 'Surely I will die surrounded by my family
   after a long, good life.
For I am like a tree whose roots reach the water,
   whose branches are refreshed with the dew.
New honors are constantly bestowed on me,
   and my strength is continually renewed.'

"Everyone listened to my advice.
   They were silent as they waited for me to speak.
And after I spoke, they had nothing to add,
   for my counsel satisfied them.
They longed for me to speak as people long for rain.
   They drank my words like a refreshing spring rain.
When they were discouraged, I smiled at them.
   My look of approval was precious to them.
Like a chief, I told them what to do.
   I lived like a king among his troops
   and comforted those who mourned.

"But now I am mocked by people younger than I,
   by young men whose fathers are not worthy to run with my
      sheepdogs.
A lot of good they are to me—
   those worn-out wretches!
They are gaunt from poverty and hunger.
   They claw the dry ground in desolate wastelands.
They pluck wild greens from among the bushes
   and eat from the roots of broom trees.
They are driven from human society,
   and people shout at them as if they were thieves.
So now they live in frightening ravines,
   in caves and among the rocks.
They sound like animals howling among the bushes,
   huddled together beneath the nettles.
They are nameless fools,
   outcasts from society.

"And now they mock me with vulgar songs!
    They taunt me!
They despise me and won't come near me,
    except to spit in my face.
For God has cut my bowstring.
    He has humbled me,
    so they have thrown off all restraint.
These outcasts oppose me to my face.
    They send me sprawling
    and lay traps in my path.
They block my road
    and do everything they can to destroy me.
They know I have no one to help me.
    They come at me from all directions.
They jump on me when I am down.
    I live in terror now.
My honor has blown away in the wind,
    and my prosperity has vanished like a cloud.

"And now my life seeps away.
    Depression haunts my days.
At night my bones are filled with pain,
    which gnaws at me relentlessly.
With a strong hand, God grabs my shirt.
    He grips me by the collar of my coat.
He has thrown me into the mud.
    I'm nothing more than dust and ashes.

"I cry to you, O God, but you don't answer.
    I stand before you, but you don't even look.
You have become cruel toward me.
    You use your power to persecute me.
You throw me into the whirlwind
    and destroy me in the storm.
And I know you are sending me to my death—
    the destination of all who live.

"Surely no one would turn against the needy
    when they cry for help in their trouble.
Did I not weep for those in trouble?
    Was I not deeply grieved for the needy?
So I looked for good, but evil came instead.
    I waited for the light, but darkness fell.

My heart is troubled and restless.
    Days of suffering torment me.
I walk in gloom, without sunlight.
    I stand in the public square and cry for help.
Instead, I am considered a brother to jackals
    and a companion to owls.
My skin has turned dark,
    and my bones burn with fever.
My harp plays sad music,
    and my flute accompanies those who weep.

"I made a covenant with my eyes
    not to look with lust at a young woman.
For what has God above chosen for us?
    What is our inheritance from the Almighty on high?
Isn't it calamity for the wicked
    and misfortune for those who do evil?
Doesn't he see everything I do
    and every step I take?

"Have I lied to anyone
    or deceived anyone?
Let God weigh me on the scales of justice,
    for he knows my integrity.
If I have strayed from his pathway,
    or if my heart has lusted for what my eyes have seen,
    or if I am guilty of any other sin,
then let someone else eat the crops I have planted.
    Let all that I have planted be uprooted.

"If my heart has been seduced by a woman,
    or if I have lusted for my neighbor's wife,
then let my wife serve another man;
    let other men sleep with her.
For lust is a shameful sin,
    a crime that should be punished.
It is a fire that burns all the way to hell.
    It would wipe out everything I own.

"If I have been unfair to my male or female
        servants
    when they brought their complaints to me,
how could I face God?
    What could I say when he questioned me?

For God created both me and my servants.
He created us both in the womb.

"Have I refused to help the poor,
or crushed the hopes of widows?
Have I been stingy with my food
and refused to share it with orphans?
No, from childhood I have cared for orphans like a father,
and all my life I have cared for widows.
Whenever I saw the homeless without clothes
and the needy with nothing to wear,
did they not praise me
for providing wool clothing to keep them warm?

"If I raised my hand against an orphan,
knowing the judges would take my side,
then let my shoulder be wrenched out of place!
Let my arm be torn from its socket!
That would be better than facing God's judgment.
For if the majesty of God opposes me, what hope is there?

"Have I put my trust in money
or felt secure because of my gold?
Have I gloated about my wealth
and all that I own?

"Have I looked at the sun shining in the skies,
or the moon walking down its silver pathway,
and been secretly enticed in my heart
to throw kisses at them in worship?
If so, I should be punished by the judges,
for it would mean I had denied the God of heaven.

"Have I ever rejoiced when disaster struck my enemies,
or become excited when harm came their way?
No, I have never sinned by cursing anyone
or by asking for revenge.

"My servants have never said,
'He let others go hungry.'
I have never turned away a stranger
but have opened my doors to everyone.

"Have I tried to hide my sins like other people do,
concealing my guilt in my heart?

Have I feared the crowd
   or the contempt of the masses,
   so that I kept quiet and stayed indoors?

"If only someone would listen to me!
   Look, I will sign my name to my defense.
Let the Almighty answer me.
   Let my accuser write out the charges against me.
I would face the accusation proudly.
   I would wear it like a crown.
For I would tell him exactly what I have done.
   I would come before him like a prince.

"If my land accuses me
   and all its furrows cry out together,
or if I have stolen its crops
   or murdered its owners,
then let thistles grow on that land instead
     of wheat,
   and weeds instead of barley."

Job's words are ended.

+ + +

Job's three friends refused to reply further to him because he kept insisting
on his innocence.

Then Elihu son of Barakel the Buzite, of the clan of Ram, became angry.
He was angry because Job refused to admit that he had sinned and that
God was right in punishing him. He was also angry with Job's three friends,
for they made God appear to be wrong by their inability to answer Job's
arguments. Elihu had waited for the others to speak to Job because they
were older than he. But when he saw that they had no further reply, he
spoke out angrily. Elihu son of Barakel the Buzite said,

"I am young and you are old,
   so I held back from telling you what I think.
I thought, 'Those who are older should speak,
   for wisdom comes with age.'
But there is a spirit within people,
   the breath of the Almighty within them,
   that makes them intelligent.
Sometimes the elders are not wise.
   Sometimes the aged do not understand justice.

So listen to me,
    and let me tell you what I think.

"I have waited all this time,
    listening very carefully to your arguments,
    listening to you grope for words.
I have listened,
    but not one of you has refuted Job
    or answered his arguments.
And don't tell me, 'He is too wise for us.
    Only God can convince him.'
If Job had been arguing with me,
    I would not answer with your kind of logic!
You sit there baffled,
    with nothing more to say.
Should I continue to wait, now that you are
      silent?
    Must I also remain silent?
No, I will say my piece.
    I will speak my mind.
For I am full of pent-up words,
    and the spirit within me urges me on.
I am like a cask of wine without a vent,
    like a new wineskin ready to burst!
I must speak to find relief,
    so let me give my answers.
I won't play favorites
    or try to flatter anyone.
For if I tried flattery,
    my Creator would soon destroy me.

"Listen to my words, Job;
    pay attention to what I have to say.
Now that I have begun to speak,
    let me continue.
I speak with all sincerity;
    I speak the truth.
For the Spirit of God has made me,
    and the breath of the Almighty gives me life.
Answer me, if you can;
    make your case and take your stand.
Look, you and I both belong to God.
    I, too, was formed from clay.

So you don't need to be afraid of me.
  I won't come down hard on you.

"You have spoken in my hearing,
  and I have heard your very words.
You said, 'I am pure; I am without sin;
  I am innocent; I have no guilt.
God is picking a quarrel with me,
  and he considers me his enemy.
He puts my feet in the stocks
  and watches my every move.'

"But you are wrong, and I will show you why.
  For God is greater than any human being.
So why are you bringing a charge against him?
  Why say he does not respond to people's complaints?
For God speaks again and again,
  though people do not recognize it.
He speaks in dreams, in visions of the night,
  when deep sleep falls on people
  as they lie in their beds.
He whispers in their ears
  and terrifies them with warnings.
He makes them turn from doing wrong;
  he keeps them from pride.
He protects them from the grave,
  from crossing over the river of death.

"Or God disciplines people with pain on their
    sickbeds,
  with ceaseless aching in their bones.
They lose their appetite
  for even the most delicious food.
Their flesh wastes away,
  and their bones stick out.
They are at death's door;
  the angels of death wait for them.

"But if an angel from heaven appears—
  a special messenger to intercede for a person
  and declare that he is upright—
he will be gracious and say,
'Rescue him from the grave,
  for I have found a ransom for his life.'

Then his body will become as healthy as a child's,
    firm and youthful again.
When he prays to God,
    he will be accepted.
And God will receive him with joy
    and restore him to good standing.
He will declare to his friends,
'I sinned and twisted the truth,
    but it was not worth it.
God rescued me from the grave,
    and now my life is filled with light.'

"Yes, God does these things
    again and again for people.
He rescues them from the grave
    so they may enjoy the light of life.
Mark this well, Job. Listen to me,
    for I have more to say.
But if you have anything to say, go ahead.
    Speak, for I am anxious to see you justified.
But if not, then listen to me.
    Keep silent and I will teach you wisdom!"

+

Then Elihu said:

"Listen to me, you wise men.
    Pay attention, you who have knowledge.
Job said, 'The ear tests the words it hears
    just as the mouth distinguishes between foods.'
So let us discern for ourselves what is right;
    let us learn together what is good.
For Job also said, 'I am innocent,
    but God has taken away my rights.
I am innocent, but they call me a liar.
    My suffering is incurable, though I have not sinned.'

"Tell me, has there ever been a man like Job,
    with his thirst for irreverent talk?
He chooses evil people as companions.
    He spends his time with wicked men.
He has even said, 'Why waste time
    trying to please God?'

"Listen to me, you who have understanding.
  Everyone knows that God doesn't sin!
  The Almighty can do no wrong.
He repays people according to their deeds.
  He treats people as they deserve.
Truly, God will not do wrong.
  The Almighty will not twist justice.
Did someone else put the world in his care?
  Who set the whole world in place?
If God were to take back his spirit
  and withdraw his breath,
all life would cease,
  and humanity would turn again to dust.

"Now listen to me if you are wise.
  Pay attention to what I say.
Could God govern if he hated justice?
  Are you going to condemn the almighty judge?
For he says to kings, 'You are wicked,'
  and to nobles, 'You are unjust.'
He doesn't care how great a person may be,
  and he pays no more attention to the rich than to the poor.
  He made them all.
In a moment they die.
  In the middle of the night they pass away;
  the mighty are removed without human hand.

"For God watches how people live;
  he sees everything they do.
No darkness is thick enough
  to hide the wicked from his eyes.
We don't set the time
  when we will come before God in judgment.
He brings the mighty to ruin without asking anyone,
  and he sets up others in their place.
He knows what they do,
  and in the night he overturns and destroys them.
He strikes them down because they are wicked,
  doing it openly for all to see.
For they turned away from following him.
  They have no respect for any of his ways.
They cause the poor to cry out, catching God's attention.
  He hears the cries of the needy.

But if he chooses to remain quiet,
   who can criticize him?
When he hides his face, no one can find him,
   whether an individual or a nation.
He prevents the godless from ruling
   so they cannot be a snare to the people.

"Why don't people say to God, 'I have sinned,
   but I will sin no more'?
Or 'I don't know what evil I have done—tell me.
   If I have done wrong, I will stop at once'?

"Must God tailor his justice to your demands?
   But you have rejected him!
The choice is yours, not mine.
   Go ahead, share your wisdom with us.
After all, bright people will tell me,
   and wise people will hear me say,
'Job speaks out of ignorance;
   his words lack insight.'
Job, you deserve the maximum penalty
   for the wicked way you have talked.
For you have added rebellion to your sin;
   you show no respect,
   and you speak many angry words against God."

✝

Then Elihu said:

"Do you think it is right for you to claim,
   'I am righteous before God'?
For you also ask, 'What's in it for me?
   What's the use of living a righteous life?'

"I will answer you
   and all your friends, too.
Look up into the sky,
   and see the clouds high above you.
If you sin, how does that affect God?
   Even if you sin again and again,
   what effect will it have on him?
If you are good, is this some great gift to him?
   What could you possibly give him?

No, your sins affect only people like yourself,
    and your good deeds also affect only humans.

"People cry out when they are oppressed.
    They groan beneath the power of the mighty.
Yet they don't ask, 'Where is God my Creator,
    the one who gives songs in the night?
Where is the one who makes us smarter than the animals
    and wiser than the birds of the sky?'
And when they cry out, God does not answer
    because of their pride.
But it is wrong to say God doesn't listen,
    to say the Almighty isn't concerned.
You say you can't see him,
    but he will bring justice if you will only wait.
You say he does not respond to sinners with anger
    and is not greatly concerned about wickedness.
But you are talking nonsense, Job.
    You have spoken like a fool."

+

Elihu continued speaking:

"Let me go on, and I will show you the truth.
    For I have not finished defending God!
I will present profound arguments
    for the righteousness of my Creator.
I am telling you nothing but the truth,
    for I am a man of great knowledge.

"God is mighty, but he does not despise anyone!
    He is mighty in both power and understanding.
He does not let the wicked live
    but gives justice to the afflicted.
He never takes his eyes off the innocent,
    but he sets them on thrones with kings
    and exalts them forever.
If they are bound in chains
    and caught up in a web of trouble,
he shows them the reason.
    He shows them their sins of pride.
He gets their attention
    and commands that they turn from evil.

"If they listen and obey God,
　they will be blessed with prosperity throughout their lives.
　All their years will be pleasant.
But if they refuse to listen to him,
　they will cross over the river of death,
　dying from lack of understanding.
For the godless are full of resentment.
　Even when he punishes them,
　they refuse to cry out to him for help.
They die when they are young,
　after wasting their lives in immoral living.
But by means of their suffering, he rescues those who suffer.
　For he gets their attention through adversity.

"God is leading you away from danger, Job,
　to a place free from distress.
　He is setting your table with the best food.
But you are obsessed with whether the godless will be judged.
　Don't worry, judgment and justice will be upheld.
But watch out, or you may be seduced by wealth.
　Don't let yourself be bribed into sin.
Could all your wealth
　or all your mighty efforts
　keep you from distress?
Do not long for the cover of night,
　for that is when people will be destroyed.
Be on guard! Turn back from evil,
　for God sent this suffering
　to keep you from a life of evil.

"Look, God is all-powerful.
　Who is a teacher like him?
No one can tell him what to do,
　or say to him, 'You have done wrong.'
Instead, glorify his mighty works,
　singing songs of praise.
Everyone has seen these things,
　though only from a distance.

"Look, God is greater than we can understand.
　His years cannot be counted.
He draws up the water vapor
　and then distills it into rain.

The rain pours down from the clouds,
    and everyone benefits.
Who can understand the spreading of the clouds
    and the thunder that rolls forth from heaven?
See how he spreads the lightning around him
    and how it lights up the depths of the sea.
By these mighty acts he nourishes the people,
    giving them food in abundance.
He fills his hands with lightning bolts
    and hurls each at its target.
The thunder announces his presence;
    the storm announces his indignant anger.

"My heart pounds as I think of this.
    It trembles within me.
Listen carefully to the thunder of God's voice
    as it rolls from his mouth.
It rolls across the heavens,
    and his lightning flashes in every direction.
Then comes the roaring of the thunder—
    the tremendous voice of his majesty.
    He does not restrain it when he speaks.
God's voice is glorious in the thunder.
    We can't even imagine the greatness of his power.

"He directs the snow to fall on the earth
    and tells the rain to pour down.
Then everyone stops working
    so they can watch his power.
The wild animals take cover
    and stay inside their dens.
The stormy wind comes from its chamber,
    and the driving winds bring the cold.
God's breath sends the ice,
    freezing wide expanses of water.
He loads the clouds with moisture,
    and they flash with his lightning.
The clouds churn about at his direction.
    They do whatever he commands throughout the earth.
He makes these things happen either to punish people
    or to show his unfailing love.

"Pay attention to this, Job.
    Stop and consider the wonderful miracles of God!

Do you know how God controls the storm
    and causes the lightning to flash from his clouds?
Do you understand how he moves the clouds
    with wonderful perfection and skill?
When you are sweltering in your clothes
    and the south wind dies down and everything is still,
he makes the skies reflect the heat like a bronze mirror.
    Can you do that?

"So teach the rest of us what to say to God.
    We are too ignorant to make our own arguments.
Should God be notified that I want to speak?
    Can people even speak when they are confused?
We cannot look at the sun,
    for it shines brightly in the sky
    when the wind clears away the clouds.
So also, golden splendor comes from the mountain of God.
    He is clothed in dazzling splendor.
We cannot imagine the power of the Almighty;
    but even though he is just and righteous,
    he does not destroy us.
No wonder people everywhere fear him.
    All who are wise show him reverence."

+ + +

Then the LORD answered Job from the whirlwind:

"Who is this that questions my wisdom
    with such ignorant words?
Brace yourself like a man,
    because I have some questions for you,
    and you must answer them.

"Where were you when I laid the foundations of the
        earth?
    Tell me, if you know so much.
Who determined its dimensions
    and stretched out the surveying line?
What supports its foundations,
    and who laid its cornerstone
as the morning stars sang together
    and all the angels shouted for joy?

"Who kept the sea inside its boundaries
     as it burst from the womb,
and as I clothed it with clouds
     and wrapped it in thick darkness?
For I locked it behind barred gates,
     limiting its shores.
I said, 'This far and no farther will you come.
     Here your proud waves must stop!'

"Have you ever commanded the morning to appear
     and caused the dawn to rise in the east?
Have you made daylight spread to the ends of the earth,
     to bring an end to the night's wickedness?
As the light approaches,
     the earth takes shape like clay pressed beneath a seal;
     it is robed in brilliant colors.
The light disturbs the wicked
     and stops the arm that is raised in violence.

"Have you explored the springs from which the seas come?
     Have you explored their depths?
Do you know where the gates of death are located?
     Have you seen the gates of utter gloom?
Do you realize the extent of the earth?
     Tell me about it if you know!

"Where does light come from,
     and where does darkness go?
Can you take each to its home?
     Do you know how to get there?
But of course you know all this!
For you were born before it was all created,
     and you are so very experienced!

"Have you visited the storehouses of the snow
     or seen the storehouses of hail?
(I have reserved them as weapons for the time of trouble,
     for the day of battle and war.)
Where is the path to the source of light?
     Where is the home of the east wind?

"Who created a channel for the torrents of rain?
     Who laid out the path for the lightning?
Who makes the rain fall on barren land,
     in a desert where no one lives?

Who sends rain to satisfy the parched ground
and make the tender grass spring up?

"Does the rain have a father?
Who gives birth to the dew?
Who is the mother of the ice?
Who gives birth to the frost from the heavens?
For the water turns to ice as hard as rock,
and the surface of the water freezes.

"Can you direct the movement of the stars—
binding the cluster of the Pleiades
or loosening the cords of Orion?
Can you direct the constellations through the seasons
or guide the Bear with her cubs across the heavens?
Do you know the laws of the universe?
Can you use them to regulate the earth?

"Can you shout to the clouds
and make it rain?
Can you make lightning appear
and cause it to strike as you direct?
Who gives intuition to the heart
and instinct to the mind?
Who is wise enough to count all the clouds?
Who can tilt the water jars of heaven
when the parched ground is dry
and the soil has hardened into clods?

"Can you stalk prey for a lioness
and satisfy the young lions' appetites
as they lie in their dens
or crouch in the thicket?
Who provides food for the ravens
when their young cry out to God
and wander about in hunger?

"Do you know when the wild goats give birth?
Have you watched as deer are born in the wild?
Do you know how many months they carry their young?
Are you aware of the time of their delivery?
They crouch down to give birth to their young
and deliver their offspring.
Their young grow up in the open fields,
then leave home and never return.

"Who gives the wild donkey its freedom?
  Who untied its ropes?
I have placed it in the wilderness;
  its home is the wasteland.
It hates the noise of the city
  and has no driver to shout at it.
The mountains are its pastureland,
  where it searches for every blade of grass.

"Will the wild ox consent to being tamed?
  Will it spend the night in your stall?
Can you hitch a wild ox to a plow?
  Will it plow a field for you?
Given its strength, can you trust it?
  Can you leave and trust the ox to do your work?
Can you rely on it to bring home your grain
  and deliver it to your threshing floor?

"The ostrich flaps her wings grandly,
  but they are no match for the feathers of the stork.
She lays her eggs on top of the earth,
  letting them be warmed in the dust.
She doesn't worry that a foot might crush them
  or a wild animal might destroy them.
She is harsh toward her young,
  as if they were not her own.
  She doesn't care if they die.
For God has deprived her of wisdom.
  He has given her no understanding.
But whenever she jumps up to run,
  she passes the swiftest horse with its rider.

"Have you given the horse its strength
  or clothed its neck with a flowing mane?
Did you give it the ability to leap like a locust?
  Its majestic snorting is terrifying!
It paws the earth and rejoices in its strength
  when it charges out to battle.
It laughs at fear and is unafraid.
  It does not run from the sword.
The arrows rattle against it,
  and the spear and javelin flash.
It paws the ground fiercely
  and rushes forward into battle when the ram's horn blows.

It snorts at the sound of the horn.
　　It senses the battle in the distance.
　　It quivers at the captain's commands and the noise of battle.

"Is it your wisdom that makes the hawk soar
　　and spread its wings toward the south?
Is it at your command that the eagle rises
　　to the heights to make its nest?
It lives on the cliffs,
　　making its home on a distant, rocky crag.
From there it hunts its prey,
　　keeping watch with piercing eyes.
Its young gulp down blood.
　　Where there's a carcass, there you'll find it."

Then the LORD said to Job,

"Do you still want to argue with the Almighty?
　　You are God's critic, but do you have the answers?"

+

Then Job replied to the LORD,

"I am nothing—how could I ever find the answers?
　　I will cover my mouth with my hand.
I have said too much already.
　　I have nothing more to say."

+

Then the LORD answered Job from the whirlwind:

"Brace yourself like a man,
　　because I have some questions for you,
　　and you must answer them.

"Will you discredit my justice
　　and condemn me just to prove you are right?
Are you as strong as God?
　　Can you thunder with a voice like his?
All right, put on your glory and splendor,
　　your honor and majesty.
Give vent to your anger.
　　Let it overflow against the proud.

Humiliate the proud with a glance;
   walk on the wicked where they stand.
Bury them in the dust.
   Imprison them in the world of the dead.
Then even I would praise you,
   for your own strength would save you.

"Take a look at Behemoth,
   which I made, just as I made you.
   It eats grass like an ox.
See its powerful loins
   and the muscles of its belly.
Its tail is as strong as a cedar.
   The sinews of its thighs are knit tightly together.
Its bones are tubes of bronze.
   Its limbs are bars of iron.
It is a prime example of God's handiwork,
   and only its Creator can threaten it.
The mountains offer it their best food,
   where all the wild animals play.
It lies under the lotus plants,
   hidden by the reeds in the marsh.
The lotus plants give it shade
   among the willows beside the stream.
It is not disturbed by the raging river,
   not concerned when the swelling Jordan rushes around it.
No one can catch it off guard
   or put a ring in its nose and lead it away.

"Can you catch Leviathan with a hook
   or put a noose around its jaw?
Can you tie it with a rope through the nose
   or pierce its jaw with a spike?
Will it beg you for mercy
   or implore you for pity?
Will it agree to work for you,
   to be your slave for life?
Can you make it a pet like a bird,
   or give it to your little girls to play with?
Will merchants try to buy it
   to sell it in their shops?
Will its hide be hurt by spears
   or its head by a harpoon?

If you lay a hand on it,
> you will certainly remember the battle that follows.
> You won't try that again!
No, it is useless to try to capture it.
> The hunter who attempts it will be knocked down.
And since no one dares to disturb it,
> who then can stand up to me?
Who has given me anything that I need to pay back?
> Everything under heaven is mine.

"I want to emphasize Leviathan's limbs
> and its enormous strength and graceful form.
Who can strip off its hide,
> and who can penetrate its double layer of armor?
Who could pry open its jaws?
> For its teeth are terrible!
The scales on its back are like rows of shields
> tightly sealed together.
They are so close together
> that no air can get between them.
Each scale sticks tight to the next.
> They interlock and cannot be penetrated.

"When it sneezes, it flashes light!
> Its eyes are like the red of dawn.
Lightning leaps from its mouth;
> flames of fire flash out.
Smoke streams from its nostrils
> like steam from a pot heated over burning rushes.
Its breath would kindle coals,
> for flames shoot from its mouth.

"The tremendous strength in Leviathan's neck
> strikes terror wherever it goes.
Its flesh is hard and firm
> and cannot be penetrated.
Its heart is hard as rock,
> hard as a millstone.
When it rises, the mighty are afraid,
> gripped by terror.
No sword can stop it,
> no spear, dart, or javelin.
Iron is nothing but straw to that creature,
> and bronze is like rotten wood.

Arrows cannot make it flee.
   Stones shot from a sling are like bits of grass.
Clubs are like a blade of grass,
   and it laughs at the swish of javelins.
Its belly is covered with scales as sharp as glass.
   It plows up the ground as it drags through the mud.

"Leviathan makes the water boil with its commotion.
   It stirs the depths like a pot of ointment.
The water glistens in its wake,
   making the sea look white.
Nothing on earth is its equal,
   no other creature so fearless.
Of all the creatures, it is the proudest.
   It is the king of beasts."

+

Then Job replied to the LORD:

"I know that you can do anything,
   and no one can stop you.
You asked, 'Who is this that questions my wisdom with such
     ignorance?'
   It is I—and I was talking about things I knew nothing about,
   things far too wonderful for me.
You said, 'Listen and I will speak!
   I have some questions for you,
   and you must answer them.'
I had only heard about you before,
   but now I have seen you with my own eyes.
I take back everything I said,
   and I sit in dust and ashes to show my repentance."

+ + +

After the LORD had finished speaking to Job, he said to Eliphaz the Te-manite: "I am angry with you and your two friends, for you have not spo-ken accurately about me, as my servant Job has. So take seven bulls and seven rams and go to my servant Job and offer a burnt offering for your-selves. My servant Job will pray for you, and I will accept his prayer on your behalf. I will not treat you as you deserve, for you have not spoken accu-rately about me, as my servant Job has." So Eliphaz the Temanite, Bildad the Shuhite, and Zophar the Naamathite did as the LORD commanded them, and the LORD accepted Job's prayer.

When Job prayed for his friends, the LORD restored his fortunes. In fact, the LORD gave him twice as much as before! Then all his brothers, sisters, and former friends came and feasted with him in his home. And they consoled him and comforted him because of all the trials the LORD had brought against him. And each of them brought him a gift of money and a gold ring.

So the LORD blessed Job in the second half of his life even more than in the beginning. For now he had 14,000 sheep, 6,000 camels, 1,000 teams of oxen, and 1,000 female donkeys. He also gave Job seven more sons and three more daughters. He named his first daughter Jemimah, the second Keziah, and the third Keren-happuch. In all the land no women were as lovely as the daughters of Job. And their father put them into his will along with their brothers.

Job lived 140 years after that, living to see four generations of his children and grandchildren. Then he died, an old man who had lived a long, full life.

THE STORIES AND THE STORY
How the Bible Works

The Bible is a gift. The Creator of all things has entered into our human story, and he has spoken. Working through all the authors of the Bible's various writings, God brings wisdom into our lives and light to our path. But his biggest intention for the Bible is to invite us into its Story. What God wants from us, more than anything else, is to make the Bible's great drama of restoration and new life the story of our lives too.

The appropriate way to receive a gift like this is to come to know the Bible deeply, to lose ourselves in it precisely so that we can find ourselves in it. In other words, the best thing we can do with the Bible is to immerse ourselves in it.

The first step on this journey of immersion is to become intimately familiar with the Bible's individual books—the songs and stories, the visions and letters. These books reflect different kinds of writing, and each book with its various parts must first be read and understood on its own terms. Your *Immerse Bible* is designed to help you easily see what kind of writing is found in each book. This will foster a better reading experience that leads to reading more and to reading in context.

But there is an even bigger goal than understanding the individual books. At its heart, the Bible is God's grand narrative of the world and his intentions for it. By reading whole books and then reading them as a collection of writings, we discover how the Bible presents God's big story—*the* Story. The true destination of Bible reading is for us to inhabit the Story. All the smaller parts of the Bible—Gospels and histories, proverbs and prophecies—take their rightful places in revealing the saving drama of God.

As we begin our journey deep into the heart of the Bible, we come across many stories. The plots and subplots of these stories fit together to tell the Bible's big Story. All the characters, communities, and covenants play a part in bringing the overall Story to its fitting conclusion. That is, they are related to each other and work together to reveal God's bigger purposes for the world.

But how are they related?

The following overview of the main stories that make up the Story will help you understand the overall flow of the Bible. It will reveal how the major stories in the Bible are really subplots of the big Story. As each new subplot is introduced, we will see how it serves the bigger narrative, particularly the story that immediately precedes it.

The Bible is a connected, multi-layered story, and Jesus the Messiah is directly at the center of it all. Sent by the Father and empowered by the Spirit, he is the One who ultimately brings resolution to all the stories. He is the thread—the beginning and the end—that ties the Scriptures together. Jesus the Messiah makes the Story's good ending possible, enabling the completion of God's one, big, saving purpose for all things.

1. The Story of God and His World

In the beginning God made everything and said it was all very good. It is evident from the rich variety of interconnected living things in his created order that God delights in flourishing life. This thriving, teeming world brings God glory and reveals his power.

When we read the Bible in its ancient Near Eastern context, something else also becomes clear. The opening song of creation shows us that God intends for the entire cosmos to be his temple, the place where he makes his home. When the Bible says God "rested" on the seventh day, it doesn't simply mean he stopped working. In the ancient world, a deity "rested" in order to take up residence within a temple. So the new world God made becomes his creation-temple, and he rules over it, bringing peace and life.

This is the Bible's first account, and it forms the frame for everything else that happens. God's creation is the stage for all the acts of the Story going forward. And the role of others in the drama will determine whether or not the Creator's plan for flourishing life will be realized.

2. The Story of Humanity

Humans come into the creation story in a special way. They are portrayed as being formed from the earth itself, establishing their permanent connection with the rest of the creation. Yet they are set apart from the beginning with a unique calling: stewardship. Out of all the creatures, only humans are made in the image of God himself and are to bring God's intentions for his creation to fruition. Their job is to rule over all things, helping life to flourish. Humanity is God's plan for managing his world. As priests in the temple of God's creation, humans—more than any other creature—will determine the success or failure of God's purposes for the world.

However, there are also other forces at work. Evil powers exist and are in a position to influence humans, drawing them away from God and interfering with his aims. God's people are lured into self-assertion and rebellion. This disrupts not only their relationship with God but also the way they function in the world. Because of humanity's bond with the rest of creation and their special vocation within it, great tragedy comes into the world. As their own humanity is twisted out of shape, guilt, pain, violence, and death begin to wreak havoc throughout God's good creation. Human beings are made for worship, created to bring glory to the Creator. But when humans direct their worship elsewhere, the damage reverberates throughout the world.

You'd think this would be enough to make God reject humans completely. But instead, God makes a promise to Adam and Eve that he will continue to work in and through human beings. In fact, it will be an offspring of the woman who will defeat the powers of evil. God will overcome the moral chaos of the world, and he will do it in partnership with humanity. In the Bible's Story, the fate of humanity and the rest of creation are irrevocably bound together.

But the question then becomes: How will God do this?

3. The Story of Abraham and His Family

The book of Genesis reveals a surprising answer: God is going to mend the world and bring his blessing to all the families on earth through one man and his descendants. God calls Abram (his name is later changed to Abraham) to leave his home and go to a new land and a new future. God narrows his focus to one family for a time as the means for bringing restoration to all the world's families.

From this point on, the big stories of humanity and of creation will hinge on what happens in the smaller story of Abraham's descendants. God intends for this family to be an agent for the renewal of the world. This plan begins with God's making promises to Abraham—to bless him, to make his family into a great nation, and to bring blessing to all nations. Over time, God makes a series of these promises, or covenantal agreements, with Abraham's family. Each new covenant moves the story forward and makes God's ultimate intentions more clear.

Early in the narrative, Abraham's descendants go down to Egypt and are eventually enslaved there. But God comes down to set them free and bring them into their own land, an event known as the Exodus. This great act of liberation becomes the template, or pattern, for all the acts of deliverance that God will bring in the future. (The nation that comes from Abraham's descendants becomes known as Israel, named after Abraham's grandson.)

As part of the Exodus, God gives his Law to the people through the great leader Moses, and this Law becomes an important part of his covenantal agreement with Israel. In revealing his mandates to Israel, God expects Israel to become a light to the nations. God wants his people to show the rest of the world what it looks like to live well under God's rule.

Another critical event in the Exodus occurs when God's personal presence comes down and inhabits the Tabernacle (a great tent set up at the center of Israel's camp). This Tabernacle becomes God's house in the midst of his people and is filled with symbols of the earth and sky. It is thus a miniature picture of the cosmos, revealing God's desire to cleanse and renew the whole creation and to make his home with us here once again.

God is present with his people in their new land, keeping the promises he made through Moses. But Israel struggles to honor its covenantal obligations. Throughout the story of Israel, the nation turns away from God again and again. This breakdown threatens the covenant itself. God is committed to working through his people. So if they fail, then his restoration project cannot move forward.

But this story is full of God's surprises. Along the way, God establishes a further covenant with Israel's king David. God assures David of a dynasty of kings on which the promises and hopes of Israel will be concentrated. The destiny of Israel as the beginning of God's new humanity is now focused here.

However, the people of Israel persist in rejecting God's covenant—worshiping idols, inflicting injustice on the poor, and looking out only for themselves. In anger and frustration, God finally intervenes. He exiles his people from their own land and withdraws his presence from them. Others now rule over Abraham's family, and Israel's role in the divine drama seems to have disappeared. A key biblical truth is revealed here: There can be no renewal, for Israel or the wider world, until evil and wrongdoing are dealt with. Judgment is part of setting things right.

The failure of Israel is critical for the overall Story. Israel was called to be the means by which God saves the world, but now the rescue party itself needs rescuing. Everything God intended for his people—indeed, for the entire creation—now seems in doubt.

God sees everything that has gone wrong. But wrongdoing, violence, and death will not get the last word—not in God's Story. He has another promise. Through his prophets, God brings a vision of a new future, one aligned with his founding purpose. He will establish a new covenant, one that completes and surpasses all the covenants that came before. God himself will return to his people and restore them. They will be the light they were always meant to be. So the people wait—praying, worshiping, longing—for one more promise to come true.

4. The Story of Messiah Jesus

By the first century AD, Israel had been suffering under foreign rule for centuries. Now subjugated by the Roman Empire, God's people are divided about what to do. Zealous factions advocate violent rebellion. Many teachers and other religious leaders are urging people to get more serious about following Israel's distinctive way of life under God's law. And those running the Temple in Jerusalem survive by making compromises with their Roman overlords.

Israel's ancient prophet Isaiah had foretold a time when a messenger would come to Jerusalem proclaiming the good news that God is returning at last, that his people are being saved. But Rome had its own version of the good news, and it wasn't about Israel's God. The empire's gospel was about the great blessings brought by their own powerful leader, Caesar Augustus. He is, they said, "a savior for us and those who come after us, to make war to cease, to create order everywhere. The birthday of the god Augustus was the beginning for the world of the good tidings that have come to men through him" (from the Priene Calendar Inscription in Asia Minor, ca. 9 BC).

Into this world a child is born in Israel. He is a descendant of King David, but he comes from a humble family. An angel speaks to his mother, Mary, before he is born. He tells her that this child will be the long-promised and long-awaited Messiah, Israel's King, the One who will fulfill their history. Remarkably, Scripture's account of the ministry of Jesus echoes particulars of Israel's history.

Before Israel's Exodus, Pharaoh killed many Israelite babies, but Israel's deliverer, Moses, escaped; King Herod also kills many Israelite babies in try-ing to kill Jesus, but Jesus also escapes. The family of Israel went to Egypt to survive a deadly famine; the family of Jesus also survives by going to Egypt. Israel passed through the Jordan River to enter the Promised Land; Jesus is baptized in the Jordan River before beginning his ministry in Israel. Israel spent forty years in the wilderness, where they struggled with temp-tation; Jesus spends forty days fasting in the wilderness and is tempted by the devil. And as Israel had twelve sons who fathered twelve tribes, Jesus chooses twelve men to be his closest followers. In all of this, Jesus is reliving aspects of the ancient narrative of Israel, but now with a different outcome. Jesus is refreshing Israel's story and renewing Israel itself—through himself.

In his opening message to the people of Israel, Jesus calls them to be the light they were always meant to be, announcing the Good News that something unprecedented is happening in Israel's story. He demonstrates in powerful words and miraculous deeds what it looks like when God comes as King—teaching, correcting, and healing. Jesus is widely recognized as a rabbi and a mighty prophet in Israel, but the current religious leaders see him as a dangerous new problem. Jesus critiques their leadership, thus threatening their positions of power.

This tension between Jesus and the Jewish religious leaders rises until Jesus travels to Jerusalem for a final confrontation. His twelve disciples now recognize him as the Son of David, the Messiah, but they still don't understand his mission. They assume Jesus is going to fight his enemies and claim the throne. But Jesus talks about fighting a different kind of battle. He says his struggle is against the powers of darkness and the spiritual ruler of this world.

Then during Israel's annual celebration of the Exodus, Jesus shares a final Passover meal with his disciples. He tells them that his death will inaugurate the new covenant promised by the prophets. He is arrested by the religious leaders and handed over to the Romans for execution. He is nailed to a cross, with a mocking sign posted above his head that reads "The King of the Jews." It certainly looks as though Jesus has lost, that he is no king after all. But three days later, Jesus is raised from the dead and appears to his disciples.

It turns out that Jesus willingly went to his death as a sacrifice for the sins of his people. Through his sacrifice, he wins a surprising victory over the spiritual powers of darkness. He takes on sin and death directly—ironically, through death—emptying them of their power over humanity, and he rises from the dead to confirm his triumph. This unexpected story of Israel's Messiah reveals God's long-term plan. All the earlier covenants were leading to this one. The life and ministry of Jesus brings all the narrative threads in the Scriptures together into a single, coherent Story.

5. All the Stories in One

So we see that the story of Jesus does not simply stand alone. The Bible presents his narrative as intimately tied to all the plots and subplots that came before him. Jesus, crucified and raised, is God's answer to Israel's previous failure, humanity's wrongdoing and death, and the curse on all creation.

Jesus fulfills Israel's story and successfully plays the role of rescuer given to Abraham's family. He is Abraham's faithful descendant and David's powerful son, the Messiah. He is the light the nations have been longing for. People from every tribe, nation, and community can now join Abraham's family through belief in Jesus the Messiah. As the true Israelite, Jesus is also a new Adam, a fresh start for the human race. He has defeated our archenemies sin and death, restoring our relationship with God and ushering us into the life that is truly life. The new covenant in Jesus introduces a new world.

Jesus opens the doorway to the true worship of God, and we recover our God-given vocation to be his image-bearers through our stewardship of the world. As the new Adam, Jesus brings flourishing life back into the world. He embodies the new creation in his resurrection, blazing a path of future renewal for everything in heaven and on earth.

Jesus also launches a new community of God's people—the church—

creating the renewed humanity that God envisioned from the beginning. This community is the focus of God's work on the way to a completely restored and healed creation. The book of Acts and the letters of the New Testament record how the earliest churches continued the ministry of God's coming reign that Jesus had begun. The context of this ministry changes over time and in location, but the ministry itself remains the same for God's new family: to embody and proclaim the Good News of God's victory through the Messiah.

In the end, the discovery of the narrative unity we find in the Scriptures is not merely for the purpose of information. The Bible is an invitation. It calls us to join the Story and take up our own role in God's ongoing redemptive drama. We read the Bible deeply and well in order to learn the true story of our lives within God's bigger Story of the world. We read the Bible to grasp the cosmic scope and meaning of Jesus' victory. And we read the Bible to know what it means to follow Jesus ourselves. The path of the cross—selfless love and sacrifice—is the path for us, too. But that path also ends in our own resurrection when the Messiah returns.

> Yet what we suffer now is nothing compared to the glory he will reveal to us later. For all creation is waiting eagerly for that future day when God will reveal who his children really are. Against its will, all creation was subjected to God's curse. But with eager hope, the creation looks forward to the day when it will join God's children in glorious freedom from death and decay. For we know that all creation has been groaning as in the pains of childbirth right up to the present time. And we believers also groan, even though we have the Holy Spirit within us as a foretaste of future glory, for we long for our bodies to be released from sin and suffering. We, too, wait with eager hope for the day when God will give us our full rights as his adopted children, including the new bodies he has promised us. We were given this hope when we were saved.
>
> From Paul's letter to the Romans

The final theme of the biblical chronicle is life, the same theme that began the Story. Through the power of the Spirit and the action of the Son, the Father's intention will be realized in a new heaven and a new earth.

I M M E R S E
The Reading Bible

Many people feel discouraged in their Bible reading. The size and scope (not to mention the tiny fonts and the thin pages) intimidate new and seasoned readers alike, keeping them from diving into and immersing themselves in the word of God. The Bible itself is not the problem; how the Bible has been presented to readers for generations is.

Our Bibles currently look like reference books—a resource to put on the shelf and consult only when needed. So we read it like a reference book: infrequently and in small pieces. But the Bible is a collection of good writings that invite us to good reading—and it's God's word! There is an urgent need today for Christians to know the word of God, and the best way to do so is by reading the Bible. However, we need to understand the Bible on its own terms. We need to become deeply acquainted with whole books by reading them at length. And we can learn how to read the Bible well by altering a few of our current Bible reading habits.

First, we need to think about the Bible as a collection of writings written in various literary forms known as *genres*. Each literary form, or genre, used in the Bible—such as a poem, story, or letter—was chosen because, along with the words, it works to communicate truths about God to real people. (See "The Literary Forms of the Bible," p. 341, for a further explanation of some of these genres.) A complete book can be composed in a single genre, or the author may use several genres to tell one story. And even when books of the Bible are made up of several different compositions, as in the book of Psalms, those components are drawn together in such a way as to give each book an overall unity as a distinct work in itself.

Second, recognizing that the Bible is made up of whole books that tell a complete story, we should seek to understand the Bible's teaching and live out its story. To help readers better understand and read the Bible as whole books, we've removed any additives from the Bible text. Those additions, while inserted with good intentions, have accumulated over the centuries, changing how people view the Bible and, therefore, what they think they're supposed to do with it.

Chapters and verses aren't the original units of the Bible. The latest books of the Bible were written in the first century AD; however, chapter divisions were added in the thirteenth century, and the verse divisions we use today appeared in the middle of the sixteenth century. So for the majority of its history, the Bible had no chapters or verses. They were introduced so that reference works like commentaries and concordances could be created. But if we rely on these later additions to guide our reading of the Bible, we often miss the original, natural structure. This also puts us at risk of missing the message and meaning of the Bible. For this reason, we have removed the chapter and verse markers from the text. (We do, however, include a verse range at the top of each page, allowing for easy reference.)

This edition also removes the section headings that are found in most Bibles. These are also not original but the work of modern publishers. These headings create the impression that the Bible is made up of short, encyclopedic sections. So, like chapters and verses, they can encourage us to treat the Bible as a kind of reference work rather than a collection of good writings that invite good reading. Many headings may also spoil the suspense that the inspired storytellers sought to create and use to such good effect. (For example, a heading that often appears in the book of Acts announces in advance "Peter's Miraculous Escape from Prison.")

So, in place of section headings, *Immerse: The Reading Bible* uses line spacing and graphic markers to simply and elegantly reflect the natural structures of the Bible's books. For example, in the letter known as 1 Corinthians, Paul addresses twelve issues in the life of the community in Corinth. In this edition, double line breaks and a single cross mark off the teaching Paul offers for each issue. Single line breaks separate different phases of the longer arguments Paul makes to support his teaching. And triple line breaks with three crosses set off the opening and closing of the letter from the main body. By contrast, the section headings in a typical Bible divide 1 Corinthians into nearly thirty parts. These divisions give no indication of which parts speak together to the same issue or where the letter's main body begins and ends.

Modern Bibles also include hundreds of footnotes and often include cross-references throughout the text. While these features provide information that can be helpful in certain settings, there's a danger that they, too, can encourage us to treat the Bible as a reference work. Constantly going back and forth between the text and the notes doesn't really qualify as being immersed in reading the Bible.

Third, the order in which the books appear is another important factor in reading the Bible well and at length. For the majority of the Bible's history, its books were not arranged in any fixed order. Instead, they were placed in a great variety of orders, depending on the needs and goals of each presentation. In some cases, books from the same time period were put together. In other cases, similar kinds of writing were set side by side. And often the Bible's books were organized according to the way the community used them in worship.

The order of books that we know today didn't become fixed until near the time of the invention of the printing press in the fifteenth century. This ordering has many drawbacks. For example, it presents Paul's letters in order of length (longest to shortest) rather than in the order in which he wrote them. Also, in this order, the books of the prophets are divided into groups by size, and the smaller books are then organized based on phrases they share. This arrangement puts them out of historical order and sends the reader swinging back and forth between centuries. And there are many other similar concerns in what we know as the traditional order.

This edition returns to the church's longstanding tradition of arranging the Bible's books to best meet the goals of a given presentation. To help readers delve deeper into the Story of the Bible, it places Paul's letters in their likely historical order. The books of the prophets are arranged in similar fashion. Furthermore, the collection of prophetic books is placed immediately after the story of Israel because the prophets were God's messengers to the people during the unfolding of that story. The remaining books of the First Testament, known traditionally as the "Writings," are placed after the prophets and arranged by type of writing. The introductions to the various groups of books in this Bible will explain more about how they are arranged and why.

Finally, some complete books of the Bible were broken into parts over time. The books of Samuel and Kings originally made up one long book, but they were separated into four parts so they would fit conveniently on ancient papyrus scrolls. The books of Chronicles, Ezra, and Nehemiah are similarly the divided parts of an originally unified composition. In this edition, both of these two longer works are put back together as Samuel–Kings and Chronicles–Ezra–Nehemiah. Luke and Acts were written as a unified story of the life of Jesus and the birth of the community of his followers. These two volumes had been separated so that Luke could be placed with the other Gospels. But since the two parts were meant to be read together, they have been reunited here as Luke–Acts.

All of this is presented in a clean, single-column format, allowing each of the Bible's basic units to be read like the books they are. The lines of Hebrew poetry can easily be seen, and stories, proverbs, letters, and other genres can readily be identified. In short, *Immerse: The Reading Bible* takes full advantage of good visual design to provide a more authentic encounter with God's sacred words.

It is our prayer that the combined effect of these changes to the visual layout of the Bible will enhance your reading experience. We believe these changes serve the Scriptures well and will allow you to receive these books on their own terms. The goal, after all, is to let the Bible be the book that God inspired so it can do its powerful work in our lives.

THE LITERARY FORMS OF THE BIBLE

Just as God's word uses existing human language, the inspired authors also employ existing human literary forms that enable words to be arranged in meaningful ways. These different types of writing are called *genres*.

Today most of us are probably more familiar with the concept of genre from watching movies. By watching the opening scene, we can identify whether it's a Western, a science fiction thriller, a romantic comedy, or a documentary. Once we know what kind of film it is, we know what expectations we should have about what can or can't happen, how things are likely to develop, and how we should interpret what is being shown. These expectations, created by previous films and respected by filmmakers, are like an agreement with the audience about how its message will be communicated and should be interpreted.

Likewise, the Bible's authors and editors, through God's inspiration, used and respected the genres of their day. We may be able to recognize some of them as similar to genres we know today, but others may be less familiar.

Since understanding genres is critical to reading the Bible well, we will describe the key types below. The compositions that reflect these genres make up either whole Bible books or smaller sections of larger books, so some Bible books are written partly in one genre and partly in another. (Many of the genres introduced here will be further explained in the introductions to books or sections of the Bible.) As indicated below, the specific genres employed in the Bible can be divided into two general categories of writing: prose and poetry.

PROSE GENRES

- **Stories.** Narrative—or stories—weave together events in a way that shows they have a larger meaning. Typically, a story situates the reader in a place and time and then introduces a conflict. This conflict intensifies until it reaches a climax, which is followed by a resolution.

  Narrative is the most common genre used in the Bible, emphasizing that God primarily makes himself known through his words and actions in specific historical events. The Bible doesn't teach about God merely in the abstract; its historical narratives are intentionally shaped to highlight key points about God and how he relates to people and the world.

The Bible features two special types of stories-within-stories. Sometimes a person will tell a story to illustrate a point about the larger narrative that person is in. These stories are called *parables* and were a favorite teaching tool of Jesus. They usually describe real-life situations but sometimes can be fanciful, like Jotham's parable in the book of Judges, which uses talking trees as the characters. People in a story may also relate *dreams* and *visions* that they've had. In this case they're not making up a story but reporting one they've seen. This subset of narrative speaks in pictures and uses symbols to represent realities.

- *Apocalypse.* Meaning "unveiling," apocalypse is an ancient genre structured as a narrative but composed entirely of *visions* employing vivid symbols which a heavenly visitor reveals to a person. These visions disclose the secrets of the spiritual world and, often, the future. The book of Revelation is a complete apocalypse, while the book of Daniel is split between narrative and apocalypse. Elements of apocalypse also appear in Isaiah, Ezekiel, and Zechariah.

- *Letters.* About one-third of the Bible's books are letters that were originally written by one person to another person or to a group. Letters in the Bible, following the form of ancient letters, have three parts: the opening, the main body, and the closing. In the opening, writers typically give their name, say who they're writing to, and offer a word of thanksgiving or prayer. The main body deals with the business of the letter. In the closing, the writer extends greetings, shares prayer requests, and offers a prayer for God to bless the recipients. Letters in the Bible are typically used by leaders to present their authoritative teaching to a community when they aren't physically present.

- *Laws.* Also known as commands, these are instructions for what to do in specific situations in order to live as God intends. Less frequently, laws are statements of general principles to follow. Many biblical laws have been gathered into large collections, but sometimes they are placed within narratives as part of the resolution after a conflict. God's instructions are most often presented in the Bible as part of his covenantal agreements with his people, contributing to his larger saving purposes.

- *Sermons.* These are public addresses to groups that have gathered for worship or for the celebration of a special occasion. They typically explain the meaning of earlier parts of the Bible's story for people living in a later part of that story. Most sermons in the Bible are found within narratives, but the book of Hebrews comprises four sermons that were collected and then sent out in the same letter.

The book of Deuteronomy is a series of sermons by Moses to the people of Israel as they were about to enter the Promised Land. Parts of it take the form of a *treaty* that high kings would make with the kings who served them. The Ten Commandments are a miniature version of that kind of treaty.

- **Prayers.** These are addressed to God and are usually offered in a public setting in the Bible, though sometimes they are private. They can include praise, thanksgiving, confession, and requests.

- **Lists.** Many kinds of lists are found in the Bible. One of the most common types, *genealogy*, is a record of a person's ancestors or descendants. The Bible also includes lists of things like offerings, building materials, assigned territories, stops along journeys, court officials, population counts, and so on. Lists in the Bible are not merely informative but usually make a theological point or provide verification of someone's connection to God's people.

POETRY GENRES

Hebrew poetry is based not on the repetition of sound (rhyme) but on the repetition of meaning. Its essential unit, the couplet, features a form of parallelism. One line states something, and the next line repeats, contrasts, or elaborates on the first line, intensifying its meaning. This feature is sometimes expanded to a triplet (three-line unit) for greater emphasis.

Poetry frequently uses metaphors and other figurative language to communicate messages with greater strength and emotion.

- **Proverbs.** These are short sayings, typically two lines in length (though sometimes longer), that teach practical lessons for life in God's world. Proverbs are not necessarily promises about how things will work out; mainly they are descriptions of wise ways to live.

- **Songs.** Poetry set to music. In the Bible, songs are used primarily for celebration or for mourning (in which case they are called *laments*). They are often found within narratives, but some books of the Bible are whole collections of songs.

  Psalms are songs used by people gathered for worship. These songs are most often addressed to God as prayers set to music.

- **Oracles.** These are messages from God delivered by prophets. In the Bible, oracles are most often recorded in poetry; originally, they may have been sung. Some oracles are in prose, but even those often use symbolic language similar to dreams and visions. Most biblical oracles are found within larger collections from the same prophet; however, the book of Obadiah consists of a single oracle.

- *Poetic dialogue.* Utilized in a number of ancient writings, poetic dialogue is a conversation in which each participant speaks in a form of poetry. In the Bible, this genre is found only in the book of Job.

Reading the Bible well starts with recognizing and then honoring each book's genre. Following this practice will help prevent mistakes in interpretation and allow us to discover the meaning that the Bible's creators originally intended.

NLT: A NOTE TO READERS

The *Holy Bible*, New Living Translation, was first published in 1996. It quickly became one of the most popular Bible translations in the English-speaking world. While the NLT's influence was rapidly growing, the Bible Translation Committee determined that an additional investment in scholarly review and text refinement could make it even better. So shortly after its initial publication, the committee began an eight-year process with the purpose of increasing the level of the NLT's precision without sacrificing its easy-to-understand quality. This second-generation text was completed in 2004, with minor changes subsequently introduced in 2007, 2013, and 2015.

The goal of any Bible translation is to convey the meaning and content of the ancient Hebrew, Aramaic, and Greek texts as accurately as possible to contemporary readers. The challenge for our translators was to create a text that would communicate as clearly and powerfully to today's readers as the original texts did to readers and listeners in the ancient biblical world. The resulting translation is easy to read and understand, while also accurately communicating the meaning and content of the original biblical texts. The NLT is a general-purpose text especially good for study, devotional reading, and reading aloud in worship services.

We believe that the New Living Translation—which combines the latest biblical scholarship with a clear, dynamic writing style—will communicate God's word powerfully to all who read it. We publish it with the prayer that God will use it to speak his timeless truth to the church and the world in a fresh, new way.

The Publishers

A full introduction to the NLT can be found at tyndale.com/nlt/process.

A complete list of the translators can be found at tyndale.com/nlt/scholars.

8-Week Reading Plan

Reading Plan Instructions: Always read to the largest break on the page where each reading ends. If there is more than one largest break, go to the last one. If no breaks appear on that page, read to the bottom of the page.

Week 1 Psalms (Book One)
Day 1   pp. A9-7
Day 2   pp. 7-15
Day 3   pp. 15-25
Day 4   pp. 25-35
Day 5   pp. 35-44

Week 2 Lamentations, Psalms (Book Two)
Day 6   pp. 165-173
Day 7   pp. 173-180
Day 8   pp. 45-55
Day 9   pp. 55-66
Day 10   pp. 67-77

Week 3 Song of Songs, Psalms (Book Three)
Day 11   pp. 181-187
Day 12   pp. 187-194
Day 13   pp. 78-83
Day 14   pp. 83-92
Day 15   pp. 92-99

Week 4 Proverbs
Day 16   pp. 195-202
Day 17   pp. 202-211
Day 18   pp. 211-218
Day 19   pp. 219-225
Day 20   pp. 226-233

Week 5 Proverbs, Psalms (Book Four)
Day 21   pp. 233-243
Day 22   pp. 243-250
Day 23   pp. 100-106
Day 24   pp. 106-114
Day 25   pp. 114-119

Week 6 Ecclesiastes, Psalms (Book Five)
Day 26   pp. 251-258
Day 27   pp. 258-265
Day 28   pp. 120-130
Day 29   pp. 130-141
Day 30   pp. 141-148

Week 7 Psalms (Book Five), Job
Day 31   pp. 148-155
Day 32   pp. 155-163
Day 33   pp. 267-272
Day 34   pp. 272-282
Day 35   pp. 282-289

Week 8 Job
Day 36   pp. 289-295
Day 37   pp. 295-302
Day 38   pp. 302-310
Day 39   pp. 310-319
Day 40   pp. 319-327

4 QUESTIONS TO GET YOUR CONVERSATIONS STARTED:

1. What stood out to you this week?
2. Was there anything confusing or troubling?
3. Did anything make you think differently about God?
4. How might this change the way we live?

More Immerse resources available at www.ImmerseBible.com/Poets.

16-Week Reading Plan

Reading Plan Instructions: Always read to the largest break on the page where each reading ends. If there is more than one largest break, go to the last one. If no breaks appear on that page, read to the bottom of the page.

Week 1 Psalms (Book One)
Day 1   pp. A9-2
Day 2   pp. 3-7
Day 3   pp. 7-11
Day 4   pp. 11-15
Day 5   pp. 15-20

Week 2 Psalms (Book One)
Day 6   pp. 20-25
Day 7   pp. 25-30
Day 8   pp. 30-35
Day 9   pp. 35-40
Day 10   pp. 40-44

Week 3 Lamentations, Psalms (Book Two)
Day 11   pp. 165-170
Day 12   pp. 170-173
Day 13   pp. 173-177
Day 14   pp. 177-180
Day 15   pp. 45-50

Week 4 Psalms (Book Two)
Day 16   pp. 50-55
Day 17   pp. 55-61
Day 18   pp. 61-66
Day 19   pp. 67-71
Day 20   pp. 72-77

Week 5 Song of Songs, Psalms (Book Three)
Day 21   pp. 181-184
Day 22   pp. 184-187
Day 23   pp. 187-190
Day 24   pp. 190-194
Day 25   pp. 78-80

Week 6 Psalms (Book Three)
Day 26   pp. 81-83
Day 27   pp. 83-87

Day 28   pp. 87-92
Day 29   pp. 92-95
Day 30   pp. 96-99

Week 7 Proverbs
Day 31   pp. 195-198
Day 32   pp. 198-202
Day 33   pp. 202-206
Day 34   pp. 206-211
Day 35   pp. 211-214

Week 8 Proverbs
Day 36   pp. 215-218
Day 37   pp. 219-222
Day 38   pp. 222-225
Day 39   pp. 226-229
Day 40   pp. 230-233

Week 9 Proverbs
Day 41   pp. 233-237
Day 42   pp. 237-240
Day 43   pp. 241-243
Day 44   pp. 243-246
Day 45   pp. 246-250

Week 10 Psalms (Book Four)
Day 46   pp. 100-103
Day 47   pp. 103-107
Day 48   pp. 107-112
Day 49   pp. 112-116
Day 50   pp. 116-119

Week 11 Ecclesiastes
Day 51   pp. 251-253
Day 52   pp. 253-256
Day 53   pp. 256-259
Day 54   pp. 259-262
Day 55   pp. 262-265

Week 12 Psalms (Book Five)
Day 56   pp. 120-125
Day 57   pp. 125-130

Day 58   pp. 130-135
Day 59   pp. 135-141
Day 60   pp. 141-145

Week 13 Psalms (Book Five)
Day 61   pp. 145-148
Day 62   pp. 148-152
Day 63   pp. 152-155
Day 64   pp. 155-159
Day 65   pp. 159-163

Week 14 Job
Day 66   pp. 267-271
Day 67   pp. 271-275
Day 68   pp. 275-278
Day 69   pp. 279-283
Day 70   pp. 283-287

Week 15 Job
Day 71   pp. 287-291
Day 72   pp. 291-294
Day 73   pp. 294-297
Day 74   pp. 297-301
Day 75   pp. 301-305

Week 16 Job
Day 76   pp. 305-310
Day 77   pp. 310-315
Day 78   pp. 315-319
Day 79   pp. 319-323
Day 80   pp. 323-327

THE IMMERSE BIBLE SERIES

IMMERSE: THE READING BIBLE comes in six volumes and presents each Bible book without the distractions of chapter and verse numbers, subject headers, or footnotes. It's designed for reading—especially for reading with others. By committing to just two eight-week sessions per year (spring and fall), you can read through the entire Bible in three years. And online video and audio support tools make it easy to read together in groups. Step into this three-year Immerse Bible reading cycle with your friends; then do it again—and again—for a lifetime of life-giving, life-changing Bible engagement!

Immerse: Beginnings includes the first five books of the Bible, known as the *Torah* (meaning "instruction"). These books describe the origins of God's creation, the human rebellion, and the family of Israel—the people God chose to be a light to all peoples. We follow the covenant community from its earliest ancestors to the time it is about to enter the Promised Land.

Immerse: Kingdoms tells the story of Israel from the time of its conquest of Canaan (Joshua) through its struggle to settle the land (Judges, Ruth) and the establishment of Israel's kingdom, which ends in a forced exile (Samuel–Kings). The nation of Israel, commissioned to be God's light to the nations, falls to division and then foreign conquest for rejecting God's rule.

Immerse: Prophets presents the First Testament prophets in groupings that generally represent four historical periods: before the fall of Israel's northern kingdom (Amos, Hosea, Micah, Isaiah), before the fall of the southern kingdom (Zephaniah, Nahum, Habakkuk), around the time of Jerusalem's destruction (Jeremiah, Obadiah, Ezekiel), and after the return from exile (Haggai, Zechariah, Malachi, Joel, Jonah).

Immerse: Poets presents the poetical books of the First Testament in two groupings, dividing the books between songs (Psalms, Lamentations, Song of Songs) and wisdom writings (Proverbs, Ecclesiastes, Job). These writings all reflect the daily, down-to-earth faith of God's people as they live out their covenant relationship with him in worship and wise living.

Immerse: Chronicles contains the remaining First Testament books: Chronicles–Ezra–Nehemiah, Esther, and Daniel. These works were all written after the Jewish people fell under the control of foreign empires and were scattered among the nations. They remind God's chastened people of their identity and calling to faithfully represent God to the nations and that there is still hope for the struggling dynasty of David.

Immerse: Messiah provides a unique guided journey through the entire New Testament. Each major section is anchored by one of the Gospels, highlighting the richness of Scripture's fourfold witness to Jesus the Messiah. This creates a fresh reading of the New Testament centered on Christ.